The Political Economy of Latin America

D0145364

This brief text offers an unbiased reflection on debates about neoliberalism and its alternatives in Latin America with an emphasis on the institutional puzzle that underlies the region's difficulties with democratization and development. In addition to providing an overview of this key element of the Latin American political economy, Peter Kingstone also advances the argument that both state-led and market-led solutions depend on effective institutions, but little is known about how and why they emerge. Kingstone offers a unique contribution by mapping out the problem of how to understand institutions, why they are created, and why Latin American ones limit democratic development.

This timely and thorough update includes:

- A fresh discussion of the commodity boom in the region and the resulting "Golden Era" in Latin America;
- The recent explosion of social policy innovation and concerns about the durability of social reform after the boom;
- A discussion of the knowledge economy and the limits to economic growth, with case studies of successful examples of fostering innovation.

Peter Kingstone is Professor of Politics and Development and co-founder of the Department of International Development (with Andy Sumner) at King's College London. He is also co-editor of the *Democratic Brazil* series (with Timothy J. Power), including *Democratic Brazil Divided* (University of Pittsburgh Press, 2017). He writes about the politics of economic reforms and democratic politics in Latin America.

'In the second edition of this admirably succinct text, Professor Kingstone develops the argument that weak institutions bear much of the responsibility for the erratic pace and uneven character of development during the past century in Latin America. The text provides cogent, impartial, and refreshingly plain-spoken analyses of import substitution industrialization, market reforms, the rise of the left, and the recent expansion of anti-poverty policies in the diverse countries of the region. Concise case studies illuminate the analyses, and Professor Kingstone gives special attention to twenty-first century international changes like the rising importance of Asian trade and investment. The text gives students the opportunity, in the space of a few class sessions, to acquire a firm grounding not only in the politics of Latin American development, but also in what institutions are, how they originate and change, and how specific institutions shape development policies and outcomes.'

– James W. McGuire, Professor and Chair, Department of Government,
Wesleyan University

'An already impressive work is now, in its second edition, a more indispensable book. Peter Kingstone has written an authoritative account of Latin America's contemporary political economy. This overview of more than 100 years of development models has been updated to cover the region's more recent turn to the left with clear assessments of what worked, what didn't, and why. Kingstone does more than synthesize scholarly polemics. He advances the argument, in lucid prose and through well-selected data, that the debate should not be between more state or more market, but rather, which institutions are needed for states and markets not to malfunction. Kingstone's updated book should be mandatory reading for any student of development.'

– Javier Corrales, Dwight W. Morrow 1895 Professor of Political Science,
Amherst College

'This is the most comprehensive and up-to-date book on Latin American political economy currently available. It is well written, intellectually provocative, and touches upon all the most pressing issues affecting the economies of Latin America today. Kingstone's institutional focus is insightful and provocative. It demonstrates the key role of socioeconomic institutions in shaping economic development, be it either state or market-led.'

– Luigi Manzetti, Associate Professor of Political Science, Southern
Methodist University

'Much has happened in the region since *The Political Economy of Latin America* was first published. The commodity boom has ended and the left is in electoral retreat, yet their legacy is still not well understood. Kingstone's timely update discusses the issues raised by these changes, broadening the book's historical scope. In the process, he shows how his original arguments about the need to find an institutional balance between well functioning markets and well functioning states, avoiding past extremes of "too much market" or "too much state," are even more compelling.'

– Philip Oxhorn, Professor of Political Science, McGill University

The Political Economy of Latin America

Reflections on Neoliberalism
and Development after the
Commodity Boom

Second Edition

Peter Kingstone

Routledge
Taylor & Francis Group

NEW YORK AND LONDON

Second edition published 2018
by Routledge
711 Third Avenue, New York, NY 10017

and by Routledge
2 Park Square, Milton Park, Abingdon, Oxon OX14 4RN

Routledge is an imprint of the Taylor & Francis Group, an informa business

© 2018 Taylor & Francis

First edition published by Routledge 2011

Library of Congress Cataloging in Publication Data
Names: Kingstone, Peter R., 1964-
Title: The political economy of Latin America : reflections on neoliberalism and development after the commodity boom /
Peter Kingstone.
Description: 2nd Edition. | New York : Routledge, 2018. | Revised edition of the author's The political economy of Latin America, c2011. | Includes bibliographical references and index.
Identifiers: LCCN 2017045292 | ISBN 9781138926981 (hardback) |
ISBN 9781138926998 (pbk.) | ISBN 9781317404477 (epub) |
ISBN 9781317404484 (WebPDF) | ISBN 9781317404477 (ePub) |
ISBN 9781317404460 (mobipocket/kindle)
Subjects: LCSH: Latin America--Economic policy. | Economic development--Latin America. | Industrial policy--Latin America. |
Neoliberalism--Latin America.
Classification: LCC HC125 .K48 2018 | DDC 338.98--dc23
LC record available at https://lccn.loc.gov/2017045292

ISBN: 978-1-138-92698-1 (hbk)
ISBN: 978-1-138-92699-8 (pbk)
ISBN: 978-1-315-68287-7 (ebk)

Typeset in Times New Roman
by Taylor & Francis Books

For the Clove – which has spread out too far and wide...

Contents

Tables

Preface

I was skeptical when Michael Kerns of Routledge first approached me roughly a decade ago and asked if I'd be interested in expanding a review article I'd written for *Latin American Research Review* into a small book. I was unsure if it was something that I'd want to do and not sure there would be any interest. I was gratified to discover that it was a project that I enjoyed very much and that it found a welcome audience. So, when he approached me about revising it, I was more than happy to take it up again.

When I wrote the first edition, Latin America was riding the crest of the commodity boom and it seemed as if the future was hopeful. Many people were concerned about what would happen when the boom ended, but it looked as if at least some Latin American countries had found a stable, successful path forward. In fact, compared to the US, which seemed incapable of confronting its own dilemmas in the wake of the global financial crisis, Latin America seemed in good shape.

Almost ten years later, the world is in a much more fragile place. I have traded my home in the US for one in the UK and discovered that it shares many of the tensions and conflicts of the US and offers almost equally disappointing politics. This book is a reflection on the hard challenges facing Latin America, but it is offered with a profound awareness of the very hard challenges facing the US and my new home of the UK and the disappointing absence of innovative ideas on the political horizon. Latin America is facing serious challenges at the end of the commodity boom, but it still seems a more innovative and experimental region than either my old or my new home. When I wrote the first book, I strongly endorsed the view that a balanced model that supports markets, includes a balanced supportive role for the state, and actively addresses poverty and inequality is the best way forward – neither markets nor states, but both working together. Nothing in the intervening years has changed my mind. I also argued that they rested on a strong institutional foundation, but social science had not offered any clues as to how a country develops that. I still stand by that assessment. In fact, in many respects, it seems as if political science, my discipline, has backed away from even trying to answer questions like that. The result is that we are very good at identifying problems and small solutions. But, we are no closer to answering the big ones. Brazil, where I have done most of my work in the past, is a tragic story of enormous potential swept away in ugly politics and corrosive corruption. Why and how Brazilians can design institutions that are more resistant to the kinds of calamities unfolding in the country is a question for which political science has no answer.

Regrettably, hard times inflict great costs, but it meant that the task of taking up the book and reflecting on what has changed was intellectually stimulating once again. Michael Kerns has moved on, but I'm grateful to Natalja Mortensen of Routledge for her support and her suggestions. I'm also very grateful to the faculty and students of the Department of International Development at King's College London, my new home. Exchanging ideas about development and democracy with the astonishing diversity of experiences, skills and backgrounds that a development department in London offers has been a great treat and is reflected in my thinking in this book. I'm also thankful to Kaidi Ru and Jazmin Rivas Chong for their research assistance. I'm also grateful to Hélène Maghin and Eva Renon, both of whom began this as research assistants, but ended up as co-authors of Chapter Five before moving on to their own post-graduate work at Sciences Po and University College London respectively.

Finally, I want to thank my family. My children have left home and are off venturing in the world, bringing back reports from the field of the way the world is changing. As always, they bring far more wealth into my life than work ever can. I especially want to thank my wife, Lisa, who is my partner, best friend and the wisest person I know.

1 Markets, States, and the Challenge of Development in Latin America

"Latin America after the Golden Era" … that was the topic of discussion when a group of leading Latin American and Iberian economic officials met in Madrid in July 2014 under the auspices of the Ibero-American General Secretariat (Secretaría General Iberoamericana, SEGIB). SEGIB coordinates meetings and summits every year, but this one centered on the bold, but somewhat worrisome idea that Latin America *had had* a "Golden Era" but it was over and there was now a "new economic reality"[1] threatening the region. The idea that Latin America had experienced a "golden age" or a "golden decade" roughly between 2003 and 2012 was actually quite common. Perhaps the most emblematic image of Latin America triumphant was the *Economist* magazine cover depicting Rio's famous *Christ the Redeemer (Corcovado)* statue rocketing into the sky with the enthusiastic caption "Brazil Takes Off."[2] But, Brazil was not alone. All through the region, Latin Americans and foreign observers shared the sense that something historically distinctive had been happening. But, a "Golden Era?" What was so special about the first decade of the 2000s that merited such a triumphant term?

The answer is that the period really did stand out as an historic period of economic, social and political changes in virtually every Latin American country. Those changes included tens of millions of people lifted from poverty and rapidly declining inequality in a region known as the global champion of inequity and exclusion for decades if not centuries. At the same time, foreign debt, budget deficits, and inflation fell, in most cases dramatically. This came in a region so engulfed and devastated by these macroeconomic troubles that the 1980s had been dubbed "the lost decade." Politically, Latin American democracies appeared in general to be strengthening and deepening as well, with new groups mobilizing and participating and formal and informal barriers to women, indigenous, racial minorities, and the poor all falling. Over the 2000s, Latin America went from the world's champion of inequality to the world's leading laboratory for innovative new social policies. After roughly 500 years, it appeared as if long-standing patterns of social and economic exclusion might instead be heading towards a new "golden" standard of inclusion.

Two exemplars widely held up as possible models of development highlight Latin America's visibility and impact on the global community. On one side, Venezuela under Hugo Chávez offered a new form of socialist change that inspired leftists all around the world, based on an explicit critique of liberal democratic capitalism. At his peak, Chávez financed sympathetic left-wing politicians and parties throughout the region, provided social assistance for programs in other countries (including subsidized fuel to low income Americans), and openly challenged US leadership in the world, delighting his admirers by calling George W. Bush "the Devil" at his 2006 address to the United Nations.[3] On the other side, Brazil, led by working class hero turned party leader and president, Luiz Inácio Lula da Silva offered a more moderate model heralded as the "Brasília Consensus" that blended support for markets with a strong state presence and progressive social programs. Lula and his admirers spread the gospel of Brazil's miracle, offering political advice to other leftist parties in the region, such as the Farabundo Martí para la Liberación Nacional (Farabundo Martí National Liberation Front, FMLN) of El Salvador, technical advice and aid to other developing countries, particularly in Africa, and marking the country's new found prominence on the global stage by winning bids to host the World Cup in 2014 and the Olympics in 2016.

But, if the era was so special, why did it come to an end? The idea that the "golden age" had reached its end by 2012–2013, and that the road beyond was filled with perils was also widely held across Latin America. Newspapers from diverse parts of the region all pointed to an end to the unusual cycle of good times, fueled by historically high commodity prices. Commodity prices across a wide range of products – from energy, to food, to minerals and metals – had risen steadily over the 2000s (even recovering very quickly from the 2008 global financial crisis), driven primarily by Chinese growth and consumption of commodities. But, by 2011, China's growth had slowed and prices began to decline at an accelerating pace. The end of the cycle was not a surprise – commodity prices are particularly volatile and prone to cycles. Indeed, observers such as the Inter-American Development Bank noted concern that Latin American governments were overly dependent on commodity export revenues, particularly for domestic spending, which had also risen sharply over the period.[4] Others noted that very few Latin American countries had taken advantage of the boom to invest in future prosperity or to create genuine stabilization funds to protect them against a downturn in commodity prices.[5] In short, the region had benefited from an incredibly favorable global economy – "good times" that gave politicians unusual room to offer new social and economic benefits.[6] With the fall of commodity prices, the good times were over.

The tensions began to show quickly, economically, socially and politically. On the economic front, growth and per capita GDP growth slowed down steadily from roughly 2012 on, turning negative on average by 2015–2016. Export revenues declined and along with them, the outstanding macroeconomic performance of the "Golden Era," including debt levels, fiscal deficits, and the threat of inflation (already pronounced in some countries like Argentina and Venezuela). The growing constraints on revenues meant that governments began to feel pressure on their ability to maintain the levels of social spending of the "Golden Era." In some countries, like Ecuador, efforts to cut spending led to open protests. In Brazil, vast expenditures to prepare for the World Cup in 2014 and the Olympics in 2016 contrasted with underinvestment in health, education and especially transport and provoked the 2013 *Vinegar Revolution* as hundreds of thousands of angry citizens took to the streets to demand FIFA (Federation Internationale de Futbol Associations) level social policy.[7] In fact, by 2017, Brazil and Venezuela, champions of their respective models of development, had descended into severe crisis, economically and politically with Brazil paralyzed by a massive corruption scandal and Venezuela an openly and increasingly repressive authoritarian regime.

Of course, Latin America is not alone in confronting economic, social and political dilemmas in the contemporary period. In the US, the 2016 presidential election brought Donald Trump to power in a context of bitter polarization, framed explicitly around identity issues. But, beneath the ugly politics lay a story of diminishing economic opportunities affecting both Democrat and Republican voters. Bernie Sanders' and Elizabeth Warren's rhetoric targeted the privileges of the top 1% of earners at the expense of jobs and public services (including education) for the rest of society. Donald Trump's angry white identity politics captured the mood in communities hit by declining opportunity and ravaged by social ills like opioid addiction that fostered a deep sense that the government and establishment elites had abandoned them. In the United Kingdom, angry working class voters shocked globalized London elite opinion by opting to leave the European Union and its guarantee of free movement of labor within Europe. The vote came after years of budget cuts that the ruling Conservative Party argued were necessary to restore growth after the global financial crisis of 2008–2009. By the time of the vote in 2016, the UK economy was growing faster than the rest of Europe, but it was growth that rested on stagnant wages, rising household debt, low wage (or no wage), low quality work, and devastating cuts to long cherished public services such as the National Health Service. The US and the UK were not unique among the rich democracies. In fact, bad economic performance, worrying social indicators, and fraught, angry politics had become one of the defining features of democratic capitalism around the world. How to promote growth and make sure society broadly shares in it has become one of the critical questions facing the world in the new millennium. And beneath that question lies the fundamental, controversial and deeply conflictual problem of whether you trust markets or the state.

In Latin America, the argument over market and state has always been present and it has always been intense. For example, in January of 2000, the residents of Cochabamba, Bolivia's third largest city, went to war with their government. The conflict was fraught with emotion and marked by profound and ultimately irreconcilable differences. It lasted several months as angry protestors barricaded buildings, blockaded streets and occupied government offices. The government declared a state of siege and met the protestors with violent repression by Bolivian soldiers and Cochabamba police. So, what was so important to the citizens of Cochabamba that they would openly battle their government? The answer was water and the seemingly innocuous question of how best to deliver it to local residents. But, this harmless question triggered one of the most successful and extensive mobilizations of citizens in Bolivian history as middle class consumers, poor peasants, indigenous groups, environmentalists and labor unions came together to form an organization called *Coordinadora por la defensa del Agua y la Vida* (Coordination for the Defense of Water and Life). The movement drew the attention and support of left-wing and anti-globalization activists all over the world. Their purpose was to fight for their way of life, as manifested in the way they obtained their water.[8]

The problem had to do with privatization – the process whereby a government sells ownership of a state owned enterprise, or alternatively licenses the right to operate it. Access to running water was under-developed and inequitable and the government lacked the resources to invest in improved capacity.[9] As a result, a hasty and poorly conceived auction took place. The winning consortium, Aguas de Tunari, led by Bechtel Corporation of the United States, promised to invest in increased capacity and in exchange was guaranteed a 15% return on their investment. Within days, Aguas de Tunari introduced rate increases of as much as 35%. Many residents drew their water from wells or from collected rainwater and believed that the contract granted Aguas the right to charge for this water as well. The threat of exorbitant prices for water and the uncertainty over who held rights to ground and rainwater stirred the uprising. Initially, President Hugo Banzer – one time general and military dictator of the country – refused to back down, defending the integrity of the contract and the necessity of the new investments. Ultimately, however, the rising anger over the use of unrestrained force against protestors involved in the struggle undermined Banzer's resolve and he relented, canceling the contract and returning water service to local control. Aguas de Tunari officials had already fled the city in fear for their lives.[10]

This so-called "Water War" captures all the elements of the major conflicts playing out throughout Latin America and much of the rest of the capitalist world: markets versus government control; private property rights versus community needs; efficiency versus social justice; centralized, technical decision-making versus democratic accountability. Seemingly simple policy choices, like how to provide water, are often at the center of great trade-offs between much larger and harder to reconcile visions of society. This book is about those policy choices and the difficult trade-offs they reflect. It is about how those trade-offs have played out in Latin America over the past thirty years and what it means for the future.

Why Latin America? Latin America is a region that often escapes global and/or US attention. It is rarely at the center of global strategic struggles (the 1962 Cuban Missile Crisis a prominent exception). Although the region contains important deposits of oil and natural gas, it is not the central actor in global struggles over strategic resources, as with the Middle East or the former Soviet Union. It has not been the center of powerful, competing ideologies, such as communism or more recently political Islam. Indeed, a common Latin American complaint is that aside from the US' periodic unwelcome interventions in national politics, American presidents actually pay little real attention to the region.[11] US governments care about drug interdiction policies, but Latin American concerns are rarely high priority matters for US foreign policy or foreign economic policy, or for the larger American public for that matter.

Yet, Latin America is an important region for both the US and the world. The US, of course, has a long and lamentable history of military and covert intervention in the region. Hugo Chávez' intense anti-US rhetoric, such as calling President George Bush "satan," may appear crazed to some US observers, but it reflects a real history of subverting democratic governments, supporting dictatorships, and financing violent insurgencies or counter-insurgencies.[12] But, the US connection to Latin America extends well beyond foreign policy. Perhaps most importantly, the US and Latin America are deeply integrated demographically and economically. By 2017, Latinos were the fastest growing minority in the country, con-stituting nearly 17% of the US population (52 million people), of whom 19 million were born in Latin America. The growing US Latino population and ongoing migration from the region have built upon the long-standing Latino population in the country, dating at least to the US seizure of roughly 1/2 of Mexico's territory in the US–Mexican War of 1846–1848. These new flows of migration have deepened the already strong bonds with the region to the south.

In turn, this flow of migration reflects the development of Latin America's economy. Economic development has been a controversial problem in Latin America for most of its modern history. Economic failures – most notably to provide meaningful opportunities and accep-table standards of living – left millions in the region in terrible straits. This misery at home with opportunity abroad played an important role in driving Latin Americans to look for work in the US. The US and Latin America are linked economically as well. Latin America is, in regional terms, one of the US's largest trading partners, accounting for roughly 20% of all imports and exports with comparable importance for Latin American countries as well.[13] So, while both the US public and politicians take Latin America for granted, what happens in the region matters a great deal.

From a global and historical perspective, Latin America matters also, most importantly because it raises intriguing questions about development and economic growth – questions that have been vital and controversial in the wake of the 2008–2009 economic crisis, the long, slow recovery and the emergence of angry populist and undemocratic politics everywhere. Latin America has been a laboratory of competing strategies for promoting growth and development for over 100 years – a region where the debate over the proper balance of markets and government leadership has continued unabated for decades. In some periods, markets have appeared predominant; in others government leadership. For roughly two decades over the 1980s and 1990s, the pro-market side, often referred to as "neoliberalism," appeared to have won. As Francis Fukuyama observed, the "end of history" – meaning the end of debate over democratic capitalism – had arrived.[14] Forrest Colburn lamented the triumph of consumerism over genuine citizenship and called it "Latin America at the End of Politics."[15] Government leadership in the economy was condemned as ineffective and inefficient – destructive of democracy and perpetuating poverty and inequality. The left in Latin America virtually disappeared.[16] As Margaret Thatcher once declared: "there is no alternative."

But, starting in 1999 and continuing into the new century, a "Pink Tide" swept the region as left-wing parties made a stunning resurgence. Voters in diverse countries supported critics of markets and US influenced approaches to the challenges of development and democracy. Indeed, as many of the world's leading economies plunged into recession, Latin America's development experiments became ever more relevant and took on renewed urgency and interest for both developing and developed countries around the world. For the left, this reversal in fortune represented a "backlash" against the reviled philosophy "neoliberalism." For such critics, neoliberalism had been an elitist project that uses markets to reward the wealthy at the expense of the poor, undermines democracy, and converts citizens into mere consumers. Voters had rightly risen up and rejected it and it appeared that they would reap rewards for doing so.

From roughly 2000 until 2012–2013, the region boomed, with the left arguably leading the way in offering new models of socially inclusive growth.[17] In the rest of the world, inequality rose in almost all rapidly growing "emerging economies" such as China or India. Over the same period, the US and Europe suffered low levels of economic growth that did little to reduce unemployment, under employment and precarious employment while the wealthiest 1% recovered quickly from the crisis. By contrast, in Latin America governments of both the left and the right began experimenting with new models for socially, politically and economically inclusive growth. Poverty and inequality fell dramatically all over the region while new social policy innovations flourished.

However, a decade into Latin America's "golden age" the leftist wave and its accompanying optimism came to an end. Economically, the region's situation began to deteriorate and with this change, governments hit the limits of their capacity to maintain or deepen the array of social benefits that had expanded dramatically in the boom times. Sluggish growth, rising unemployment, falling real wages, and threats to newly acquired social rights had political consequences, including rising protests, electoral losses for the left, and worrisome efforts to hold on to power by undermining democratic rules. Perhaps most dramatically, an impeachment in Brazil plunged the country into division, rancor and deep political and economic crisis. Many on the left saw this as a "coup" – the revenge of neoliberalism and the global capital elites that promoted it against the poor and their political champion.

Not surprisingly, advocates of neoliberalism advanced a different view which was that left governments had spent money irresponsibly during the boom times. When the boom ended, leftist parties paid the price for their dismissal of the consequences of their "macroeconomic populism."[18] Neoliberals argued that economies work best with minimal government involvement. This view held a near hegemonic position in the world's leading economic powers and international economic institutions, such as the World Bank or the International Monetary Fund (IMF). This view set the tone for US policies beginning with Ronald Reagan in 1980 and for British policies beginning with Margaret Thatcher in 1979. Since that time, neoliberal recommendations about the proper balance between markets and states shaped policies in Europe and Japan as well as the former Communist nations and the developing world.

Yet, the economic crisis of 2008–2009 – arguably a result of poorly regulated financial markets – called into question the wisdom of simply relying on markets. Even in the United States, one of the leading advocates of free markets in the world, the balance between markets and government shifted under first the Bush administration and then even more under the Obama administration. Even so, polarized politics ensured that state involvement in the economy remained very modest as Republicans and many Democrats opposed increased government spending and regulation. In Europe, the Euro area countries, led by Germany, and the UK clung steadfastly and obstinately to orthodox austerity policies designed to cut debt, even in the face of devastating unemployment and increases in poverty in Southern Europe, and serious concerns over precarious employment and under-employment elsewhere.[19] In both the US and Europe, limited efforts to address the impact of the crisis helped spur new nationalist, populist, and xenophobic politics. Angry identity politics feed on grievances and particularly take root when there is underlying economic pain. In short, even in the wealthy Organization for Economic Cooperation and Development (OECD) countries, the crisis cracked open a question that appeared to have been firmly settled and as of 2017 has no clear answer anywhere in the world.

Latin America largely escaped the worst effects of the global financial crisis of 2008–2009, suggesting that indeed the new "Golden Era" was real and durable. The subsequent decline and return to pessimism about the power of the state to promote growth and social inclusion have led to renewed calls for market discipline and government spending restraints. As of 2017, neoliberal economics seems entrenched in the US and Europe and on the rise again in Latin America. But, the promotion of markets across all of them rested uneasily on roiling politics, worries about the health of democracy, and threats to protecting and deepening social inclusion. Rather than "the end of history," the 2000s have shown that "history" is very much alive and the question of how to promote growth and ensure it is widely shared is still an open and sharply contested one.

Markets Versus States and Neoliberalism in Latin America

The question of the proper balance between markets and government intervention is a crucial one for promoting economic growth and for larger developmental goals such as reducing poverty and inequality. Economic growth does not settle all societal problems. It says little about whether or how the benefits of growth are invested back into society. It says little about whether society invests in the health and education of its citizens thereby producing human capital – the set of skills and attributes that leverage improved productivity and societal returns and the basis of long-term growth. Economic growth says little about the distribution of the gains: who wins and who loses. It says little about poverty and inequality – it is certainly possible for small minorities to capture all or most of the gains of economic growth. But, it is also true that in the absence of economic growth, all these other developmental goals are elusive if not impossible. Economic growth affords societies the opportunities to solve larger developmental goals. How to best manage economic growth is a matter that profoundly affects the character of a society.

But finding a clear answer to markets or government or even the proper balance between the two has proven elusive. At the heart of the debate over the proper balance between markets and government are fundamental differences in beliefs about how societies prosper. Market advocates firmly believe in the inherent creative, dynamic and entrepreneurial spirit in all individuals. For these scholars and policy-makers, government involvement creates a wide array of impediments and inefficiencies that limit the potential of individuals in a society. Government involvement produces distortions in the economy that send the wrong signals and create the wrong incentives for societal actors. An economy burdened with excessive government intervention suffers from waste, inefficiency and, often, pervasive corruption. For advocates of a stronger role for government, the problem of the pro-market position is that it fails to recognize the way that those with economic power may simply use their influence (both economic and political) to accumulate more for themselves at the expense of the rest of society. In addition, it fails to recognize that countries may find themselves disadvantaged in the global economy in ways that limit development absent explicit government intervention.

There is of course a middle ground. At the extremes, both positions present problems and in fact most economies in the world combine both markets and government intervention. In the real, empirical world all market economies include a government role and no serious analyst envisions its complete disappearance. The challenge is how to find the correct balance between the two.[20] On the whole, the role of the state in the US economy is much smaller than the rest of the OECD countries. Yet, even with a more moderate position, where the line gets drawn has both economic and political consequences – who wins and who loses within a given society. As a result, it is not a simple, technical discussion. It has been historically, and continues to be, a difficult, conflict-riddled, and sometimes even violent debate.

While the debate has sparked again with renewed vigor in the developed world, the topic has never ceased being an open question in Latin America. Even before the crisis of 2008–2009, the question of how to manage the economy was a controversial issue in Latin America. Neoliberalism (sometimes also referred to as the "Washington Consensus") has been at the center of enormous controversy since its first appearance in Latin America. It was first implemented in 1973 (even before Reagan and Thatcher) under the auspices of the Chilean dictator Augusto Pinochet and his band of US trained economic advisors, the "Chicago Boys." By the late 1980s/early 1990s, it had swept through the region, at least in part due to the catastrophic results of a debt crisis that turned the 1980s into the "lost decade." For many critics, neoliberalism was a set of policies that served the interests of developed countries' firms and financiers at the expense of Latin Americans. The program was foisted on vulnerable Latin American governments by the IMF, World Bank, and Washington, except of course in Chile where it was foisted on the population by a brutal dictatorship.[21]

By contrast, neoliberalism's advocates argued that the region had been floundering under a closed, government led, import-substitution regime (ISI) that was not sustainable financially and was not an effective growth strategy in any event. ISI protected a narrow group of highly privileged industrialists, a limited middle class, and to a lesser extent a narrow labor aristocracy that earned wages and benefits out of line with its productivity. The cost of this highly inefficient economic strategy was intractable poverty, declining state capacity, and ultimately the external debt that triggered the crisis of the 1980s.[22] Neoliberalism was not an elitist project that served the interests of the US, the global financial community and their privileged interlocutors in Latin America. It was a program that offered the hope of renewed growth and more sustainable development by "getting prices right."

Roughly forty years after neoliberalism first became hegemonic in the region, the debate shows little sign of slowing. Years of leftist government and experiments with new models of political economy offered hope of a post-Washington Consensus pathway. Yet, the end of the "Golden Era" has led to a return of the right, reinvigorated neoliberal critiques and renewed calls for neoliberal policies. But, even neoliberalism's strongest supporters conceded that it had not lived up to its earlier promises on growth and opportunity.[23] Clearly neoliberal policies were not *the* answer for the region either. If neither the Pink Tide nor neoliberalism offer good models, what is the solution? Finding a new path, however, is challenging because critics and supporters do not agree on the basic facts or their interpretations.

The Institutional Dilemma

One thing is clear: Latin American nations continue to wrestle with many of the same problems they have wrestled with for decades: uneven growth with persistent poverty and inequality, even after the gains of the "Golden Era"; ineffective state institutions that deliver limited benefits, often to a highly restricted minority of the population; and political institutions that frequently fail to translate citizens' needs and concerns into compelling mandates for elected officials.[24] Latin American economic problems have remained very similar: through authoritarianism and democracy, and through state-led import substitution industrialization and market-led neoliberalism, and through both the triumphant rise and fall of the "Golden Era."

The disappointment of the end of the "Golden Era" is particularly acute. The rise of the left coincided with widespread efforts to address long-standing inequalities in the region. Ultimately, governments of both the left and the right introduced policies in diverse realms, including health, education, non-contributory pensions and social assistance, and gender and race discrimination among others. Poverty and inequality declined all over Latin America. At the same time, the region seemed to offer new forms of political inclusion. Radical critics of capitalism and liberal democracy saw countries like Venezuela, Ecuador or Bolivia promote more participatory forms of politics that brought many new citizens into politics while attacking or reforming the institutions of liberal democracy. Countries like Brazil, Chile and Uruguay appeared to offer moderate forms of social democracy that worked within existing political institutions to preserve liberal capitalism while finding ways to extend benefits and improve participation for wide swathes of the citizenry. Ultimately, however, these shifts proved themselves dependent on the unusually strong commodity boom from 2003–2012. As of 2017, it is not clear what will happen to the extraordinary gains of the boom years. One critical question is, to what extent were the gains just the result of an unusually auspicious global economy, and to what extent do they rest on real and meaningful changes? With the end of the boom times, the question is, what happened to the region? Did Latin American governments capitalize on the boom to forge a more secure development path?

The limitations of the gains of the 2000s suggest that at root lies a failure to develop an institutional infrastructure that supports democracy and development. The problem is not "too much market" or "too much government." Rather, it is poorly functioning markets and poorly functioning governments. Both markets and governments need effective institutions to perform well. Governments need to be able to design good policies that really address the problems and challenges facing individuals in the economy. They need to be able to collect reliable information. They need to be able to monitor performance. They need to be able to sanction misbehavior or defiance of rules and regulations. They need to be able to enforce contracts and protect rights holders. They need to be accountable to the public. If they cannot, the consequences can be very destructive. For example, governments that cannot find reliable information may pass laws that have little to do with realities on the ground.[25] Laws that do not correspond to the challenges of life as people really live it are ignored. Illegality is a profound problem affecting Latin America – from simple acts such as ignoring stoplights at night, to widespread smuggling of even basic consumer goods, to illegal, informal housing and commerce, to a variety of measures to avoid labor regulations. Political corruption scandals plague the region. All across Latin America, laws are passed and routinely ignored because they make little sense to people who have to live with them or they impose costs that are unaffordable, or they seem unfair or unjust.

Good public policy also depends on effective institutions. Even good intentions can go awry when government institutions do not function effectively. For example, in 1996, the Bolivian government under President Gonzalo Sánchez de Lozada tried to create a pension called a *bonosol* for all Bolivians, regardless of whether they had contributed to a pension plan or not (non-contributory). It was an innovative plan to address widespread poverty in the country and a recognition that most poor Bolivians did not in fact contribute to some kind of old age savings account through formal payroll taxes. Ultimately, the plan foundered for a number of reasons, but perhaps foremost among them was the simple logistic failure of producing a real list of eligible recipients – an inability of the government to simply keep track of its own population. Over the next twenty years, every Latin American country began to experiment with new kinds of social assistance and non-contributory pensions and indeed Bolivia resurrected the *bonosol* in a new form.[26] State officials across the region had learned a great deal over that time (from experience and from each other) and the quality of policy making improved considerably. Yet, even the most successful programs struggled to identify eligible citizens or to decrease barriers to citizens enrolling for the benefit, such as getting official ID cards or birth certificates. For example, Ecuador's *Bono de Desarrollo Humano* (Human Development Bond, BDH) developed through the 2000s into one of the most successful assistance programs in the region at finding and registering the eligible poor, yet only reached 65% of the bottom 40% of society.[27] These limitations to otherwise innovative policy ideas rested on limits to state capacity and the institutions needed to govern.

These institutional weaknesses undermine the functioning of the market as well. At the very least, markets depend on governments to protect the rule of law so that contracts will be enforceable and property rights secure. But, institutional weaknesses mean that often contracts are unreliable and in some instances unenforceable while property rights are insecure. Unreliable contracts and property rights lead to informal practices to get around the institutional failures – practices that can be highly inefficient and destructive of the competitive process that is key to markets working well.[28] In short, both markets and governments need effective institutions to produce the results that societies want them to produce. But, which institutions, and what explains why they work well or do not? These are crucial questions that as yet we do not understand as well as we need to foster real development in addition to growth.

Confronting Complexities

The Diversity of Latin America

This is a book about economic development in Latin America. But, treating Latin America as a single region with a common set of challenges poses some problems. The first challenge is simply deciding which countries constitute "Latin America." There is no set definition and different accounts treat the region differently. Some count only the Spanish and Portuguese speaking countries, excluding Belize, Surinam, French Guiana and Guyana as well as much of the Caribbean. Some accounts exclude the Caribbean. More inclusionary accounts treat the Caribbean, Central and South America and Mexico as one region. This book limits its discussion to the 17 Spanish and Portuguese speaking non-Caribbean countries (therefore excluding Cuba and the Dominican Republic). The Spanish and Portuguese speaking countries share a similar colonial heritage as well as cultural affinities. Furthermore, as a book on growth and development, excluding the small, mono-crop island economies limits the already important variations in the region in terms of development dynamic. The countries included are: Argentina, Bolivia, Brazil, Chile, Colombia, Costa Rica, Ecuador, El Salvador, Guatemala, Honduras, Mexico, Nicaragua, Panama, Paraguay, Peru, Uruguay and Venezuela.

Even this more restrictive group is not monolithic and the degree of diversity is enough to warrant considerable caution when discussing it as one. Among other things, Latin American countries display enormous differences in terms of race, ethnicity, religion, and language, not to mention climate and geography. For example, tiny Costa Rica with oceans on either side is thrown in with land-locked mountainous countries like Bolivia or nearly temperate, highly urbanized ones like Argentina. In racial/ethnic terms, the Latin American region is tremendously varied: black, white and mulatto Brazil with its complex racial mix of black, multiple official and unofficial designations of mulatto, indigenous, white and every possible combination of them; mestizo Mexico, with indigenous pockets primarily in the south; almost entirely white, European Argentina and Uruguay; finally, societies like Ecuador or Bolivia where European origin minorities share nationality with large majority mestizo and indigenous populations. Careful discussions of Latin American history also have to take into account that the region has a varying political history, from Costa Rica which has been democratic continuously since 1948, to places like Argentina which has violently swung back and forth between democracy and dictatorship.

In particular, two critical differences stand out for the purposes of this book. First, Latin American nations cover a range of sizes from small countries like Costa Rica or Honduras with populations of only a few million to countries like Argentina or Mexico with populations in the tens of millions to the continent sized Brazil – the fifth most populous country in the world. Population size, in turn, has a substantial effect on the economy and the possible development path of the various countries in Latin America. Smaller Latin American countries have, for the most part, depended on the export of a limited number of commodities such as bananas, sugar or coffee. Countries like Guatemala or Honduras made only limited efforts to promote industry and instead have relied almost exclusively on the volatile prices of commodities on international markets for economic growth.[29] This stands in sharp contrast to the economic paths of the larger countries in Latin America, notably Argentina, Brazil, Colombia, Chile, Mexico or Venezuela. In these countries, large-scale, government-led industrialization programs transformed their economies and societies, beginning with the Great Depression and continuing through the post-War period. These represent two economic poles with Latin American countries arrayed between them, with Brazil at the high end of industrialization, and countries like Honduras or Guatemala at the low end. Brazil produces goods like cars, airplanes, and sophisticated software. Its industrial development sustained the growth of the largest middle class in the developing world. In countries like Guatemala, much of the population continues to work in plantation agriculture and suffers with very low standards of living and quality of life.

Despite the differences, Latin American nations share some important common traits. For one, they are linked by the three common, central economic challenges of the region: poverty, inequality and uneven development. The "Golden Era" led to declines in all three, yet they remain persistent problems and are even more of a concern with the end of the commodity boom. Latin America's poverty rate declined dramatically and Latin America fares better on poverty than many other parts of the developing world (see Table 1.1). But, as of 2012, one in four Latin

Table 1.1 Poverty Head Count (%) at $3.10 per day, PPP, Regional Comparisons

Country Name	1996	1999	2002	2005	2008	2010	2011	2012	2013
China	71.5	67.18	56.4	41.76	32.96	27.24	22.24	19.05	11.09
East Asia & Pacific	68.1	64.8	54.81	42.84	35.22	28.72	24.66	22.05	15.98
Europe & Central Asia	18.43	20.04	14.39	10.79	7.36	7.35	7.14	6.91	6.47
Latin America & Caribbean	27.28	26.19	25.61	21.37	15.43	13.83	12.83	11.93	11.33
Low income	85.25	85.03	83.96	80.65	78.54	76.76	75.54	73.73	72.01
Middle income	60.25	58.96	54.31	47.18	41.97	38.02	34.6	32.37	28.92
Sub-Saharan Africa	76.53	76.84	76.53	73.06	70.28	69.13	67.86	66.5	64.99
Upper middle income	50.45	48.13	40.76	30.62	23.58	19.82	16.64	14.55	9.91

Source: Data available at World Bank, www.worldbank.org

Americans was still poor (defined as earning less than US$ 4 per day) while 11.5% were extremely poor (defined as earning less than $3.10 PPP (Purchasing Power Parity) per day). Poverty rates are high in virtually all countries of Latin America, although there is substantial variation between countries like Argentina, Chile and Uruguay on the one hand, and the extreme poverty of the small Central American countries Guatemala, Honduras or Nicaragua. While the picture as of 2017 is much better than in 2000 and dramatically better than 1990, the prospects for lifting more citizens out of poverty and protecting those that have only barely risen above are limited. Income from labor is the most important factor in lifting households out of poverty and with growth slowed or negative in much of the region, millions will continue to wrestle with living in poverty. Unfortunately, poverty has been a remarkably resilient feature of the Latin American landscape through both economic booms and busts of the past.[30]

But, if the region is not the global leader in poverty it is still the global champion of inequality. Africa, Asia and Eastern Europe all wrestle with issues of poverty. But, Latin America's poverty levels stand in stark contrast to the extraordinary wealth in its midst, even with the improvements during the "Golden Era." The Gini coefficient, the standard measure of inequality, for Latin America fell from 57 in 2000 to 52 in 2012 – a remarkable achievement in its own right.[31] But, even so, it remained higher than any other region. The Sub-Saharan African nations came closest to Latin America with an average Gini coefficient of 44.7. By contrast, the coefficient for the rich economies averaged 32.2.[32] Middle class Latin Americans live lives that are easily recognizable to middle class North Americans. Young people gather in shopping malls that are nearly indistinguishable from their US equivalents, listening to iPods and texting each other on smart phones that work as well or better than they do in the US. They drive in similar cars, eat in restaurants and go to clubs that are similar to those in the US. Many attend excellent universities and entertain life ambitions similar to their US counterparts. If they get sick or injured, they have access to doctors and hospitals that are comparable to what middle class Americans enjoy. The crucial difference is the vast sea of poverty and the enormous distance socially, economically and politically between members of the middle and upper classes in Latin America and the poor. The US has high levels of poverty and inequality compared to most OECD countries. But, the poor do not constitute nearly as large a portion of the population and the physical separation of middle class America and the poor is greater than in Latin America where they often live side by side. The closeness of poverty and privilege sharpens the contrast between the different worlds each side inhabits.

This dualism is part of the region's uneven development. Latin Americans live in two separate worlds: one is a world that has benefited from economic growth and change and enjoys the services and institutions that function for them, although often only because of personal connections or the unjust exclusionary way that law and rules apply in Latin America.

The other is a world of poverty, but also of fear and uncertainty. This is a world in which the law and the legal system are often weapons that violate the rights of its denizens rather than protection. It is a world of tenuous or no access to basic health care or decent education. The great Brazilian anthropologist Roberto da Matta has noted the hierarchical nature of social relations between these two worlds and the ways in which supposedly universal rules are subverted to benefit those of higher status – "persons" rather than the "individuals" of democratic, law bound societies.[33]

The physical contours of these two worlds are immediately apparent and dramatic in their differences. Roughly 50% of Guatemalans still live in countryside villages, with houses made of sticks or adobe and looking as they probably did centuries ago. Seemingly light-years away, young upper and middle class Guatemalans in expensive cars cruise the rows of fancy restaurants in Guatemala City's upscale Zona 10. The voyage takes less than an hour, but the worlds seem utterly unconnected. In Bolivia, La Paz sits in a bowl shaped canyon that drops from the *altiplano* – the plateau over 12,000 feet high in the Andes. At the rim, a vast, informal city of over 1 million inhabitants has formed – El Alto. It is a municipality replete with unpaved roads and unfinished, haphazardly built buildings, many without windowpanes and lacking basic services like lighting or water. The informal settlement falls down the canyon rim towards the center where it meets the downtown and the higher income neighborhoods, with large boulevards and public squares and glass and steel high rises. Indigenous women wrapped in shawls and with round, bowler like hats – part of a relatively recent wave of migration from the countryside – illuminate the clash of two worlds confronting each other in the modern districts of the city. In Rio de Janeiro, poor shantytowns, *favelas*, tumble down the mountainsides – collections of colorful, creatively assembled shanties with water collection and sanitation ditches dug into the mountain, often side by side. The *favelas* fall into the famous wealthy neighborhoods of Leblon and Ipanema or Copacabana, with high-rise buildings on beautiful, tree lined avenues and abutting among the finest beaches in the area. Although they are often treated as "marginals," these informal and impoverished settlements constitute a vast, underprivileged economic base on which the more developed economy rests and depends. The "myth of marginalization" obscures the indignities and indecencies of economies that simply have not grown enough to absorb into the formal labor market millions who have been left behind or left out of the process of economic development.[34]

Latin America has undergone profound changes since the 1930s, many of them impressive and progressive, and especially so over the 2000s. Many more Latin Americans today enjoy the benefits of improved access to health care and maternity care, running water and proper sanitation. Incomes have improved over the decades and large middle and working classes have grown, economically and politically, especially between 2003 and 2013. But, growth in Latin America lags behind other regions. As Table 1.2 shows,

Table 1.2 Comparative Growth Rates, 1990–2016

Country Name	1990–1995	1996–2000	2001–2005	2006–2010	2011–2014	2015	2016
Argentina	6.7	2.66	2.35	5.79	3.14	2.65	−2.29
Bolivia	4.11	3.46	3.1	4.6	5.63	4.86	4.26
Brazil	3.09	2.16	2.88	4.47	2.14	−3.77	−3.59
Chile	8.71	4.2	4.21	3.52	4.35	2.25	1.59
Colombia	4.14	1.25	3.63	4.55	5.03	3.05	1.96
Costa Rica	5.56	4.98	4.11	4.68	4.16	4.72	4.33
Ecuador	2.98	1.14	4.87	3.41	5.38	0.16	−1.47
El Salvador	6.19	3.06	2.35	1.45	1.94	2.3	2.37
Guatemala	4.28	3.95	3.03	3.67	3.77	4.14	3.07
Honduras	3.57	3.07	4.66	3.66	1.74	3.64	3.61
Mexico	2.18	5.1	1.66	2	2.89	2.63	2.3
Nicaragua	1.81	5.03	3.17	2.54	5.14	4.85	4.7
Panama	5.54	4.65	4.34	7.92	8.89	5.78	4.88
Paraguay	4.45	0.44	1.93	5.14	5.42	2.96	4.09
Peru	5.33	2.61	4.3	6.94	5.13	3.25	3.88
Uruguay	4	2.96	0.34	5.97	4.27	0.37	1.45
Venezuela	3.53	0.84	3.08	3.84	1.79	NA	NA

Table 1.2 (continued)

Country Name	1990–1995	1996–2000	2001–2005	2006–2010	2011–2014	2015	2016
Average	4.48	3.03	3.18	4.36	4.17	2.74	2.2
China	13.0	8.63	9.8	11.32	8.11	6.9	6.69
India	6.11	6.09	6.73	8.33	6.49	8.01	7.1
Upper Middle Income	2.26	4.14	5.58	6.46	5.09	3.34	3.46
Lower Middle Income	2.94	3.84	5.93	6.55	5.41	5.42	5.12
Lower Income	0.39	3.47	4.29	5.71	5.37	4.58	4.09

Source: Data available at World Bank, www.worldbank.org

average GDP growth lagged significantly behind key competitors like India and China and the regional average was below the median for all Middle Income countries. In per capita terms, growth in Latin America from 1995 to 2014 was only 2.1% and even during the boom years of 2003–2012, it was only 3% – well below rates of growth in Asia. Growth does not solve all problems. It is not sufficient to lift people out of poverty and reduce inequalities. But, it is necessary. Latin American growth has been solid, but not spectacular. Latin American nations have experimented with new, innovative policies and millions of citizens enjoyed greatly improved lives as a result. But, to date, their depth and breadth have been insufficient. The insufficiency points to a second complexity.

Growth versus Development

As noted earlier, economic growth is not a sufficient condition for improving the quality of life. Millions can be and have been left out systematically from the benefits of economic growth. One important way of thinking about development comes from the economist Amartya Sen who framed it as the expansion of human capabilities, that is to say the enlargement of citizen's abilities to live the lives they choose to live, rather than the expansion of income.[35] Sen's ideas were important in the development of the United Nation's widely used measures of "human development." The human development index (HDI) captures elements that affect the quality of life such as access to health care, education, and basic services like potable water. Like all measures, it has flaws and detractors, but the HDI captures important features that shape the life chances that individuals face. It reflects the construction of human capital – health and education primarily – that allow individuals to live productive lives and to leverage greater wealth for themselves and their families. It reflects the measures that keep children from dying in infancy from malnutrition or diarrhea. In comparative terms, Latin America's HDI is high compared with the global bottom in Sub-Saharan Africa or South Asia. Latin American governments have managed real improvements in indicators like life expectancy, infant mortality, and access to health care and education. But, the region lags well behind the OECD and East Asia, and Eastern Europe, and is comparable to the relatively underdeveloped Middle East and North Africa.

Guillermo O'Donnell, offers another way to think about development and democracy.[36] O'Donnell, among the leading theorists of democracy in the world, has argued that real democracy can only rest on a Sen type understanding of the fullness of citizens' capabilities. Thus, democracy requires civil and political rights consistent with common definitions. But true citizenship requires social rights that are well enough developed for citizens to participate meaningfully in society. Hunger, poverty, illiteracy or poor education, uneven or unfair application of the law, as much as freedom of the press or assembly, all contribute to the fullness of citizens' capabilities. Thus, Sen and O'Donnell together offer a broad conception of development that has critical implications for the kind of lives people live. This broader view depends on governments that are responsive to the needs of their citizens and on laws that are fairly and universally applied. Growth can occur with little to no improvement in the quality of life of much of society. Good social policies can actually improve the quality of life with only moderate growth – arguably exactly what happened over the 2000s in the region. Democratic governance depends to some extent on both growth and human development. All three, however, rest on developing effective institutions. Therefore, in this book, development refers to the mix of economic growth, quality of life and effective institutions. On this score, Latin America performs far less well than hoped for when the 1980s brought a third wave of democratization to the region and neoliberal reforms to restore growth.

Unbundling Labels and their Usage in the Book

Talking about economic development over the past 40 years inevitably turns to the terms "neoliberalism" or "leftist." There are two issues to consider when discussing these terms. First, they are highly controversial. Observers mean different things when using these labels. For example, some scholars use neoliberalism to denote a broad philosophy about state–market relations and differentiate it from "market-oriented" reforms that became pervasive in Latin America in the 1990s. Others see it as a philosophy and a political agenda. Others use it to describe a set of linked policies designed to enhance the role of markets. Similarly, scholars argue over the definition of the left and even more so how to classify parties of the left. For some, the term left is reserved only for parties that have specific voter bases or policy goals. Others use the term broadly and include a class of politicians common in Latin American history that used anti-elite rhetoric and various mechanisms of compensation to mobilize "popular" sectors behind a more conservative or nationalistic program. Such "populists" – a controversial term itself – are not considered leftists by those who believe left parties are genuinely committed to social justice and/or redistributive policies.

Examining neoliberalism and leftist alternatives requires explicit choices about what we mean when we use them. It is important to remember, however, that both these umbrella labels refer to a collection or a bundle of separate and separable policies or organizations. In this book, I use the term neoliberal to refer to a set of policies that were prescribed together to enhance the role of markets in economic development. In that sense, it is a very narrow and thin conception of what neoliberalism means. That definition sums up the policy program, but does not take a position on the deeper and critical questions about the motives behind the reforms, the politics underlying their implementation, or the economic and political effects. Choosing to define neoliberalism this way does not prejudge the political questions or preclude the possibility that it is a political project led by elites to assert or reassert their dominance. Nor does it take the underlying political agenda as a given. Instead, using the term this way permits considering variations in who supports and who benefits the set of policies.

The market oriented policies that are part of the neoliberal program include privatization of state owned assets, liberalizing trade and finance, deregulating business activity, minimizing macroeconomic imbalances such as inflation, debt and deficits; as well as privatizing social services. No country in Latin America applied the full set of neoliberal reforms and all countries, even among the left, applied some. The book does not explore each policy separately, but they do have different economic and political logics and economic and political consequences.[37]

By contrast with the use of neoliberalism, this book uses the term the left very broadly and permissively, meaning political parties with broadly defined commitments to improve social justice and equity and includes both moderate reformers as well as more revolutionary figures. The left in Latin America is very diverse, in their programs, strategies, and constituencies. In general, the direct connection between social classes and voting in Latin America is weak or absent so we cannot point to a consistent or uniform pattern of leftist party support or specific positions that relate to defined social bases.[38]

Organizations on the left vary on their bases of support as well as on the range of policies they emphasize. Policies on the left can include a variety of measures to distribute or redistribute wealth to lower income groups, social policies to redress inequities, as well as policies to use state power to regulate the influence of business and/or promote economic development. Once again, these are separable policies and all Latin American countries, even the most neoliberal, implemented elements of them. All capitalist countries mix market and state oriented policies. Whether they are left or neoliberal in the end depends on some discretionary judgments.

Overview of the Book

Latin America experienced important changes since the first edition of this book came out. At the time, the prospects for the region appeared bright, despite some clear challenges for both democracy and economic development. As of this writing in 2017, the terrain seems much more difficult. As a result, the second edition differs from the first in three ways. The first edition framed the contemporary problem around the emergence of two contrasting models, one more radical in the reforms it promoted and one more moderate. This seemed an effective way of understanding the emergent trend and the prospects for the future, despite the difficulties of classifying cases. The second edition recognizes that this contrast still exists, but it offers less analytical leverage than it appeared to in 2010. Instead, the book's central focus is on the commodity boom and its related "Golden Era" and the consequences of its end. While Chapter Two and Three are largely the same, the remaining chapters have all been revised to reflect the shift in focus and conclusions.

A second change is that Chapter Four does not have the paired comparison of Brazil and Venezuela as the exemplars of the two lefts, as the two now exemplify some of the greatest dangers rather than two alternative models of development. Brazil has descended into angry, divisive politics, driven by the eruption of a massive corruption scandal that has implicated most of the political class. The impeachment of President Dilma Rousseff in 2016, the indictment of her predecessor, Luiz Inácio Lula da Silva, and the mountain of evidence implicating the interim president, Michel Temer, have left the country divided between large majorities fed up with the political establishment on one side and warring, polarized camps on the other. In the meantime, the promise of inclusionary growth has receded both because of the conjunctural economic crisis and the deeper structural dilemmas the Brazilian economy faces. At the same time, Venezuela in the wake of Hugo Chávez' death in 2013 has fulfilled all the worst fears of the harshest regime critics. From the celebrated leader of the anti-US hegemony bloc, Venezuela under Nicolás Maduro has become an overt dictatorship in which the government uses control of the courts to undermine elections and subvert the legislature, relying on violence to support its destruction of any resemblance of rule of law. At the same time, severe economic mismanagement, coupled with declining oil prices and exports, has led to widespread shortages of basic goods and pervasive hunger in a country once perceived as one of the most stable in the region. The third change is a new chapter that focuses specifically on the "Golden Era" and tries to ascertain the extent to which changes were durable. It does so by looking at the two sides of the story of change: the realm of social policy and performance, and the realm of economic performance, and particularly the factors that affect the possibility of advancing the high value-added, high labor productivity knowledge economy.

The book advances a series of claims. First, there has been a tendency to swing too sharply between market-led and state-led policies and back again. When these pendular swings have occurred historically, there has been a tendency to dismiss the prior model as a failure. This write-off of the past is unfortunate. As much as the neoliberals decried state-led import substitution industrialization and the contemporary left condemns neoliberalism, both models had important and impressive accomplishments, as well as flaws. In short, they were neither as bad as their critics said, nor as good as their advocates promised. Second, beginning in the 1990s and extending into the 2000s, a new more flexible and pragmatic model emerged in the region. This approach appeared to balance markets and the state in a way that offered promise for the future – what Javier Santiso labeled "Latin America's Political Economy of the Possible."[39] Experiences varied widely across the region, but positive examples appeared on both the left and the right, benefiting from the commodity boom, but also trying to build something sustainable for the future. By contrast, some of the most radical cases, exemplified by Venezuela, benefited from the commodity boom, but did little beyond that to promote new, sustainable models of development. Nevertheless, it is not clear that any Latin American government did enough during the "Golden Era" to ensure a sustainable path of development. Finally, the end of the commodity boom in 2012–2013 shows that even a new, balanced model is not sufficient. In the final analysis, full development – growth with equity, quality of life, and democratic governance – depends on the quality of institutions. Latin America still has a long way to go with this last challenge. By the late 1990s, advocates of development across the ideological spectrum agreed about this basic point. Unfortunately, we still have only limited understanding of where good institutions come from and how to foster them in developing societies.

Chapter Two offers a brief examination of the historical background to the initiation of neoliberal reforms in the region as a way to better understand them. The chapter reviews the rise of import substitution industrialization (ISI) and discusses its achievements as an economic development strategy. It explains the underlying political logic of ISI and the resulting political and economic benefits. It examines the record of ISI to provide a fair balance of what it did well – and the ways Latin America changed as a result – and what it did poorly. It then looks at how the combination of inherent flaws and conjunctural causes came together to end it as a viable strategy for development.

Chapter Three explores more fully the origins and character of the neoliberal reform program. One of the complaints neoliberal advocates make is that their critics distort the original policy agenda, for example arguing that neoliberals did not care about poverty or social policy. By contrast, neoliberal advocates tend to underemphasize the exaggerated promises made early on as well as the fact that *some* neoliberal policy makers carried out their reforms in undemocratic ways, or under considerable duress from external pressure. Neoliberal advocates are, in fact, a diverse group. As it turns out, so are the critics and their criticisms come from a variety of perspectives. This chapter provides a balanced assessment of the myriad positions that come out of both diverse groups. The chapter concludes with a paired comparison of Chile and Bolivia. The two countries pursued some of the deepest neoliberal reforms in the region with almost polar opposite results, highlighting the weak link between neoliberal reforms and development success or failure.

Chapter Four examines the shift to the left, often referred to as the "Pink Tide," that began in Latin America beginning in 1998 with the election of Hugo Chávez. It considers the reasons for the region's shift and explores the shortcomings of the neoliberal model that pushed voters to support alternatives. It then considers what difference leftist victories have made to the region. The chapter pays careful attention to the emergence of two ideal types on the left, one more radical and the other more moderate and contrasts them with the right. The review of the data shows that overall Latin American experiences varied a lot within these broad categories and it is hard to make strong claims for better performance in any of the three categories. Yet, in general, it does suggest that governments that pursued a more balanced approach, combining macroeconomic stability, social inclusion and a state role to support the market, offer more promise for the future.

Chapter Five moves away from considering partisan differences and focuses more specifically on the changes across the whole region during the "Golden Era" to consider the extent to which the enthusiasm rested on real, meaningful and durable changes. The chapter examines both the social realm and the economic realm to probe the nature of the shifts. Indicators of social inclusion, such as poverty and inequality, are very sensitive to the performance of the economy in general. As a result, the chapter explores a variety of ways to draw conclusions about the depth and sincerity of government efforts to promote equity and social and economic rights. On the economic side, the chapter reviews the good fortune produced by the commodity boom, but focuses on the lack of changes at the micro level to understand why Latin America's economic prospects after the boom did not improve. The chapter ends with a discussion of two exemplary industrial clusters to show how good state–private sector cooperation can enhance the possibility for development.

Finally Chapter Six opens by surveying the political scene in the wake of the end of the commodity boom. All across the region, democratic politics seems more fragile than it had even a few years before. The problems arise from below and from above in terms of growing citizen disenchantment as well as from politicians undermining the rules of democratic politics to entrench their own power. The problem lies in the inadequacy of the region's institutions for policy-making and political representation. The institutional problems in Latin America range from missing and/or weak institutions to institutions that on paper look like western ones, but do not function the same way. The end result is that institutions meant to improve representation, responsiveness, and accountability do not always serve those ends, and policies (neoliberal or otherwise) appear undemocratic. In the same vein, growth-supporting institutions (market or state) also function poorly, with significant consequences for development. Political economists have begun to pay more attention to institutions as key components of democratic development. But, to date, we still lack good explanations for institutional development and performance.

Notes

1 "América Latina después de la decada dorada." Available online at http://segib.org/america-latina-despues-de-la-era-dorada. Accessed August 1, 2017.

2 *Economist*, November 12, 2009.
3 "Chávez Calls Bush 'the Devil' in U.N. Speech," *New York Times*, September 20, 2006. Available online at http://www.nytimes.com/2006/09/20/world/america s/20cnd-chavez.html?mcubz=3. Accessed August 1, 2017.
4 Andrew Powell, "Rethinking Reforms: How Latin America and the Caribbean Can Escape Suppressed World Growth." Inter-American Development Bank, 2013 Latin American and Caribbean Macroeconomic Report. Washington DC. Available online at http://www20.iadb.org/intal/catalogo/PE/2013/11625en.pdf. Accessed August 1, 2017.
5 For example, see Jack Campbell, "How can Latin America overcome its dependence on commodities." *World Economic Forum*, May 8, 2015. Available online at http://www.weforum.org/agenda/2015/05/how-can-latin-america-over come-its-dependence-on-commodities. Accessed on August 1, 2017. Also, Diana Tussie and Pablo Heidrich, "A Tale of Ecumenicism and Diversity: Economic and Trade Policies of the New Left." In *Leftovers,* Jorge Castañeda and Marco A. Morales, eds. (New York: Routledge, 2008).
6 Daniela Campello, *The Politics of Market Discipline in Latin America: Globalization and Democracy* (New York: Cambridge University Press, 2015).
7 Alfredo Saad-Filho, "The Economic Context of Social Protests in 2013." In *Democratic Brazil Divided,* Peter Kingstone and Timothy J. Power, eds. (Pittsburgh: University of Pittsburgh Press, 2017).
8 Robin Broad, ed., *Global Backlash: Citizen Initiatives for a Just Local Economy* (New York: Roman and Littlefield, 2002).
9 Benjamin Kohl and Linda Farthing, *Impasse in Bolivia: Neoliberal Hegemony and Popular Resistance* (London: Zed Books, 2006).
10 Michael Reid, *The Forgotten Continent: The Battle for Latin America's Soul* (New Haven: Yale University Press, 2007): 141–142. The "Water War" is an intensely controversial event with sharply conflicting views and one has to be very careful parsing through the alternative sources on the subject.
11 For example, see Peter Hakim, "Is Washington Losing Latin America?" *Foreign Affairs*, January/February 2006.
12 This is highlighted by President Donald Trump's threat to use force to intervene in Venezuela's unrest and descent into authoritarianism under Chávez' successor, Nicolás Maduro. Trump's only other engagement with Latin America in his first year in office was his insistence on building a wall on the border and his persistent demand that Mexico should pay for it.
13 United States Trade and Industry Commission statistics, retrieved at http://www.trade.gov/mas/ian/tradestatistics/index.asp June 2010.
14 Francis Fukuyama, "The End of History?" *The National Interest*, Summer 1989.
15 Forrest D. Colburn, *Latin America at the End of Politics* (Princeton: Princeton University, 2002).
16 See the extended discussion of the disappearance of the left in Jorge Castañeda, *Utopia Unarmed: The Latin American Left after the Cold War* (New York: Vintage Books, 1993).
17 The role of the left as the leader of progressive change is a controversial one, explored in greater depth later in the book. The key argument that the rise of the left was the essential necessary force pushing social and economic inclusion is in Evelyne Huber and John D. Stephens, *Democracy and the Left: Social Policy and Inequality in Latin America* (Chicago: University of Chicago Press, 2012). For an alternative that gives more weight to electoral politics and the need to appeal to the informal sector poor, see Candelaria Garay, *Social Policy Expansion in Latin America* (New York: Cambridge University Press, 2016).
18 The term comes from Rudiger Dornbusch and Sebastian Edwards, eds., *The Macroeconomics of Populism in Latin America* (Chicago: University of

Chicago Press, 1991), a study that focused on leftist governments in Latin America that had emphasized distribution and redistribution while minimizing the risks of inflation.

19 For a study of the emergence of this new economic class, see Guy Standing, *The Precariat: The New Dangerous Class* (London: Bloomsbury Academic, 2014).

20 Even the advocates of market reform in Latin America did not want the state to disappear, only to become leaner and more efficient. See Javier Corrales, "Markets," in *Constructing Democratic Governance*, Jorge Dominguez and Michael Shifter, eds. (Baltimore: Johns Hopkins University Press, 2003).

21 See the account of neoliberalism's origins in David Harvey, *A Brief History of Neoliberalism* (New York: Oxford, 2005).

22 This very different account of the problems facing Latin America due to excessive state involvement can be found in Pedro Pablo Kuczyinski, *Latin America Debt* (Baltimore: Johns Hopkins University Press, 1988).

23 For example, John Williamson, "An Agenda for Restarting Growth and Reform." In *After the Washington Consensus: Restarting Growth and Reform in Latin America*, John Williamson and Pedro Pablo Kuczynski, eds. (Washington DC: Institute for International Economics, 2003).

24 Guillermo O'Donnell, "Human Rights, Human Development and Democracy." In *The Quality of Democracy: Theory and Applications* (Notre Dame: University of Notre Dame Press, 2004).

25 Roberto G. MacLean discusses the problem of law making in Latin America. He defines good laws as a "record of compromise" among varied interests in society. To record a compromise, laws have to identify the actors with a stake in an issue and assign rights and obligations in a manner that fairly reflects the balance of interests. Unfortunately, in Latin America laws are frequently copied from abroad regardless of their fit with local interests. Moreover, law making is compromised by limited transparency and accountability and low quality information. The result is laws that do not reflect society accurately and are subsequently ignored. Hon. Roberto G. MacLean, "The Social Efficiency of Laws as an Element of Political and Economic Development," *NAFTA: Business and Law Journal of the Americas* 4, no. 2, 1998.

26 Katharina Muller, "Contested Universalism: From Bonosol to Renta Dignidad in Bolivia," *International Journal of Social Welfare*, 18 (April 2009), 163–172.

27 Chloe S. Rinehart and James W. McGuire, "Obstacles to Takeup: Ecuador's Conditional Cash Transfer Program, The *Bono de Desarrollo Humano*," *World Development*, 97, 2017, 165–177.

28 For example, Robert Sherwood documents the perverse impact on technological innovation that stems from the weakness of intellectual property right protections. Firms are reluctant to invest in innovations when they cannot be sure that other firms will not steal them. The result is underinvestment and inefficient and costly ad hoc mechanisms to protect intellectual property. Robert M. Sherwood, "Intellectual Property for Latin America: How Soon Will it Work?" *NAFTA: Business and Law Journal of the Americas* 4, no. 2, 1998.

29 And in turn, these contrast with similarly small Costa Rica which has used its greater homogeneity, income and educational equality and political stability to push a development path based on foreign direct investment and local participation in eco-tourism and creating new "Silicon Valleys." See Luciano Ciravegna, *Promoting Silicon Valleys in Latin America* (Abingdon, Oxon: Routledge, 2011).

30 Nancy Birdsall and Miguel Székely, "Bootstraps, not Band-Aids: Poverty, Equity and Social Policy." In *After the Washington Consensus: Restarting Growth and Reform in Latin America*, John Williamson and Pedro Pablo Kuczynski, eds. (Washington DC: Institute for International Economics, 2003).

31 Renos Vakis, Jamele Rigolini and Leonardo Lucchetti, "Left Behind: Chronic Poverty in Latin America and the Caribbean" (Washington DC: World Bank Group, Latin American Development Forum, 2016).

32 Nora Lustig, "Poverty, Inequality and the New Left in Latin America," *Woodrow Wilson Center Update on the Americas,* October 2009.

33 Roberto da Matta, "Do You Know Who You're Talking To?!: The Distinction between Individual and Person in Brazil." In *Carnival, Rogues and Heroes: An Interpretation of the Brazilian Dilemma,* Roberto da Matta (Notre Dame: University of Notre Dame Press, 1991). In addition, see Guillermo O'Donnell's rejoinder "And Why Should I Give a Shit? Notes on Sociability and Politics in Argentina and Brazil." In *Counterpoints: Selected Essays on Authoritarianism and Democracy,* Guillermo O'Donnell (Notre Dame: University of Notre Dame Press, 1999) which further explores the nature of hierarchical social relations and compares among Argentina, Brazil, and the US. Another important addition to this discussion is Alberto Carlos Almeida's exploration of the persistence of hierarchical values in "Core Values, Education and Democracy: An Empirical Tour of DaMatta's Brazil." In *Democratic Brazil Revisited,* Peter Kingstone and Timothy Power, eds. (Pittsburgh: University of Pittsburgh Press, 2008).

34 Janice E. Perlman, *The Myth of Marginality: Urban Politics and Poverty in Rio de Janeiro* (Berkeley: University of California Press, 1980).

35 Amartya Sen, *Development as Freedom* (New York: Knopf, 1999).

36 Guillermo O'Donnell, "Human Rights, Human Development and Democracy." In *The Quality of Democracy: Theory and Applications* (Notre Dame: University of Notre Dame Press, 2004).

37 By disaggregating the term neoliberalism, I am however making a decision to eschew more radical critiques, such as of David Harvey, which see neoliberalism as one single capitalist project to reassert domination, whereas disaggregating the term opens the door to arguing that there are separate and separable political logics driving individual policies, upon which different segments of elites may well disagree and which may have quite different consequences as well.

38 Ryan E. Carlin, Matthew M. Singer and Elizabeth J. Zechmeister, *The Latin American Voter: Pursuing Representation and Accountability in Difficult Contexts* (Ann Arbor: University of Michigan Press, 2015).

39 Javier Santiso, *Latin America's Political Economy of the Possible: Beyond Good Revolutionaries and Free Marketeers* (Cambridge: MIT Press, 2006).

2 Import Substitution Industrialization and the Great Transformation in Latin America

The choice between market-led and state-led development is not new in Latin America. In fact, it dates back to the early 20th Century as Latin American societies and economies grew more complex. In that context, the simple commodity export model that had prevailed since colonial times appeared inadequate to meet the social and political goals of rising new classes. The state-led development process known as import substitution industrialization (ISI) emerged out of the political conflicts of that period. In turn, the character of the ISI model shaped the subsequent challenges facing Latin America, and the way Latin American nations responded to those challenges produced the turn to neoliberalism. In essence, the models of development pursued in the region have been consistently direct responses to the failures of the pre-existing models. As Kurt Weyland has noted, one consequence of this style of policy making is to exaggerate the defects of the previous model and overestimate the benefits of the new one.[1]

This chapter explores the antecedent politics and economic development leading up to the shift to neoliberalism. The central argument is that the ISI model was fundamentally flawed, but not as dysfunctional as its most ardent critics suggest. Import substitution industrialization led to a profound transformation of the region's economy, politics, and social structure. It was a period that witnessed rapid economic growth and the development of new technological capacity within a model that emphasized the expansion of internal markets. Along with that process of economic development, the urban population grew dramatically bringing with it new social policies that built social capital through increased access to education and health. The politics of the period was volatile. Few countries in Latin America remained democratic through the period. The 1960s to the 1980s witnessed an array of the most brutal dictatorships in the region's history, including in Argentina, Brazil, Chile, Peru and Uruguay among others. But the legacy of economic development, urban growth and social capital production is a civil society that today is more capable of demanding and defending democracy than at any time in the past.

Unfortunately, the positives of the ISI model are offset by some important limitations. A key one was that the model was too exclusionary. In many Latin American countries, the benefits of ISI were limited to a minority of the population. Even the most successful Latin American economies left vast segments of the population behind. Too often, the divide had racial or ethnic character – such as Afro-Brazilians or the indigenous in countries like Guatemala, Ecuador, Bolivia or Peru. In almost all countries, the divide grew between the growing urban population and the rural population. Brazilians frequently refer to their country as being characterized by "two Brazils" – one developed (or at least developing), with higher standards of living and better access to health, education, and social welfare (such as pensions) while the other lives with much lower standards of living and lacks health care, education and basic social services. Although it is a Brazilian expression, it is apt for most of Latin America as well. To a large extent, this gap between distinct "haves" and "have nots" is a function of ISI's limited capacity to create jobs and wealth for the whole of society.

An additional flaw of ISI is that it was not financially self-sustaining. In essence, ISI policies led to greater consumption of resources than the savings generated by the economy permitted. As a consequence, governments following ISI sought sources of financing in a variety of ways: exchange rate manipulation, printing money, and borrowing abroad for example. In the final analysis, the methods governments employed to finance economic development had a number of perverse consequences including debt, inflation, and frequently recurring balance of payments difficulties among other painful problems. Over time, the financial imbalances that ISI helped to produce weakened the capacity of Latin American states to govern the economy.[2] The cluster of problems surrounding ISI's financial concerns are the most direct cause of the rise of neoliberalism as a reaction.

The question we might ask is whether ISI's problems were inevitable. ISI's limitations were considerable and there is no question that countries had to make adjustments to its basic tenets. But, it is probably also true that the tendency to hew too strongly to one course (state-led, internal market emphasis over market-led export markets) overstated the weaknesses of the ISI program. As John Sheahan has noted, balanced programs were possible.[3] Sustainable economic policies need to balance policy elements and their economic effects. However, the politics of the period often made such balanced programs hard to sustain. The end result is that ISI tended to lend itself toward political choices that exacerbated the model's limitations. That tendency, unfortunately, recurred with neoliberalism and continues to pose a problem in some cases in the more recent shift to the left. Thus, ISI almost certainly needed significant adjustments. It is not clear, however, that it needed to be discarded. As in much of the process of development in Latin America, the story is as much political as economic.

In the Beginning

Latin America's economic development, beginning in colonial times, was governed by mercantilist principles. In other words, economic activity was organized by and for the Crown, with the explicit permission of the Crown, and built around the extraction and export of natural resources. There were variations in the colonial experience. For example, the Portuguese Crown maintained looser control of Brazil than the Spanish Crown did of the rest of Spanish America. The administration of the Spanish Crown itself changed under the liberal reforms of the Bourbon dynasty beginning in the late 18th Century.[4] Nevertheless, despite the variations in administrative control, the central economic activity remained natural resource extraction and plantation agriculture. The central administration remained limited in its promotion and guidance of economic activity. Manufacturing did not emerge to any meaningful degree anywhere in the region due both to colonial policy and to the absence of any real incentive to invest in it. Land tenure was highly concentrated and inaccessible to most colonists. Labor was cheap – in many cases virtually slave labor through the *encomienda* system.[5] The extraordinarily unequal distribution of wealth and land, the very small size of the consumer classes, and the very low wages of rural workers meant that there really was no internal market that might encourage investment in manufacturing.

Independence produced considerable turmoil, but ultimately did not result in significant changes in the basic structure of production in Latin American economies.[6] The wars of independence from the 1810s into the 1820s were exceptionally disruptive in Spanish America, causing ample loss of life, destruction of physical capital, and provoking capital flight as loyalists fled back to Spain. The period following the wars of independence was one in which landowners sought to consolidate and protect their land holdings in the face of continuing violent conflicts and regime instability. In most Latin American nations, successive warlords competed for control of the country, rarely holding on to power for any significant amount of time. The region stagnated economically throughout this period.

Change came for most Latin American countries in the latter half of the 19th Century as landowners teamed with strongmen to establish firm political control and to reinsert their economies into international markets. Newly established "liberal" republics featured political parties, elections and the basic constitutional features of US style presidentialism, although in practice they were "republics" only in name. The landowning class and the regimes that represented their interests invited foreign investment into their countries to rebuild the infrastructure necessary for the export of natural resources. That included railroads and other areas of transport, telegraph (and later telephone) lines, port facilities, and eventually critical utilities like electricity. Foreign corporations were invited in to invest in critical extractive sectors where domestic capacity did not exist. That included oil in places like Venezuela, silver in Mexico, copper in Chile, or guano in Peru.

Fernando Henrique Cardoso and Enzo Faletto identified two variations in the pattern of foreign investment in Latin America: enclave and nationally controlled economies.[7] In the latter, domestic elites maintained control of the national economy and the insertion of the domestic economy into international markets turned on cooperative interaction between foreign and domestic capital. For example, Argentina's cattle ranching or Brazil's coffee production remained in domestic hands while depending on foreign investment in keys areas such as transportation. In such cases, small internal markets did develop because domestic control of production contributed to the growth of small urban middle and working classes. By contrast, enclave economies represented areas of foreign investment in the central sectors of the economy that were largely divorced from the rest of the economy and society and were almost completely controlled and regulated by the foreign companies themselves. In enclaves, as in Central American agriculture, Mexican silver or Chilean copper, foreign owners paid rents that benefited governing elites, but had almost no benefits for the larger population. For Cardoso and Faletto, these two different types of economies had consequences for later development, but in neither case did a strong incentive to develop manufacturing exist. In both forms of post-colonial economic development, internal markets remained small and domestic savings remained inadequate to finance investment – private or state.

As a result, manufacturing remained a limited activity and state involvement in the economy continued to be restricted to the most basic functions, such as issuing currency, or coercively maintaining control over labor.[8] The lack of manufacturing did not represent a limit on national wealth in the 19th Century. It did, however, undermine the possibility of more significant economic development into the late 19th and 20th Centuries. In fact, data on per capita growth rates comparing Latin America and other regions of the world shows only a small gap between Latin America and the West into the early 20th Century. Between 1870 and the onset of the Great Depression, Latin America enjoyed rapid growth rates and increases in per capita GDP, based almost exclusively on the export of natural resources.[9]

But, manufacturing matters for a number of reasons. First and perhaps foremost is the problem of the terms of trade.[10] Classical economics arguments for free trade state that aggregate welfare improves if countries follow their comparative advantage and produce what they can produce most efficiently and trade for the rest. A typical example used in economics textbooks is English wool and Portuguese wine. Even if England can produce both more efficiently than Portugal, both countries are better off if England produces wool (its comparative advantage) and Portugal produces wine (where its comparative advantage lies) and the two trade with each other. The problem is that that is a relatively equal trade, but as economies become more sophisticated, those producing cars or consumer electronics enjoy significant advantages over producers of commodities. For example, Portugal does not need to sell much wine to purchase a comparable amount of wool. Yet, it takes a vast amount of coffee to purchase a single car. The ratio of prices is inherently uneven. Commodity prices are highly volatile, and in periods of high demand exporters may obtain high prices for their goods, improving the *relative* terms of trade. But, even sizable increases in commodity exports lead to relative declines in national wealth over time if one country is exporting coffee and buying cars. Thus, the terms of trade mean that those countries that continue to export primary products will fall farther and farther behind as their trade partners become more and more industrialized.

In addition to relative decline due to unfavorable terms of trade, manufacturing is also important in that it tends to lead to higher value added and higher productivity labor and, as a result, higher wages. Manufacturing also tends to spin off many more opportunities for investment in the domestic economy than agriculture (linkages). Over time, manufacturing lends itself to the development of large internal markets, greater production and diffusion of wealth, and larger domestic savings. In addition, the development of manufacturing drives the growth of key social classes for the development of democracy, namely the middle and working classes.[11] That does not mean that agriculture is not important or that natural resource exports cannot contribute to the production of wealth. It does however make it harder to generate and sustain economic and political development over the longer term. Argentina in the 1920s was one of the richest nations in the world largely on the back of beef and grain exports. By the mid 20th Century, it had fallen far behind.

As of the late 19th Century, Latin American elites had little incentive to develop manufacturing and little incentive to expand the state's role beyond its minimal functions. Landowners made handsome returns on the export of their agricultural goods. Foreign enterprises operating in sectors like mining generated resentment, but they also paid rents that filled government coffers and economically benefited elites both directly and indirectly. Similarly, governments earned revenues from taxes on trade. There was no defined political constituency calling for an industrialization program, and as sham republics, there was no political responsiveness to anyone but the agricultural elite anyway. Considering that in its early phases manufacturing would require aggressive state support to succeed against the much more competitive established producers in the West, industrialization was not feasible politically. Consequently, Latin American economies boomed, but with little change in the basic economic or political structure of the countries.

The Social Question and Latin American Change

Yet, the rapid economic growth of the late 19th Century and early 20th Century provoked social changes that proved increasingly incompatible with the political economy of the post-independence liberal republics. The economic boom triggered a wave of immigration, principally from Europe but from the Middle East and Asia as well. The population of the region grew substantially, with the most notable changes in the acceleration of urban growth and the emergence of larger urban middle and working classes.[12] Although not entirely typical for the region as a whole, Argentina's development illustrates the breadth of the changes taking place as a result of the insertion into the international economy.

Argentina's economy exploded towards the end of the 19th Century. Grain production increased 1,600% between 1860 and 1914, while exports increased 2,000% in the same period. The quantity of land under cultivation grew from 1.5 million hectares in 1872 to 25 million by 1914. Herd stocks grew by 50% between 1890 and 1920. Foreign investment poured into the country to develop the infrastructure for exports. For example, there were 6,500 kilometers of track laid in the country in 1889. By 1914, there were 31,500 kilometers. Capital formation grew by 5% per year over the 1870 to 1914 period while productivity increased 5% per year as well. Income grew by 150% between 1890 and 1920.

Socially, the country changed as well. With immigration running at roughly 200 thousand immigrants arriving per year beginning in the 1880s, Argentina had more than 3 million new permanent residents by 1914. The population of the capitol, Buenos Aires, grew 786% between 1870 and 1914. The percentage of white-collar workers grew from 6% of the city's population to 21% while the middle class swelled to 600 thousand people by 1914. The diverse middle class included doctors, lawyers, government bureaucrats, teachers, professors, insurance and banking, export-import commerce, small-scale manufacturing, as well as small-scale commerce including restaurants and shops. Blue-collar workers were concentrated in vital areas connected to the export of beef, especially ports, processing and refrigeration, and the railways. In short, Argentina was a very different place in 1914 than it was in 1880 as a cattle-rancher dominated, commodity exporting, sham republic.[13] Argentina's changes were on the high end of the scale. But, changes of this nature were emerging all throughout the region.

Not surprisingly, the social changes provoked political tensions as the newly emerging social classes pressed for political inclusion and for alternative economic policies that better matched their preferences.[14] For members of the rising middle class, a minimal state that oversaw a commodity export based economy did not provide adequate opportunities for employment and investment (especially given the very low level of domestic savings and the commitment to low tariffs on manufactured goods). For the rising working class, the state's coercive behavior in the interest of exporters and foreign investors did little to "incorporate" workers into the model of political economy prevailing in the period. The opposition to the republics expressed itself both in new political movements and parties challenging the largely sham elections of the time and in growing mobilizations of workers demanding political and economic rights. The early 20th Century witnessed growing challenges to the established order across the region.

Political conflicts, at times violent, began to emerge as both the middle class and workers demanded greater inclusion in the political system and workers mobilized for the right to unionize and to demand better working conditions. It was not until the onset of the Great Depression, however, that the basic model of political economy began to change decisively. The new economic model that emerged out of the uncertainty and disorder of the Great Depression was called "import substitution industrialization."

Import Substitution Industrialization

The Background – Depression and War

Until the Great Depression, Latin American economies functioned reasonably well on the back of a liberal trading regime in which Latin America exported commodities and imported manufactured goods. Latin American GDP growth rates averaged between 3% and 4% between 1900 and 1929, driven largely by the expansion of land and labor involved in natural resource exploitation.[15] Dependence on commodity exports – often a single commodity – was a defining characteristic of the period. For example, coffee accounted for 92% of all exports from El Salvador as late as 1938, while petroleum accounted for the same percentage from Venezuela. Even larger, more diversified economies suffered from commodity export dependence. For example, Brazil's coffee sales accounted for 45% of all exports.[16] When the stock market crashed in 1929, triggering the Great Depression, demand for commodities fell as consumption and investment in the developed world declined precipitously. As a consequence, prices for natural resources fell and along with them, government revenues from export and import taxes and profits for the land-based elites of Latin America. For example, sugar prices fell from 22.5 cents in 1920 to 1.5 cents by 1930 while coffee prices fell by 40% from 1929 to 1930.[17] Collapsing government revenues and profits for elites altered the politics of the period and undermined the support for preserving the export based, liberal trading model. Throughout the region, oligarchs sought relief for the first time from the state while the newly emergent middle and working classes saw new opportunities for mobilization.

The largest economies in the region witnessed an emergent political alliance that linked urban middle classes with the working class behind a state-led industrializing project. For the middle classes, the new project opened the doors to political power and the chance to reshape economic policy in favor of national development. These new middle class led parties constructed coalitions with workers, primarily employed in industries owned by foreign enterprises, through a mixture of what David Collier and Ruth Berins Collier refer to as *inducements* and *constraints*.[18] The inducements included rights to organize, state-subsidies for unions, the right to collectively bargain and strike as well as the beginning of welfare benefits such as pensions. Constraints included the right of the state to intervene in unions, including control of union funds and replacement of union leadership, as well as state controls over wage bargaining and strike activity. The Colliers refer to this period as "the incorporation" of the working class, and observe that the pattern of inducements and constraints varied across the region depending on the balance of power among the various social classes. In some cases, such as Argentina, both a very powerful working class and landed elites led to greater reliance on inducements, while the very weak working class in Brazil led to fewer inducements and much greater constraints on labor autonomy.

These incorporation movements represent some of the most familiar and important moments in modern Latin America. In Mexico, Lazaro Cardenas' reform efforts were crucial to the institutionalization of the 1910 Revolution. His efforts to mobilize workers and peasants and link them formally to the governing party was the key to decades of political and economic stability in Mexico. Getulio Vargas' *Estado Nôvo* produced the crucial and permanent shift from a coffee and sugar dominated export economy to the largest industrial economy in the developing world. Juan Peron's populist connection to the working class and to small domestic industries set the stage in Argentina for decades of struggle between an urban, industrializing alliance and the powerful, export dependent cattle ranchers. Other notable incorporation periods include Jorge Battle in Uruguay, the rise of the Acción Democratica and the Punto Fijo Pact in Venezuela, or the reform efforts of Juan José Arevalo and Jacobo Arbenz Guzman in Guatemala. For the Colliers, incorporation turned on the terms of the political pacts between nationalist, middle class political parties and organized workers. In economic terms, however, the key to these new alliances was ISI and the changes it provoked in the domestic political economy.

The Domestic Economic Response

Import substitution industrialization (ISI) was a logical – and often ad hoc – response to the combination of collapsing demand and prices for Latin American commodities and the disruption of the supply of manufactured goods (especially with the onset of World War II and the diversion of production into war time manufacturing). The severe shock from the international economy forced Latin American governments to look inward for sources of economic growth. With Latin American landed elites clamoring for price supports – minimum prices paid by government to guarantee profits for producers – governments in the region became involved in the economy in a way and to an extent few had been before. But disruptions to supply (and limited foreign exchange due to declining exports) meant that Latin American governments also had to help find new sources of supply of manufactured goods for domestic consumers.

The answer for policy makers was to subsidize local production of those goods that had been previously imported – therefore "import substitution industrialization." The central strategy was for policy makers to identify items that consumers were importing and support the initiation of local, domestic manufacturing to take the place of the imports. A benefit of this strategy is that it overcomes one of the most important weaknesses of state involvement in the economy. One of the great strengths of markets is that they efficiently determine demand for goods and services in an economy and create powerful incentives for investing in those areas and not others and at the right level to meet, but not exceed, existing demand. By contrast, state officials cannot efficiently determine *a priori* the level of demand for goods in a society and therefore the best sectors in which to invest.[19] The danger of state officials directing investment decisions is that they may choose sectors in which there is little or no demand and the resulting supply may be inappropriate (too little or too much). ISI avoided this risk by having state officials examine the import list to see what the existing demand actually was and then directing investment into those sectors for which there was already existing and known demand.

An additional challenge facing state officials was the competitive weaknesses of local producers. The disruption in the international economy opened a window of opportunity for investment in manufacturing. But, international competitors had inherent competitive advantages that were a threat to new, domestic producers once the global economy stabilized. Foreign firms benefited from longer experience producing the newly substituted goods, including greater access to technology, better production techniques, and greater economies of scale. The fact that foreign firms sold their goods on competitive global markets was a reflection of the substantially greater quality and lower price of their products. Given the choice to buy a low quality, high-priced locally made product or a high quality, cheaper foreign product, consumers invariably opt for the latter. Consequently, domestic capitalists needed inducements and protection to take on investments and production in areas where they had little to no comparative advantage and limited capacity to become competitive with large-scale global exporters.

A final challenge facing state officials seeking to promote domestic production is that many of the basic inputs required for industrial production were beyond the capacity of domestic producers, even with protection and inducements. Utilities like telephones or electricity required very large-scale investments, as did many mining sectors or petroleum extraction. Products like steel required extensive investments and stable, guaranteed markets to turn a profit. Domestic producers were not able or willing to undertake these investments, even with government inducements and support. In these cases, only foreign firms had the necessary technology, access to capital, and certainty of markets worldwide. Yet, the strong nationalist sentiment of the period militated against continued reliance on foreign firms. As a result, the state itself became a major investor and producer – in many instances opening new sectors to state production (such as the development of a steel industry at Volta Redonda in Brazil) or alternatively nationalizing existing foreign owned firms (perhaps the most famous instance of which is Mexico's nationalization of the oil industry and the creation of PEMEX).

The challenges facing decision makers pursuing inward-looking industrialization led to the reliance on a specific set of key policy instruments: protection for domestic industry, through both tariff and non-tariff barriers; state subsidies for domestic investors, particularly cheap and ready financing; state owned enterprises (SOEs) in both newly nationalized sectors and new areas of investment; limits on participation of foreign firms in the domestic economy; and manipulation of the exchange rate to help finance urban, industrial development.

Protecting Domestic Industry: The new sectors of domestic production suffered considerable disadvantages in the face of foreign producers. In essence, these new domestic firms were "infant industries" – industries at the earliest stage of development and therefore requiring protection and promotion. Most importantly, established foreign producers had extensive distribution networks and were able to produce with large economies of scale (i.e. large enough volume to amortize the fixed costs of production and thereby keep the price of their goods low). These firms benefited from their technological know-how and their access to capital. Given those advantages, domestic producers needed protection if they were to grow and succeed. Beginning in the 1950s and 1960s, Latin American governments recognized the need to invite multinational corporations (MNCs) back into their countries to promote investment in more capital-intensive sectors. Despite their global scale and competitiveness, protection was also offered to MNCs as inducements to invest in the domestic economy.

The most prevalent form of protection was through the use of high tariffs on imported goods, making them prohibitively expensive. For example, the average nominal rate of protection for durable consumer goods in Brazil in 1960 was 328%. Brazil represented the high end of protection, but average nominal rates of protection for other import substitution industrializers ranged from a low of 24% for Uruguay to 266% for Argentina. By contrast, the average rate of protection on consumer durables for the European Community at the time was 19%. Even the raw inputs of industrial production were protected. The average nominal rate of protection of industrial raw materials for Brazil in 1960 was 106%, while by contrast it was only 1% for the European Community. Across all product categories (nondurable consumer goods, durable consumer goods, semi-manufactured goods, industrial raw materials, and capital goods), average nominal protection for Brazil was 168% at the high end and 21% at the low end. By contrast, the average rate for the European Community was 13%.[20] The effective rate – the real level of protection once the tariffs on all inputs are included – was considerably higher. For example, the effective rate of protection on fertilizers and insecticides in Mexico in 1970 was over 600%.[21]

In addition to tariff walls, state officials used non-tariff barriers to promote and protect investments. One of the most powerful non-tariff barriers was to create a market-reserve – in effect a complete prohibition on imports. Brazil again represents the extreme end of protection. For example, Brazilian government officials believed that establishing a domestic computer industry was a development and strategic priority and that the only way to do it was to completely reserve the market for a domestic producer. Other non-tariff barriers included restrictions on foreign participation in mineral extraction or bidding on state contracts, such as for construction. In both cases, the barrier to investment and/or imports was intended as an inducement to domestic investors and protection against typically more established, competitive firms.

State Subsidies for Domestic Production: Protection, however, was not sufficient to spur industrialization. As noted above, most Latin American countries had little to no industrial investment to begin with. Even those that did, such as Argentina and Brazil, had only very small scale, low technology production and not much of that. Furthermore, Latin American countries lacked financial markets or pools of domestic savings to tap into to finance industrial investment. Thus, to a large extent, promoting industrial investment required creating an industrialist class and that meant providing access to capital necessary for investment.

The most direct form of subsidy consisted of loans, often provided at highly discounted rates (at one point, the Brazilian government offered loans at interest rates below the rate of inflation – effectively *free* money). Several Latin American countries established state banks and/or development banks to channel these loans into targeted sectors. Chile's CORFO (the Corporación de Fomento de la Producción – Corporation for the Promotion of Production) or Brazil's BNDES (Banco Nacional de Desenvolvimento Econômico e Social – National Economic and Social Development Bank) played leading roles in determining key sectors necessary for economic development and providing the financing to support them.[22] State officials also used tax incentives to encourage and support key areas of investment.[23]

Exchange Rate Manipulation: Another crucial policy tool available to state officials was manipulation of the exchange rate to support industrialization. In a free market economy, the exchange rate floats freely, reflecting the actual market demand for currency. Fluctuations in the exchange rate affect the competitiveness of exports (higher valued currency makes exports more expensive as more foreign currency is required to purchase the goods), as well as the cost of imports (higher valued currency makes imported goods cheaper as less domestic currency is required to buy foreign goods). In a poor, heavily rural, commodity export dependent economy, a weaker currency is a boon to exports and economic growth.

But, state officials wanted to encourage industrial development, which ironically depended heavily on continued (and in fact, at least initially, increasing) imports of manufactured goods – principally the capital and intermediate goods necessary to produce the consumer durables which were the first stage of substitution.

The solution was to artificially maintain fixed exchange rates that kept the domestic currency strong relative to foreign currencies. The artificially strong currency made industrial imports relatively cheaper to import and therefore constituted another form of financial subsidy to domestic industrial producers. In many countries, state officials further controlled foreign exchange through import licensing requirements. In these cases, importers could not bring in foreign goods without explicit permission from state officials. State officials freed up scarce foreign capital only for imported goods that were necessary for industrial development and were not available locally. Thus, control of exchange rates was also an important tool of industrial policy.

State Owned Enterprises: The final critical element of the import substitution tool basket was the creation of a large number of state owned enterprises. State owned enterprises emerged for several reasons and served several different purposes. The most important reason for state officials to support their creation was to fill a need in the market place that could not be met through private, domestic investors. Public utilities such as telecommunications or electricity were vital for industrial development, but required very large-scale investments. The only private investors capable of the necessary investment were foreign firms, but the strong nationalist sentiment of the period prevented state officials from allowing multinational corporations to operate in these key sectors (or in the many cases of nationalization, continuing to operate in these sectors). Sectors such as oil, gas, water, transportation or sewers all came under state ownership. In addition, many Latin American countries designated mineral resources as strategic assets of the nation and therefore closed to foreign investment. But, private domestic investors rarely had the resources to invest. As a result, mining also came under state ownership in many countries.

Regardless of the original reasons for the creation of SOEs, they came to play important roles in most Latin American economies, both as instruments of industrial policy and to some extent social policy. SOEs were critical to industrial development through their provision of the infrastructure necessary for industrialization and ultimately as suppliers of vital inputs to industry. For example, in several Latin American countries, SOEs entered into sectors such as steel, iron, petrochemicals, or aluminum. SOEs were able to supply inputs at subsidized prices to domestic industrialists. In addition, SOEs became important consumers of domestic production. So, for example, domestic producers of small-scale products like glass, plastic, ball-bearings, or later in the period machine tools and capital equipment, found large, stable, rich buyers among the country's

SOEs. SOEs also served the country's larger social goals as providers of employment to large numbers of workers. As public agencies, rather than for profit private firms, state officials could use SOEs to hire tens of thousands of workers without efficiency or competitiveness considerations, pay them higher scale salaries than their productivity warranted, and offer generous benefits. SOEs became central tools in state officials' efforts to manage unemployment and distribute wealth in society.

The Economic Rationale

While many of the policies of ISI emerged initially as ad hoc responses to the disruptions of the Great Depression and World War II, leading economists and policy-makers eventually developed a theoretical framework justifying ISI as a model of development. The most important figure in this intellectual endeavor was Raúl Prebisch, an Argentine economist who came to head the United Nations Economic Commission on Latin America and the Caribbean (ECLAC – or more commonly known by its Spanish Acronym, CEPAL – Comisión Economica para America Latina).

CEPAL and Raúl Prebisch

Prebisch's economic theories grew out of his experiences in Argentina during the Great Depression. Most importantly, he noted the dramatic impact that falling commodity prices had on the economy and their impact on the ability of the Argentine government to service foreign debt in the context of falling export revenues. Looking further afield, it became clear to Prebisch that commodity export growth was simply inadequate to develop Latin American economies. One important consideration was that Latin American countries were characterized by large pools of surplus labor that kept wages low regardless of the growth of agricultural exports. The tiny land-owning elite could maintain its individual wealth, but not spur the development of the local economy. Low wages and inadequate employment meant that the population accumulated little wealth. This in turn translated into inadequate domestic savings to finance investment and no real internal market to generate incentives to invest in production for the local market. The problem for Prebisch was that the world was divided into two: rich, developed countries in the *center* that produced manufactured goods, and poor developing countries in the *periphery* that were trapped as low wage, commodity producers. The key was to break the cycle of poverty by using the power of the state to develop a domestic industry through import substitution industrialization. Prebisch published his new theory of development, *The Economic Development of Latin America and its Principal Problem*, in 1949 – one year after the establishment of CEPAL.[24] What began as ad hoc policy responses to crisis then gelled into a well-developed theoretical framework supporting and encouraging the model.

The logic of import substitution industrialization was further developed over the years after 1949 by a growing number of economists who rejected neoclassical arguments about comparative advantage. Albert Hirschman, one of the leading economic historians of the period, argued that industrialization played a crucial role in development by encouraging *backwards* and *forward* linkages.[25] Linkages represented the areas of production that grew up in response to existing producers, both backwards and up the production chain. For example, auto producers have powerful linkage effects backwards and forwards. Auto producers encourage investments in the many parts suppliers, machines and equipment needed to produce cars. In turn, auto producers spur the opening of businesses like car dealers, mechanics, or gas stations, not to mention road construction. Each of these businesses in turn creates incentives to supply the materials necessary for their functioning. Thus, a state policy to support a particular industry has substantial multiplier effects as private investors respond to new markets. Of course, along with all this investment comes employment and newly employed workers earning better and better wages (an auto worker earns considerably more than a peasant picking coffee) constitute an important new domestic market of consumers. In short, Prebisch and those he influenced saw state leadership in fostering industry as the key mechanism for breaking the cycle of poverty in the region. A coherent, well-thought out and well-supported argument lay behind the strategy of state-led economic development.

Too Rich to Prosper

State-led, inward looking industrialization may have also been the only real industrialization option available in Latin America. The inward-looking model of industrialization is often contrasted – and usually unfavorably – with outward-looking export-oriented industrialization. The most successful East Asian economies (South Korean, Taiwan and Japan for example) were often held up as followers of this model. Under export-oriented industrialization, domestic producers enjoyed state support and incentives but were pressured to export to global markets instead. Exports meant that local producers had to become efficient and competitive. The logic behind this industrialization strategy was that firms would identify niches where they could compete in global markets and then use their success to continuously invest in improvements in competitiveness and eventually move into new sectors.

In an important article, however, James Mahon argued that that strategy was unavailable in Latin America.[26] Owing to the region's earlier experiments with democracy, workers had gained the rights to organize and collectively bargain long before their counterparts in East Asia. One consequence was that wage rates were considerably higher in Latin America than they were in East Asia. High wages made industrial production uncompetitive in Latin America and therefore closed off the export-oriented strategy. In addition, the disruption of trade and the development of domestic industrialists with economic and political clout made a shift to export orientation (and the devaluation necessary to do so) politically unpalatable. As Mahon observes, Latin America was simply too rich to follow what turned out to be a more effective strategy for economic development.

The Political Logic

Mahon's observation about labor costs and domestic industrialists' gains points to the need to understand ISI not only as an economic model, but a political one too. As noted earlier, ISI was introduced as a strategy in a period of great political instability. The sham republics of the commodity export period gave way to a rising urban coalition with a desire to participate in politics and a different set of economic preferences. ISI became established economically in no small measure because it turned out to be good politics as well.

For the rising urban, middle class, ISI turned out to be an extraordinary boon. At the most obvious level, the state's investment in and promotion of industry helped to produce new classes of industrialists out of the urban middle classes. In turn, urban, industrial growth increased the opportunities for a wide variety of middle class occupations: from urban professionals such as doctors, lawyers, teachers, professors, or journalists to urban businesses like banking, insurance or commerce (such as shop owners). Even more importantly, the rise of ISI led to an extraordinary increase in the size of the state.[27] State involvement in the control of tariffs and financing, SOEs, regulation of labor, or planning, development or regulation of the economy meant huge increases in employment opportunities at good wages and good benefits for the middle class.[28]

Similarly, the working class benefited as well. Promoting industrialization led to sharp increases in the number of industrial workers and the employment opportunities for rural migrants into the cities. Protection of domestic industry meant that employers could provide high wages and stronger benefit packages than the wealth of the economy really supported. While labor regulation imposed controls on union activity, state support also created new opportunities for bargaining and leveraging higher wages and benefits than before ISI.[29]

The groups that did not explicitly benefit from ISI were the land-owning elite and the peasants that continued to work on their land. The emphasis on urban, industrial growth forced landed elites to purchase lower quality, higher cost domestic goods where before they had been able to import manufactured goods. Furthermore, the state directed its resources into urban development and neglected development of the rural sector. Finally, manipulation of the exchange rate hurt domestic landed elites' profits and acted as a kind of indirect tax to support urban industrialists. In some cases, the landed elites tolerated the new policy as long as their political control of the countryside was left alone. Such was the case, for example, in Brazil or Colombia. In some cases, landed elites were pushed off the land, as was the case in Bolivia in the 1952 revolution or under the Peruvian military dictatorship beginning in 1968. In some cases, landed elites fought against the policy change. For example, Argentina became locked into a destructive cycle of wild policy swings from favoring domestic, industrial producers to favoring commodity exports. The instability of economic policy in Argentina is at least partially responsible for the country's dramatic decline from one of the richest nations in the world in the 1920s. Finally, in some countries – principally in Central America, but including Bolivia and Paraguay – ISI either did not take off or did so later in the face of entrenched landed elite power. Countries like Guatemala, Honduras or El Salvador continued to rely heavily on commodity exports controlled by a small number of families and with limited industrial development well into the ISI period.

For the peasants working the land, little changed in most countries in the region. Rural poverty remained (and arguably remains to this day) the scourge of the region. In a few instances, ISI oriented, nationalist governments sought to organize the rural working class and improve their conditions, particularly through land reforms. Generally, these initiatives achieved little in the ISI period. Chilean and Brazilian working class efforts to organize the rural working class helped bring on military coups in 1973 and 1964 respectively. Mexico's land reforms of the 1930s helped consolidate the nationalist, ISI regime, but had limited scope in the rural sector and did little ultimately to prevent deepening rural poverty. Venezuela's nationalist, leftist party, the Acción Democrática, backed off rural organizing as part of its moderation in the context of stabilizing democratic politics through the 1958 Pact of Punto Fijo – the power sharing agreement among the leading parties of the country that consolidated democratic rule until the recent rise of Hugo Chávez.

ISI then was not a political or economic panacea for the region and it did not lead to a stable political equilibrium. In this, it stands in sharp contrast with Western Europe where the tensions that arose out of the "social question" were resolved in favor of stable capitalist democracies. Nevertheless, ISI fueled the growth of the urban middle and working classes – the two social classes most commonly associated with the demand for democracy.[30] Those Latin American countries that did not pursue ISI vigorously did not experience as much change as the larger ones, though the winds of political reform did reach them. Even places like Bolivia or Guatemala experienced political changes associated with slowly emergent middle and working classes. Manufacturing growth tended to come at different periods. Manufacturing growth averaged around 5.5% per year from 1945–1972 and around 4.5% per year for 1972–1981. Many of the larger countries saw rapid expansion in the earlier period, but not in the 1970s. For example, Chilean manufacturing expanded 6.1% from 1929–1945 and then again 5.2% from 1945–1972, but then shrank to 0.4% in the 1970s. Peruvian manufacturing grew 7.3% from 1945–1972, but only 2.1% from 1972–1981. By contrast, Bolivia and Paraguay experienced limited growth from 1945–1972 (3.2% and 3.9% respectively), but expanded substantially in the 1970s (9.3% and 10% respectively).[31] Thus, the time periods differed but eventually the embrace of ISI virtually everywhere led to a dramatic transformation of the region.

The Great Transformation

As noted earlier, there is a tendency in policy makers and politicians to discount the past. Reformers are inclined psychologically to dismiss all previous efforts as failures (while simultaneously overestimating the potential of the new policies).[32] To some extent, this has occurred with import substitution industrialization as well. The shift to neoliberalism in the region occurred in the context of severe economic problems and in that context it was easy to argue that ISI was simply a failure. ISI did run into severe problems by the late 1970s and into the 1980s. Between the 1930s and 1980, however, Latin America underwent a profound transformation.

One of the most vigorous reminders of that success comes from Albert Hirschman, one of the leading economic historians of Latin America.[33] While eschewing the role of "prophet" for the ISI period, Hirschman provides ample evidence of the great successes from 1945–1980 – a period he compares to the period of exceptional performance in France that the French themselves refer to as "les trentes glorieuses" (the thirty glorious years). Over the ISI time period, GDP grew at an annual average rate of 5.5% leading to a quintupling of GDP for the region between 1950 and 1980. Per capita GDP more than doubled in the region while the total population grew at an annualized rate of about 2.7%. In 1950, the population of Latin America stood at 155 million people with an average life expectancy in the low fifties and per capita income (on an annualized basis in 1970 dollars) of only $420. By 1980, life expectancy had risen to the mid sixties and per capita income across a population of nearly 400 million people had risen to close to $1,000 (again on an annualized basis in 1970 dollars).

Moreover, the structure of society had changed as well. In 1950, the largest economies of the region, such as Brazil or Mexico, were still predominantly rural – roughly 60%. By 1980, the urban population of the larger economies was roughly 70%. Along with the dramatic growth of the urban population came significant improvements on a number of indicators, including school enrollments, access to and improvements in health care, and access to clean water and sanitation.[34]

The transformation of the region was not limited to good news however. Perhaps the most visible negative side of the ISI changes was the substantial and visible growth of urban poverty. Poverty existed in the countryside before ISI and continued to be severe in much of Latin America as of 1980. But, rural poverty coupled with urban growth triggered a large-scale migration of workers into the cities in search of employment beginning in the 1950s and into the 1980s. Unfortunately, the ISI model could not generate enough jobs to satisfy the rapidly growing demand. Urban unemployment and underemployment led to the swelling of shantytowns and a dramatic surge in the size of the informal sector. Shantytowns and informal sector employment were the most visible manifestations of what was essentially a second, under-privileged society growing up in parallel to the formal, legal world of business and employment. Shantytowns, unlike formal neighborhoods, lacked access to water and sanitation. Residents lacked legal title to the homes and land on which they resided, depriving them of the means to use their assets to leverage capital. They lacked access to any other forms of financing as well, relegating them to a virtually inescapable life of poverty. They lacked access to electricity or good public transportation. Moreover, informal sector workers suffered from limited or no access to healthcare. Nor did they receive pensions or any other form of protection from disability. As a result, informal sector employment meant you worked until you died. Shantytowns lacked schools, meaning again that poverty and the informality trap was inter-generational. For many residents of the formal world, these shantytowns housed "marginals" – the unwanted, marginalized people outside of society. By contrast, Janice Perlman argued forcefully that "marginalization" was a myth that glossed over the ways in which formal society depended on the labor of "marginals" to maintain their lifestyle and their wealth. In short, the benefits of the ISI formal society were constructed on the backs of those who had been left out, but whose cheap labor was necessary to maintain the system.[35] Brazilians acknowledged this separation by referring to the "two Brazils" or "BelIndia."

The profound social injustice revealed in the cities by urban poverty and informal employment also pointed to the limitations of the state. The ISI model led to profound changes and impressive achievements. But, the formal economy and the state were not capable of keeping pace with the demands and needs of society. Basic needs like electricity, water, sanitation, healthcare, or schooling were highly unequally distributed. By 1980, it was apparent that the state was simply unable to invest adequately in these critical services and sheltered, inefficient industry was incapable of generating enough employment to absorb the inflow of migrants from the countryside. To some extent, this was a function of the ISI model itself. But, it also reflected political choices about how to overcome obstacles to economic development that ultimately proved destructive to Latin America's political economy.

The Debt Crisis and the Beginning of the End

ISI's shortcomings began manifesting themselves quite early. Already by the 1940s, policy makers confronted problems that arose directly from the economic model. These problems had policy solutions – ISI was not inherently destined to fail. But, virtually all the policy solutions entailed difficult political choices. The regimes that came into power in the wake of the Great Depression generally lacked the strength and legitimacy from key constituents to make those difficult choices. Smaller economies confronted the problems earlier, generally, than the larger ones. Thus, Brazil and Mexico were able to manage the inherent conflicts and challenges of ISI longer than Chile for example. But, ultimately, all countries industrializing on the basis of import substitution ran into a similar set of problems and similar difficulties addressing them. The key problems were the way in which ISI's emphasis on urban industrialization tended to weaken agricultural production; the growing difficulties of managing the balance of payments, exacerbated by the weakening of agriculture; the emergence of inflation as a consequence of rapid industrialization; the limits of ISI as a growth model for industrialization; and finally the turn to unsustainable mechanisms of financing growth, especially external debt. Together, these problems combined to cause a collapse in the viability of ISI and the turn to neoliberalism in the region.

Agricultural Uncompetitiveness

As noted above, many Latin American countries manipulated the exchange rate in order to facilitate industrial imports necessary for the growth of manufacturing. An artificially strong domestic currency meant that less of it was necessary to purchase the expensive machinery and equipment that were essential building blocks of an industrial economy. However, the same overvalued currency made commodity exports artificially expensive – i.e. more foreign currency was needed to purchase commodities than if the currency was less valuable. As a result, commodity exports suffered from their uncompetitiveness. Further, governments typically controlled foreign exchange transactions and frequently used multiple exchange rates as a way to indirectly tax commodity export profits in order to subsidize domestic industrialists' imports. Landowners responded to declining profits by reducing their investments and decreasing rural wages. The decline in rural investments and wages had perverse consequences for the economy and society. For one, declining wages led to an increase in rural poverty and were an important driver of migration to the cities. Thus, to some extent the rapid growth of urban slums is connected to ISI's treatment of agriculture. The second important effect was to drive down export earnings necessary for the import of industrial goods. It is one of the ironies of ISI that a program designed to overcome dependence on both agricultural exports and manufactured imports really could not do either. ISI in its initial stages actually increased the volume of manufactured imports as the rapid increase in domestic investment demanded rapid increases in industrial goods needed for the growth of industry.[36] In turn, the principal source of financing for investment and imports was commodity exports. Thus, the ways ISI helped to weaken agriculture actually threatened the ability of the state to finance the economic model.

Balance of Payments Difficulties

The growing imbalances between export revenues and the capital need for imports and foreign debt payments led to growing difficulties in the balance of payments. The end of the Great Depression and World War II opened financial markets anew and, coupled with sovereign lending and lending from international institutions, Latin American states were able to borrow money abroad to finance their operations. But, interest payments on loans and the import bill both depended on Latin American governments being able to draw in foreign currency. The nationalist sentiments of ISI had closed the door to multinational corporations, therefore foreign direct investment was not initially an important source of foreign currency. Commodity exports suffered from poor terms of trade (although they were improving in relative terms for much of the post-War period), exacerbated by growing weaknesses in the agricultural sector. By the late 1950s into the 1960s, Latin American governments were facing increasing pressure from foreign lenders over their inability to meet their international financial obligations. Pressure from abroad led a number of Latin American countries to turn to the International Monetary Fund (IMF) for assistance. IMF assistance came with a price – an insistence on reductions in state spending and state support for domestic industry and labor (frequently referred to as "austerity programs" for their austere and sometimes even draconian policy requirements). Indeed, the political consequences of turning to the IMF contributed to government failures, such as with Carlos Ibañez in Chile, or regime breakdown as with Arturo Frondizi in Argentina.

Inflation

Arguably the most serious economic consequence of ISI was inflation. Inflation – technically simply the rate at which prices are rising – is a corrosive and destructive problem. It systematically erodes the purchasing power of the currency, eating at the standard of living of those who cannot store their wealth in assets that do not lose their value (such as property or often off-shore bank accounts in strong currencies). Inflation falls particularly hard on the poor who depend almost exclusively on cash for their transactions. The problem in the 1940s and 1950s was how to explain the causes of inflation and therefore apply appropriate remedies. Orthodox, mainstream theories of inflation argued that the problem stemmed from excessive government spending, due to the extensive growth of the state, printing money to cover rising spending obligations associated with ISI led development, as well as from policies that pumped money into domestic businesses and supported high wages. The appropriate response for the conservative "monetarists" or market liberals of the period was an austerity program that sharply cut government expenses and curtailed the investment and purchasing power of businesses, the middle class and workers. Needless to say, this was neither politically popular nor politically easy for governments pursuing ISI.

The alternative theory developed at the time was often referred to as "structuralist" and was associated with Raúl Prebisch and CEPAL.[37] Structuralists argued that inflation was an inherent outgrowth of promoting industrialization in a rural, underdeveloped society. For them, inflation was a supply-side problem, not a demand side. In brief, inflation rose because the supply of goods, especially food, could not rise to meet the demand in the growing urban populations of Latin America. Supply was limited because of the weaknesses of the infrastructure of the region and because the rural agricultural elites were not good capitalists. The infrastructure problem was largely inadequate transportation, so goods could not get from one part of the country to another. For example, food produced in the countryside did not move efficiently to the cities. The resulting bottleneck created an artificial shortage of supply relative to demand and therefore drove prices up. In addition, rural producers were more concerned with their status as oligarchs than they were with the market and therefore did not respond to the price signals of rising demand for food for the internal market. For structuralists, the problem was not enough state spending rather than too much. State spending was necessary to develop the country's infrastructure and to use state owned enterprises to overcome the weakness of the country's producing classes (rural and urban industrial). This entailed accepting some inflation as a cost of industrialization.

The fundamental dispute played out in Latin America from the 1940s into the 1980s. Most of the rapid industrializers suffered the highest rates of inflation, notably Argentina, Brazil, and Chile (although Colombia and Mexico – until 1970 – were more committed to macroeconomic balance and tended to have lower rates of inflation by comparison). Governments in the high inflation states alternated between periods of structuralist approaches to inflation and more austere monetarist ones. Some of these policy shifts came in the context of such intense conflict that they caused regime or government changes to occur. For example, Brazil's left-wing, democratic president João Goulart (1961–1964) deepened state spending and support for workers' wages. The inflationary spiral that ensued drove inflation to over 60% per year and was at least a proximate cause of the 1964 coup that ushered in 21 years of military rule beginning in 1964. In contrast to Goulart, the military initiated a period of harsh cuts in wages, support for domestic business, and government spending in a bid to squeeze inflation out of the Brazilian economy. By 1967, military officials decided to permit the economy to expand again, but they had only contained inflation, not eliminated it.

The problem for policy makers in this period is that inflation had both monetarist and structuralist causes.[38] The fact that both theories had kernels of truth to them meant that policy programs designed to address one set of concerns, but not the other had limited chance of working. Monetarist programs contained inflation without reducing it to acceptable levels while at the same time throwing the economy into recession. Structuralist programs allowed the economy to grow but underestimated the ability of the economy and society to cope with the rising inflation that ensued. Inflation would continue to haunt the region throughout the ISI period. By the 1980s, inflation would emerge as a profound threat and an important cause of the end of ISI in Latin America.

Exhaustion of the Easy Phase of ISI and Limited Dynamism

Another critical flaw of the ISI program was its limited dynamism and built-in bottlenecks.[39] The limited dynamism was due to the fact that industry remained sheltered from the competitive forces that normally lead firms to the actions required to become more efficient, more productive, and more innovative. Markets work through competitive pressure. That has several important implications for private companies: they must choose to invest in areas where they can produce at a competitive price and avoid investing in products that they cannot produce competitively; they need to invest in equipment, production methods, and training that increases their productivity; they need to streamline production and cut excessive costs, including employing too many workers or having bloated management structures; finally, they need to innovate to gain the competitive edge of introducing new technology. Efficiency and productivity free up resources to use in new ventures and lead to rising wages and wealth for a society. Inefficiency wastes the resources of a society, limiting the wealth that the economy creates and the opportunities it can create for work or investment.

In a closed economy, the potential for growth is limited by the size of the internal market. Protection prevents new firms from entering to compete with existing ones or from cheaper imported goods putting pressure on local producers. Protected firms enjoy guaranteed markets and as a result do not feel the need to invest in new technology or become more efficient or more productive. Instead, they can be content to earn their profits on high prices for the low volume of goods they sell. In effect, protectionism acts as a societal subsidy for business owners, allowing them to earn high profits while avoiding investments. It allowed domestic firms, for example, to hire family members regardless of their skills, leading to bloated management with limited competence. Protectionism also allowed governments, for political reasons, to push firms to hire more workers than necessary and pay them wages above the real level of their productivity because the lack of competition allowed businesses to pass on their costs through higher prices. Thus, ISI also subsidized the minority of unionized, formal sector workers at the expense of the rest of society. But, these anti-competitive and inefficient forces sharply limited the competitive and productive dynamism of the economy. With high levels of protection in place, ISI relegated much of the economically active population to underemployment and employment in the low wage, low security, no benefits informal sector. Estimates of the size of the informal sector ranged as high as 60–70% of the labor market in some Latin American countries. ISI was a direct cause of persistent, deep poverty. This stands in sharp contrast to the very positive effects on poverty from the industrialization process in the West and in the export oriented East Asian countries (labeled the East Asian Tigers in the 1980s and 1990s for their rapid growth rates).

ISI did not have to produce this outcome, however. Even Prebisch, the intellectual father of ISI, believed that protectionism should be a temporary measure to foster new industries, but that protection should then fall as firms become capable of investing in competitive improvements. The problem with the theory in this case is that it runs into the real world problem of political power. Once domestic industries emerged across the region, they used their political influence to prevent liberalization of trade and therefore preserve their positions. Thus, ISI did not have to produce this outcome. But, political realities led to economies that could better the lives of millions, but leave millions more behind.

ISI ran into another problem beginning in the 1950s and into the 1960s. ISI's easy phase of investment involved substitution of low technology, labor-intensive consumer durables that required little know-how and little capital to begin production. By the 1950s, Latin American governments had exhausted the possibilities for these easy substitutions. Instead, they needed to move to the next stage of industrial development: capital goods, i.e. the machinery and equipment necessary to produce other industrial goods. Capital goods required higher levels of technological know-how, greater security of markets (due to higher minimum economies of scale), and higher capital investments than the easy phase. In Latin America, confronting the exhaustion of the easy phase everywhere led to declining growth rates as new investment opportunities dried up. Officials believed that domestic industrialists were unwilling or unable to move into these more difficult areas of investment. Ultimately, MNCs were invited back into Latin America to move industrial production into the next level. As noted earlier, MNCs were induced to invest with the same set of perverse protections and subsidies as local industrialists. Thus, MNC investment sparked a new round of growth, but still one based on inefficient production and exclusion of large segments of the population.[40]

MNC investment brought with it its own set of problems.[41] MNCs competed directly with local industrialists in some countries, entirely displacing them. Some countries devised means to protect local industrialists, such as local ownership requirements as in Mexico or local content requirements as in Brazil. In these two countries, the largest internal markets in the region, the "triple alliance" of state, local capital and MNCs formed a successful base for further growth. In others, the tensions between MNCs and local capital were much harder to manage. MNCs also brought with them new demands for control of labor. Whereas the early phase of ISI facilitated the formation of urban coalitions between local capital, the middle class, and the working class, the new round of investment also increased tension with workers. These tensions, combined with the pressures of inflation and balance of payments crises, helped spark a wave of regime collapses, ushering in dictatorships in Argentina, Bolivia, Brazil, Chile, Ecuador, Guatemala, Peru and Uruguay. Ultimately, these dictatorships oversaw the final stages of ISI and finally collapsed with it. The most proximate cause of both transitions – the "dual transition" of democratization and market reforms, was the debt crisis that stemmed from the financial limitations of ISI.

Financial Constraints, the Debt Crisis and the End of ISI

As noted earlier, one of ISI's principal problems was that it was not self-financing. As a program of industrialization oriented towards the internal market, it depended on commodity exports to generate the revenues it needed to finance industrial development. Commodity exports, especially as they declined in competitiveness, were simply incapable of sustaining the program. Over time, Latin American governments borrowed from official international financial institutions (IFIs) and from sovereign lenders. They relied on foreign aid. Beginning in the 1950s, they were able to rely on foreign direct investment through MNCs. All of these sources were limited and most Latin American governments spent much of the period struggling with the resulting balance of payments difficulties.

That changed after 1973. The 1973 OPEC (Organization of the Petroleum Exporting Countries) oil shock created an unusual situation for most of Latin America. On one hand, sharply rising oil prices increased the import bill and constituted a drag on economic growth as well as a source of inflationary pressure. On the other hand, it led to an entirely new source of financing. Since the Arab oil producers that had triggered the shock had few if any investment opportunities at home, they recycled their revenues back into the Western banking system. Western banks needed borrowers for the recycled "petro-dollars." Western lenders were eager to earn returns on the hundreds of billions of dollars floating back into their coffers. Latin American governments were eager to borrow funds that freed them from MNCs or from the constraints of IFIs and sheltered them from the need to make painful economic adjustments in response to oil price increases. Aggressive, eager lenders met naïve, eager borrowers and within a few short years, Latin American governments, especially the big three of Argentina, Brazil and Mexico, owed hundreds of billions of dollars. Latin American governments embarked on spending sprees – payoffs to political consti- tuencies and "pharaonic" projects – often with little accountability. To this day, much of the money remains poorly accounted for.

Unfortunately, the loans were at floating interest rates and short-term maturities. When prices for oil shot up again in 1979, Western economies were plunged into deeper recession with rising inflation. Paul Volcker, the Chairman of the US Federal Reserve Board at the time, raised interest rates to combat inflation in the US. For Latin America, the crisis caught the region in a pincer. Global recession led to declining demand for com- modities and declining prices and as a result plunging export revenues. Short-term loans with floating interest rates and denominated in US dollars led to sky-rocketing interest payments. The combined effect broke the back of ISI and the state's capacity to lead the economy. The turning point came in 1982 as Mexico, crippled by capital flight and a balance of pay- ments crisis, formally defaulted on its debt. By the mid 1980s, the shift to neoliberalism began sweeping through the region.

Notes

1 Kurt Weyland, *The Politics of Market Reforms in Fragile Democracies* (Princeton: Princeton University Press, 2004). Weyland, drawing on psychological theories of learning and decision-making, notes that leaders tend to have a "prior-option" bias. That is to say that even as things may be going wrong, leaders remain com- mitted to the policies they began with – a bias in favor of pre-existing policy sets. New leaders entering into office are able to learn from past mistakes, but often are drawn to the riskiest and most extreme rejections of the past, especially in times of crisis. The result is a tendency to more dramatic swings of policy than necessary.

2 See for example the discussion of the decline of state capacity and the desire to resurrect it among neoliberals in Javier Corrales, "Market Reforms" in *Con- structing Democratic Governance*, Jorge Dominguez and Michael Shifter, eds. (Baltimore: Johns Hopkins University Press, 2003).

3 John Sheahan, *Patterns of Development in Latin America: Poverty, Repression and Economic Strategy* (Princeton: Princeton University Press, 1987).

4 James Mahoney, *Colonial and Postcolonial Development: Spanish America in Comparative Perspective* (New York: Cambridge University Press, 2010).

5 The *encomienda* system was widely practiced throughout mercantilist, colonial Latin America. Under the terms of the system, *encomenderos*, colonial elites licensed by the crown, were granted authority to seize tribute and/or labor from a defined group of indigenous. Mahoney notes that at one point in Colonial Mexico in the 1520s, one group of 30 *encomenderos* commanded authority over 180,000 indigenous. To say that the system was brutal is something of an understatement.

6 Leslie Bethell, ed, *The Independence of Latin America* (New York: Cambridge University Press, 1987).

7 Fernando Henrique Cardoso and Enzo Faletto, *Dependency and Development in Latin America* (Berkeley: University of California Press, 1979).

8 Victor Bulmer-Thomas provides an account of the early origins of very small-scale, light manufacturing in response to growing urbanization in the early 20th Century, but notes that it was almost entirely handicrafts rather than modern manufacturing. *The Economic History of Latin America since Independence* (New York: Cambridge University Press, 2003): 127–128.

9 Michael Reid, citing Angus Maddison, in *The Forgotten Continent* (New Haven: Yale University Press): 33–34.

10 In fact, the terms of trade and their declining value for commodity exporters from Latin America was the central concern of Raúl Prebisch, the intellectual father of the "structuralist" policies, such as ISI, that dominated policy-making in the region after the 1930–1940s.

11 Barrington Moore, *The Social Origins of Dictatorship and Democracy: Lord and Peasant in the Making of the Modern World* (Boston: Beacon Press, 1993); Dietrich Rueschemeyer, Evelyne Huber Stephens and John D. Stephens, *Capitalist Development and Democracy* (Chicago: University of Chicago Press, 1992).

12 This period of transformation is discussed extensively in Cardoso and Faletto, 1979 as well as Ruth Berins Collier and David Collier, *Shaping the Political Arena* (Princeton: Princeton University Press, 1991).

13 Thomas Skidmore, Peter Smith, and James Green, *Modern Latin America* (New York: Oxford University Press, 2009).

14 This section draws on Collier and Collier, 1991.

15 Rosemary Thorp, *Progress, Poverty, and Exclusion: An Economic History of Latin America in the 20th Century* (Baltimore: Johns Hopkins University Press, 1998): 87; 318.

16 Patrice Franko, *The Puzzle of Latin American Economic Development* (Oxford: Rowman and Littlefield, 2003): 37.

17 Franko, 2003: 39.

18 Collier and Collier, 1991.

19 While there is a large literature debating the merits of markets versus state, Adam Przeworski's discussion in *Capitalism and Democracy: Political and Economic Reforms in Eastern Europe and Latin America* (New York: Cambridge University Press, 1991): ch. 4, offers a unique and particularly clear discussion of their strengths and weaknesses, examining them as blueprints and in practice.

20 Bulmer-Thomas, 2003: 271.

21 Franko, 2003: 59.

22 For a brief discussion of CORFO's past policies see Roy Nelson, *Harnessing Globalization: The Promotion of Nontraditional Foreign Direct Investment in Latin America* (University Park, PA: Penn State Press, 2009). On the BNDES, see Roy Nelson, *Industrialization and Political Affinity: Industrial Policy in Brazil* (London: Routledge Press, 2005).

23 These included export incentives, though those met with little success in general. Franko, 2003: 64.

24 Prebish's contributions are reviewed in Ronald V. A. Sprout, "The Ideas of Prebish," *CEPAL Review* 46 (April 1992).

25 Albert O. Hirschman first set out his highly influential ideas about the role of linkages in development in *The Strategy of Economic Development* (New Haven: Yale University Press, 1958).

26 James E. Mahon Jr., "Was Latin America Too Rich to Prosper? Structural and Political Obstacles to Export-Led Growth," *Journal of Development Studies* 28, no. 2 (1992).

27 The expansion of the state and the range of new institutional roles is reviewed in Thorp, 1998.

28 See Anne O. Krueger, "Government Failures in Development," *Journal of Economic Perspectives* 4, no. 3 (Summer 1990) for an argument about the risks of government's role in the market stemming from (among other things) the tendency for bureaucrats to overvalue policies requiring bureaucratic involvement. Pedro Pablo Kuczynski's critique of the role of the state in Latin America identifies as well the problem of corruption, in *Latin American Debt* (Baltimore: Johns Hopkins University Press, 1988).

29 Bulmer-Thomas, 2003: 221.

30 The claim for the middle class' connection to democracy dates as far back as Marx, but perhaps is most commonly associated with Barrington Moore. The strongest advocates of the position that the industrial working class is the principal carrier of democratic demands are Rueschemeyer, Stephens and Stephens. Ruth Collier's *Paths Toward Democracy: Working Class and Elites in Western Europe and South America* (New York: Cambridge University Press, 1999) argues forcefully that both classes played critical roles through a variety of possible paths with multiple possibilities for bargaining and coalition formation.

31 Thorp, 1998: 322.

32 Weyland, 2004.

33 Albert O. Hirschman, "The Political Economy of Latin American Development: Seven Exercises in Retrospection," *Latin American Research Review* 22, no. 3 (1987).

34 A review of key changes in Latin America over the period is in Thorp, 1998, ch. 1.

35 Janice E. Perlman, *The Myth of Marginality: Urban Politics and Poverty in Rio de Janeiro* (Berkeley: University of California Press, 1980).

36 In fact, policy analysts at CEPAL recognized the problem, but Latin American governments faced constraints in reversing the policies for reasons discussed by Mahon, 1992.

37 H. W. Arndt, "The Origins of Structuralism," *World Development* 13, no. 2 (1985).

38 See Sheahan, 1987 for an account of the multiple underlying causes of inflation and the political difficulty of balancing responses.

39 See Hirchman for a diagnosis and prescription for ISI bottlenecks, "The Political Economy of Import-Substituting Industrialization in Latin America," *Quarterly Journal of Economics* 82, no.1 (1968).

40 Franko, 2003: 61–63.

41 Guillermo O'Donnell, "Tensions in the Bureaucratic-Authoritarian State and the Question of Democracy," in *The New Authoritarianism in Latin America*, David Collier, ed. (Princeton: Princeton University Press, 1979).

3 Neoliberalism and its Discontents

It is hard to overstate the destruction wrought by the debt crisis on the Latin American landscape. With Mexico's default on its debt in 1982, international lending to the region dried up. The combination of high debt, exorbitant interest rates, and declining commodity prices put tremendous pressure on Latin American countries to find the resources to manage their debt obligations. Unable to roll over their debt further, Latin American governments were forced to squeeze their own societies to extract the finances necessary to make their interest payments. That meant cutting government spending, both on jobs and services as well as on state investments. It also meant withdrawing support from domestic businesses and freezing workers' wages. These "structural adjustment programs" occurred frequently under the aegis of the IMF and the World Bank. For neoliberals and IFIs, they were a necessary first step to address the macroeconomic imbalances of the ISI period and the debt crisis. Over the 1980s, these "austerity measures" coupled with poor rates of growth, declining real wages, and severe struggles with inflation and debt led to the label "the lost decade" in Latin America.

The struggles with the macroeconomic crisis also profoundly eroded the legitimacy of ISI as a growth model. The disastrous results of the late 1970s and early 1980s made it hard to offer any reasonable defense of a model that seemed to lead inexorably to such dismal failures. In that context, "liberal" advocates of markets as the key to economic growth resurfaced as powerful political players in the region. Where the structuralists had pointed to the state as the solution to Latin America's economic troubles, the new liberals – or "neoliberals" – pointed to the state as the central culprit. The answer, then, was to withdraw the state from the economy and to enhance the role of markets.

But this new liberal approach to the economy (and by extension politics) was exceptionally controversial. At least three questions have dogged neoliberalism since its first appearance in the region. First, what is neoliberalism and what is its agenda? At the extremes, right wing advocates argue that it is a radical reorganizing of politics and the economy for the purpose of unleashing the innovative and entrepreneurial energy within society and for safeguarding individual liberties. On the left, neoliberalism is seen as a right-wing political movement akin to a conspiracy in which an intellectual framework has served, intentionally or unintentionally, as a cover for an unbridled power grab and redistribution of wealth to economic elites. A second question relates to the implementation of neoliberal policies and democracy. For advocates, neoliberalism was embraced domestically and supported by voters in repeated electoral contests. Neoliberalism's defense of individual liberties protects democratic rule from corrupt state practices that more often than not hurt the poor. For the left, neoliberalism was imposed on the region by international financial institutions in collusion with domestic elites without political deliberation and often by suppressing domestic opposition. For critics, neoliberalism not only does not protect democracy, it destroys citizenship. Finally, critics and advocates disagree on the effects of neoliberal economic policies. Neoliberals argue that the set of policies they advocated have had important benefits, including controlling inflation and renewing growth in the region. While most neoliberals concede that the program did not work as well as hoped, they reject the arguments for returning to state led economic development and dispute charges of adverse consequences of neoliberalism. Critics tend to acknowledge that neoliberal policies brought down inflation, but see little real improvement otherwise, including very modest growth coupled with declining social spending and increased poverty and inequality.

In short, neoliberalism provokes sharply polarized views of the region. Reconciling them is hard as the views are virtually mirror images of each other with limited overlap. Is neoliberalism an elitist project that benefited the wealthy at the expense of the poor while also debilitating democracy? Is it a necessary, but incomplete reform process that is building a base for economic renewal and democratic governance? Or does the answer lie somewhere in between? This chapter explores the arguments for and against neoliberalism and considers the record of performance. Ultimately, the central claim is that a balanced view between the two polar opposite positions is the most reasonable position. Neoliberalism is a complex set of programs that at times were implemented undemocratically and at times democratically. Well-intentioned politicians and policy-makers embraced neoliberalism for its potential to spur growth, but sometimes external forces (primarily IFIs and Wall Street) closed off alternative choices, or even debate about alternatives, and economic elites benefited particularly well from neoliberal policies. Finally, neoliberalism oversold itself, delivering some genuine, but insufficient benefits to the population at large. Neoliberalism's record, however, is better than its critics suggest. Ultimately, neoliberalism's performance points to the power of markets to produce economic benefits, but their limits to overcoming the deep-seated challenges facing the region.

The Origins of Neoliberalism

Neoliberalism appeared in Latin America in Chile with the 1973 coup that brought General Augusto Pinochet to power. His team of pro-market, civilian, US-trained economic advisors (the "Chicago Boys") embarked on a project of radical restructuring of the country's economy. A second, short-lived and unsuccessful experiment in pro-market restructuring began under military rule in Argentina from 1976 until the military's ouster in 1983. It was not until the late 1980s and into the 1990s, however, that neoliberal reforms really swept the region. Neoliberal ideas began to really take hold in the region in the context of the debt crisis and the "lost decade."

The Neoliberal Diagnosis

Why follow neoliberal policies? The best answer lies in the obvious collapse of the ISI regime under the weight of unsustainable debt. A key statement of the neoliberal diagnosis of the Latin American economic problem came from Pedro Pablo Kuczynski, the current president of Peru and an economist with a prior background in both government and the private sector.[1] Kuczynski argued that Latin America's growth model through the ISI period was financially unsustainable. At the heart of its failure was the state and the external debt accumulated over the course of several decades of economic mismanagement. Other nations had external debts, but Latin America's singular problem with external debt in the 1980s was different from foreign debt in other regions in several aspects. First, unlike other regions such as East Asia, Latin American debt was significantly higher. Latin American debt in 1983 – 85% of which came from the largest economies in the region (Argentina, Brazil, Chile, Mexico, Peru and Venezuela) – was roughly equal to the outstanding foreign debt in all other developing countries. Together, Latin America had accumulated 351 billion US dollars in foreign debt while the rest of the developing world owed 383 billion US dollars. But, Latin America's debt problem was more serious because its debt was largely denominated in US dollars, which made it vulnerable to exchange rate risk – i.e. if the US dollar appreciated the debt burden would increase. In addition, most of Latin America's debt was borrowed from commercial banks (about two thirds) at floating interest rates, subjecting Latin American governments to yet another risk. By contrast, other developing countries borrowed more from international institutions and by issuing sovereign bonds (about two thirds) at fixed interest rates. Some 79% of Latin American debt was in dollars and 67% was at floating interest rates. By contrast, only 57% of other developing countries' debt was dollar denominated and only 34% of it was at floating interest rates. Latin American governments borrowed heavily on much riskier terms than governments in other regions. As a result, Latin America was caught in the early 1980s by sharp increases in US interest rates and an appreciating

US dollar following the 1979 oil shock in a way that the rest of the developing world was not.[2]

The most telling indicator of Latin America's debt problem, however, lay in the capacity to service the debt – the ratio of export revenues to interest payments. In 1983–1984, Latin America and the rest of the developing world faced roughly equal interest payments due on their external debt – about 44 billion US dollars. But, Latin American export earnings totaled only 98 billion US dollars while the rest of the developing world earned 270 billion US dollars. Latin American interest payments consumed roughly 50% of the region's export earnings in contrast to the 16% ratio for the rest of the developing world. The consequence of this extraordinary debt burden was deep recession and a debilitation of the state as government officials were forced to cut spending on state employment as well as necessities like infrastructure investment and social policies in order to make their interest payments.

One could argue that Latin America's debt problem was a consequence of bad borrowing decisions – commercial paper at floating interest rates versus fixed rates and official lenders – and bad luck (the oil shock). But, for Kuczynski the problem was structural rather than accidental or contingent. It resided in the character of the Latin American ISI model and the political decisions made by state officials over the course of the 1940s into the 1980s: deliberate policy choices that favored production for the internal market weakened agriculture, kept industry uncompetitive, and limited potential export earnings. Over time, the political strength of the urban middle and industrial classes entrenched these policies and pushed state officials to keep manipulating exchange rates to favor imports over exports so that urban middle classes could continue to produce and consume like US middle classes. Unfortunately, this model of development depended on a very large public sector and extensive state role in the economy. It is this expansive state presence that lies at the heart of the neoliberal diagnosis.

As noted in Chapter Two, Latin American states played several crucial roles in the ISI model. States were vital sources of employment, investment, and regulation. But, the state – and by extension state enterprises – is easily politicized and subverted. The list of ways that state involvement in the economy perverts economic performance is long. Industrialists, for example, engage in rent-seeking, i.e. investing resources to shape regulations that protect them from competition and divert state resources to them rather than focusing on becoming efficient, competitive entrepreneurs. State enterprises employ far more people than they need in order to absorb unemployed labor. State enterprises set prices to support domestic industry and tariffs for middle and upper class consumers, such as for electricity, or steel or telecommunications, without regard for efficiency or profitability. Government officials raid state enterprises' profits rather than allow them to invest in improvements in efficiency and productivity, turning the best

SOEs into cash cows instead of productive generators of growth and inno-vation. State officials produce regulations to control investment, production and employment, usually for political reasons and without regard for the way they may generate perverse incentives or distort prices. For neo-liberals, the problem was a bloated, financially broken state protecting an inefficient, unproductive economy. The question was how to renew growth.

The "Washington Consensus"

Neoliberalism is a broad label and encompasses a wide array of free market advocates who could and did disagree amongst themselves. One set of policy prescriptions, however, has widely come to be seen as "the" neoliberal program. It was set out in a paper by John Williamson, an academic economist with important stints in agencies like the World Bank, in which he presented a set of policy prescriptions that came to be known as "the Washington Consensus."[3] Williamson was careful to note that advocates of more market-oriented policies did not necessarily agree on the full set of goals or on the policies to attain them all. Instead, the "Washington Con-sensus" represented merely the minimum set of policies and goals on which Washington officials could largely agree. This group of officials included representatives of the US government (such as the State or Treasury departments), international financial institutions (such as the World Bank, International Monetary Fund, or the Inter-American Development Bank), and leading policy think tanks associated with free market advocates (such as the American Enterprise Institute).

In Williamson's words, the consensual goals were "growth, low inflation, a viable balance of payments and an equitable distribution of income."[4] Williamson then identified ten policies that constituted the minimal con-sensual program: control fiscal deficits; reorient public expenditure priorities, reform taxes, allow markets to determine interest rates, allow markets to determine the exchange rate, liberalize trade, liberalize finances (especially foreign direct investment), privatize state owned enterprises, deregulate the economy, secure property rights. The total effect of these reforms might be summed up as "get prices right." Following this reform agenda promised to remove the state's distortionary effects on prices and thereby allow markets to signal efficiently the best areas for investment and production. Allowing markets to function freely would stimulate entrepreneurial activity and discourage uncompetitive, inefficient and wasteful investments.

Fiscal Deficits: For the Washington Consensus, deficits themselves were not inherently a problem. Neoliberals did not argue that government spending was unacceptable or that governments had to run balanced budgets.[5] As Williamson noted, small deficits that financed productive investment were acceptable.[6] Public sector deficits in the order of 17% of GDP, like Brazil's in 1983, were indicative of serious policy failures and the lack of political courage to make hard choices.[7] Most importantly, they revealed that governments lacked the political will and courage to match spending to the actual level of resources available in the economy. In short, Latin American countries were living well beyond their means because states had been trying to finance an economic program and a standard of living in excess of the wealth of the economy.[8] The region's budget deficits were central culprits in the depth and the resilience of Latin American inflation and balance of payments struggles as well as a cause of capital flight. The neoliberal response was that governments needed to find the political courage to make cuts to government spending.

Reorienting Public Expenditure Priorities: One way to cut government spending is to identify the correct priorities for public expenditure, maintaining those while cutting the wasteful portions. For Williamson, public spending that creates human capital (health and education) is warranted as is investment in public infrastructure (although what areas specifically is subject to some debate). The problem in Latin America is that health and education spending tended to be low and highly unequal in its character. For example, Latin American governments spent disproportionately on higher education, particularly financing free university education for the 2–5% of the population that went to university, almost exclusively from the economic classes that did not need subsidized schooling. By contrast, primary and secondary education in all Latin American countries were severely underfunded.

Latin American government spending went instead to a wide array of subsidies: for agriculture, for industry, for telephone service or gasoline. These subsidies represented highly inefficient allocations of resources that hurt public enterprises (for example by preventing them from charging realistic prices for services like telecommunications) and almost invariably were highly unequal in their benefits. Middle class and upper class citizens tended to benefit from state subsidies while the poor were almost entirely excluded from them.

Tax Reform: Washington Consensus technocrats agreed that Latin American governments needed to increase their tax revenues. Across the whole region, Latin American governments struggle to tax income from high earners and face widespread evasion from businesses. The former problem is a political one – Latin American states have never been able to tax their economic elites. The latter problem is due to high taxes on production, leading businesses to move into the informal sector or to understate income. The end result is low tax revenues that add to the weakness of the state and the persistence of budget deficits. While neoliberals agree that the tax base should be wide and marginal rates moderate, there was considerable debate over the most effective and efficient approach to tax reform.

Interest Rates: Interest rates throughout the ISI period were managed by the state to serve political purposes. Those included explicitly developmental ones – essentially industrial policies to encourage investment in desired sectors of the economy (or conversely discourage investments in others). They also reflected political pressures from key interest groups and/or economic classes and therefore did not even serve a nominally developmental purpose. In either event, neoliberals criticized state control of interest rates because it led to inefficient allocations of credit. In short, markets should pick winners in the economy, not government officials. For neoliberals, industrial policy should be avoided because it depends on government to make choices that individual officials simply cannot make effectively. In effect, markets get prices right and therefore signal efficient uses of resources. Government's politically motivated intervention in key prices like interest rates promotes inefficient and unproductive investments.

Exchange Rates: Exchange rates pose much the same problem as interest rates. For decades, Latin American governments manipulated exchange rates to serve political purposes, mainly to promote the growth of domestic industry (at the expense of competitive exports). Neoliberals disagreed amongst themselves on whether exchanges had to be set by the market or could be set by government. But a strong consensus existed on the need to establish an exchange rate that was competitive enough to support exports while at the same time still attracted foreign capital. Williamson observed that this "equilibrium" point between the two macroeconomic goals is difficult to reach in practice and therefore Washington Consensus officials do not necessarily agree on the best approach.

Trade Liberalization: Another area of distortion and therefore misallocation of resources derived from the extensive protection of manufactured imports. Neoliberals particularly criticized licensing systems that required importers to seek permission to import manufactured goods. For the Washington Consensus officials, licensing encouraged extensive corruption as state officials controlling these decisions wielded considerable leverage to extort bribes and local producers had strong incentives to bribe officials to prevent importation of potentially competing "similar" products. In addition to licensing, neoliberals pointed to the high rate of tariffs and their dispersion (the differences in rates among different products/sectors). For neoliberals, modest and neutral tariffs were an acceptable form of protection (and revenue collection), but not ones that advanced industrial policy goals by selectively favoring one sector over another. Similarly, high rates simply removed any competitive pressure from domestic producers and acted as a kind of subsidy for businesses at the expense of the restricted consuming class. In essence, protection is a kind of tax on consumers to benefit producers.

Foreign Direct Investment: The onset of the ISI period restricted the participation of foreign firms in many areas of the economy. Unfortunately, multinational corporations typically enjoyed better technology and production knowledge, better access to capital, and generally greater economies of scale. By the 1960s, many Latin American countries that had restricted foreign capital relented in the face of the need to spur growth and needed investments. Nevertheless, restrictions remained, especially in areas where state owned firms exercised monopoly control of "national patrimony." Thus, oil in Mexico, Venezuela, Brazil, or Bolivia, or gas in Bolivia, or copper in Chile were all sectors in need of investment but closed to multinational corporations on nationalist grounds. For neoliberals, removing these restrictions was critical for renewed growth in the region.

Privatization: For neoliberals, SOEs were an integral element in the problem of the state in the economy. SOEs employed too many people. They provided inputs to domestic producers at unreasonably low, subsidized prices. They set unrealistic tariffs for public utilities like water, electricity or telephones. They underinvested in necessary infrastructure. They borrowed heavily on international financial markets and contributed to unsustainable debt. Finally, they were hotbeds of political influence and corruption. For neoliberals, privatization of SOEs was critical because private managers are driven by market principles – the bottom line. Market principles force firms to invest in order to be competitive. They force firms to function efficiently. SOEs – even the best ones – always face the risk of political interference to serve political purposes.[9] Even socially progressive interventions, such as maintaining employment, ultimately fail as the cost of inefficiency affects the whole economy and society. By the 1980s, SOEs extended well beyond basic inputs and utilities and included even things like hotels. Privatization promised to renew investment in key sectors of the economy, reduce corruption by withdrawing the state's presence, reduce the fiscal burden of inefficient and corrupt enterprises, and provide a one-time revenue benefit from the sale of the asset.

Deregulation: Latin America's extensively regulated economies constituted another important source of distortion and inefficiency. Controls on imports, access to credit, and discretionary uses of taxes have been noted already. But, Latin American governments also controlled prices and investments and even trivial matters like the number of colors on canned goods labels. In addition, extensive labor market regulations protected workers, but at the cost of making them very expensive to hire and even more expensive to fire (encouraging firms to avoid formal labor and full time contracts and exacerbating the region's problems with employment and underemployment).[10]

Securing Property Rights: The last item on the Washington Consensus agenda was to secure property rights. Secure property rights are critical for investment as individuals and firms will not sink resources into an endeavor if they believe the state will appropriate their assets. This includes things like property (such as land) or economic sectors like mining or oil. It includes administrative expropriation where state regulators set tariffs at unprofitable rates for private producers of services like water or telecommunications. Finally, it includes intellectual property, where private investors in technology may face losses from private firms or individuals that copy patented information. Latin American governments have a history of all three forms of weak property rights protection.

The Washington Consensus position is that this minimum policy set was necessary to remove distortionary state intervention and by getting prices right build a base for renewed and sustainable economic growth. The Washington Consensus policy set was not exhaustive. Free market advocates differed in the importance of various social policy goals and how best to achieve positive economic and social goals. Over the 1990s for example, the IMF retained a primary focus on financial health and the ability to manage debt. IMF officials continued to express confidence in the basic neoliberal model despite growing doubts about the resilience of poverty and inequality in the region and the corrosive effects of debt. By contrast, the Inter-American Development Bank and the World Bank became increasingly concerned about poverty and inequality and tended to recognize that the minimal set needed to be complemented with a fuller range of policies to address social concerns. Bank officials tended to work more with local officials and as a result became more flexible in their approach to economic reforms and increasingly interested in working with non-governmental organizations. Nevertheless, neoliberalism's strongest critics saw little practical difference among the various neoliberal constituencies. Instead, they argued that neoliberalism represented a power grab by the economic elites of society.

Neoliberalism's Discontents – the Leftist Critique

For left-wing critics, such as James Petras or David Harvey, neoliberalism was above all else a political movement that reasserted the power of capital against state efforts to contain it.[11] According to this view, neoliberals believed that individual rights and liberties (particularly property rights) were coming under attack by the encroachment of an ever larger and ever more interventionist state. For neoliberals, markets, rather than the state, are the best guarantors of individual rights and freedoms and are the most effective mechanism to generate wealth. Neoliberals, inspired by economists such as Friedrich Hayek and Ludwig von Mises of the Austrian School of Economics, saw the rise of the welfare state during the Great Depression as an attack on markets and the owners of capital who were the key to investment, production and ultimately the accumulation of wealth in society. The period following World War II was an ongoing assault on individual rights and the economic elites as the state grew larger and larger throughout the developing and developed world. Those assaults consisted of higher and higher tax rates on the wealthy, growing numbers of regulations on corporations (such as environmental or work place safety regulations),[12] rights granted to labor unions (especially inclusion in policy making deliberations in countries like Sweden or West Germany), and state ownership of production.

The 1970s, however, were a turning point for the global economy as a number of the key tenets and institutions of the global economic order came under pressure. The Vietnam War challenged the financial strength of the US dollar and its role as the world's currency, culminating in the end of the Bretton Woods currency system when Richard Nixon took the dollar off the Gold Standard – a policy that had been the undergirding of financial stability in the post World War II world. The end of the Gold Standard provoked rising uncertainty and volatility in global currencies, as a new casino mentality took hold, with investors gambling on currencies that were no longer tightly connected to the strength of their domestic economies and no longer stabilized by their link to a US dollar backed by gold. The OPEC oil-shock of 1973 was even more destabilizing than the end of the Bretton Woods system. The Arab oil embargo pushed oil prices from roughly $3 per barrel to roughly $12 per barrel through 1973 and into 1974. The quadrupling of oil prices drove the global economy into crisis with recession and inflation leading to the coining of the new term "stagflation" to describe the uncommon pairing of the two.[13] Every oil importing country in the world had to make a decision on how to respond. Governments in the developed world varied substantially in their choices, depending on their own domestic political dynamics. Those choices led to very different degrees of success, spawning a debate about the advantages of states versus markets in the organization of capitalism.[14]

Neoliberal thinkers saw the crisis as evidence of the need to reign in state power and restrain the anti-market policies that accompanied excessive state growth. But for critics such as David Harvey, Gérard Duménil and Dominique Lévy, or James Petras, the intellectual blueprint was less important than the class project of the upper classes – primarily holders of financial assets. These economic elites of the advanced industrial economies saw the turmoil of this period as the opportunity to reassert the power of "the upper fractions of the owners of capital"[15] and to restore the conditions for the accumulation of capital, primarily to the benefit of economic elites. This project received critical support from US institutions such as the Federal Reserve Board and international financial institutions such as the International Monetary Fund. The neoliberal program was first implemented in 1973 in Chile with the military coup of General Augusto Pinochet. Pinochet's government drew on a pool of economists trained by the US' leading neoliberal thinker, Milton Friedman, at the University of Chicago. These "Chicago Boys" led a full scale assault on the state apparatus, unconstrained by democratic politics and supported by an enthusiastic US (which had funded the training of the Chicago Boys in the first instance as part of a program to counteract the left in Latin America). Success in Chile was followed by the turn to neoliberalism in England under Margaret Thatcher and in the US under Ronald Reagan.

Neoliberal policies in the developed world included sharp cuts in taxes on the wealthiest in society, austerity measures to eliminate inflation (and therefore protect the value of financial assets), and attacks on union power. Tax cuts on the wealthiest individuals had marked effects. For example, Ronald Reagan's tax cuts reduced the marginal tax rate on the highest earners from 70% to 28% – only slightly above the lowest income bracket. As a consequence, the share of income claimed by the top 0.1% of earners in the US rose from 2% in 1978 to over 6% in 1999 with similar trends in Britain and other OECD countries. By 1999, the top 1% controlled roughly 15% of all assets. Taxes on the middle and working classes changed little if at all. At the same time, Thatcher and Reagan's union breaking tactics helped to weaken labor power. One result was an astonishing shift in the returns for owners/managers versus labor. In 1970, the median CEO salary was 30 times higher than the median worker's salary. By 2000, it had risen to 500 to 1. For Harvey, Petras and similar critics, this brutal shift of wealth from the poor and the middle classes to the wealthiest in society was the overt purpose of the neoliberal forces. As David Harvey stated, "Redistributive effects and increasing social inequality have in fact been such a persistent feature of neoliberalization as to be regarded as structural to the whole project."[16]

It is hard to argue with the evidence in the developed world. The growth of the financial sector and the deepening of inequality throughout the advanced industrial world has been a steady feature since the 1980s. The struggles of President Obama to pass meaningful financial sector reform over 2009 and 2010 are clear indicators of the continued political power of finance, even in the wake of the collapse of the US economy. The election of Donald Trump in 2016 has opened the possibility for a full reversal of even the most seemingly unobjectionable Obama reforms.[17] For Petras or for Duménil and Lévy, the increase in wealth and growth in power of the financial sector has been the point of neoliberalism all along. It has been abetted by national and international institutions and supported by US power. As a project, it has exploited the working class of both the advanced industrial countries and the developing world. Harvey makes a sharper distinction between the blueprint – a "utopian" intellectual project promoted by neoliberal thinkers – and the political program, promoted by economic elites and key national and international institutions. But, for Harvey, the neoliberal blueprint contains within it important contradictions that make it untenable in practice and in practice the political agenda has dominated over the intellectual blueprint. In fact, he argues that where the *utopian* project of promoting economic growth has clashed with the needs of the political project's emphasis on restoring class power, the political project consistently has won out. In that sense, neoliberalism as an intellectual project is both untenable in practice and naïve politically.

The intellectual agenda also suffers from a lack of integrity or arrogance. Duncan Green, for example, discusses the unwillingness of the International Monetary Fund or World Bank to seriously consider criticisms of the neoliberal economic project. Both internal and external reviews repeatedly found that Fund sponsored programs performed poorly, particularly because IMF officials typically arrived in the host country promoting their generic blueprint with little regard for specific local conditions. The resulting programs often suffered because of their inadequate accounting of the local context.[18] For Green, the most damning criticism, however, came out of an initiative funded by the World Bank to review the Structural Adjustment Programs (SAPs) that were the centerpiece of the Bank's neoliberal reforms. SAPRI, the Structural Adjustment Participatory Review Initiative, brought together a network of thousands of NGOs, unions and academics to evaluate programs conducted jointly between the Bank and host governments. The SAPRI report, published in 2002, was highly critical of the SAPs. Rather than address the criticisms, however, the Bank buried the report and closed down the SAPRI initiative.[19]

Green is an overt critic – a policy analyst at CAFOD, the Catholic Aid Agency for Overseas Development, but the criticism of unwillingness to engage outsiders comes even from people that one could expect to be more sympathetic to the reform agenda. Javier Santiso, a financial insider as Chief Economist of the OECD Development Centre and previous work as chief economist in private banking, has chronicled the ways in which the free market ideologues of the World Bank, the IMF and Wall Street close ranks and resist any external points of view.[20] Santiso identifies two dynamics that make it hard to incorporate criticisms. First, for Wall Street investors, the abundance of information and the speed at which it flows makes it hard for actors in the financial sector to integrate new information and evaluate conflicting points of view. As a result, they are forced to take their cues from a limited number of sources and a limited number of indicators as short cuts that allow them to manage the pace of information flow and the amount of information available. Naturally, they tend to rely on key financial organizations committed to the market reform process, such as the IMF or Bloomberg New Services and a very limited set of indicators, such as inflation levels or budget deficits. A second critical limitation on serious engagement with criticism is that the financial world is very much a closed network where insiders only speak with each other. The fact that all these insiders have common sources of information, use the same informational short cuts, and follow the same economic paradigm closes out alternative viewpoints or conflicting evidence.

Critics of neoliberalism, then, make a number of quite damning statements about the neoliberal project. Intellectually, it is a flawed blueprint for development that does not take into account its own internal contradictions or the tensions between a generic framework and the local context. Insiders in the financial world at the very least have difficulty integrating critical perspectives and at worst actively work to silence dissenting viewpoints. Politically, left-wing critics argue that neoliberalism is a class project to restore the economic and political power of the wealthiest segments of society at the expense of the poor and working classes of the advanced industrial countries and of the developing world generally.

The Politics of Neoliberal Reform: Imposition or Home Grown? Democratic or Authoritarian?

If the origins and purpose of neoliberal reforms are controversial, the question of how they were implemented throughout the region is even more controversial. Neoliberalism swept through the region, beginning slowly with Chile and Argentina in the 1970s, but then with increasing intensity through the 1980s into the 1990s. Neoliberal experiments varied also by intensity with some countries implementing drastic, rapid reforms and others pursuing more gradual ones. For example, Bolivia, facing catastrophic inflation in 1985 embarked on a radical and rapid reform process. By contrast, Brazil initiated neoliberal reforms beginning in 1990, but at a gradual pace. Countries did not pass all the neoliberal reforms at once. Most countries initially implemented only so-called "first stage" reforms or IMF and World Bank sponsored "structural adjustment programs." The purpose of these initial reforms was to address fiscal imbalances and facilitate new lending to the country and as a result involved budget adjustments, privatization and trade liberalization. More complex reforms, such as deregulation of labor markets, development of regulatory institutions, social policy reforms (such as of social security) or reorganization of the financial sector typically came afterward. In either event – rapid or gradual – the onset of neoliberal reforms has generated considerable disagreement about the relationship between neoliberalism and democracy as well as the effect of neoliberalism on democracy.

Critics of neoliberalism's connection to democracy focus on at least four different elements that reveal the undemocratic character of the reform program. First, critics charge that neoliberalism was often imposed on Latin American countries by international financial institutions, such as the IMF or the World Bank. At best, a small cohort of economic and technical elites supported the reforms domestically, but otherwise the program was imposed against the preferences of the majority of the population. A second criticism is that the governments that implemented neoliberal reform programs relied on "delegative democracy" – democratic rule in which executives acted without supervision, participation or consultation with the legislature. Instead, neoliberal reforms emerged out of closed-door discussions among technically trained bureaucratic elites without accountability or transparency. A third criticism is that when social forces, such as unions, protested against the imposition of reforms without transparency or accountability, their voices were suppressed – often violently. For critics, neoliberalism hollowed out civil society and degraded the meaning and value of citizenship. Finally, critics also expressed concern that neoliberalism eroded the integrity of electoral politics as politicians campaigned against market reforms and then enacted the program upon being elected. Susan Stokes labeled this "neoliberalism by surprise."[21] Stokes defended the practice as a legitimate, albeit suboptimal form of representation, but many other observers have been more perturbed by neoliberalism's electoral performance, including both "bait and switch" tactics as well as use of "neopopulism" as a way to appeal to low-income voters.

By contrast, others have offered views of neoliberalism and politics that present a more compatible relationship with democracy. Defense of neoliberalism's compatibility with democracy rests on three plausible bases. First, public opinion research has shown that voters are more receptive to market reforms than the critical view suggests, particularly when disaggregated into component policies. For example, Andy Baker's work shows high levels of support for commercial liberalization, despite greater resistance to privatization (the most unpopular element of neoliberal reforms).[22] Neoliberalism, therefore, has been more successful politically in open, fair contests than the critical view suggests. Second, detailed country and policy studies suggest stronger congressional involvement and greater concern with important voting bases than the more critical views would suggest. For example, Sebastián Etchemendy's illuminating work on neoliberal re-structuring in Argentina, Chile and Spain explores how different patterns of state–business and state–labor relations led to alternative models for reform. Reformist governments modified reforms offering diverse forms of benefits and compensations for the old ISI coalition as a way to forge new coalitions to support the reform process.[23] Finally, some scholars offer work that challenges the view of neoliberalism as destructive of civil society, noting instead the continuous process of organizing and resisting that developed over the course of the 1990s among groups opposed to market reforms.[24] Indeed, the late 1990s witnessed the beginning of a decided turn to the left in electoral politics based on growing discontent with neoliberalism's performance. If anything, the electoral rejection of parties associated with neoliberal reforms gives testament to the strengthening of democratic governance.

Neoliberalism against Democracy

Developing by countries, virtually by definition, rely on foreign capital to promote economic growth and development. Poor countries lack large pools of domestic savings on which to draw, deep financial markets to support small business investments or long-term home mortgages. Governments are unable to generate significant revenues on taxes alone. As a result, foreign investment and external borrowing are critical elements in fostering economic growth and development. But, dependence on external sources of financing makes developing countries susceptible to pressure to adjust their economic policies to suit foreign institutions and foreign creditors. From the 1940s into the 1980s, Western lending and investment in developing countries supported state led development. International financial institutions made loans available to developing countries without requirements that borrowing nations tailor their domestic priorities to IFI principles. Commercial lenders also were willing to lend without insisting that the developing nations follow free-market principles. In part, this was because state involvement in the economy was acceptable to global financial elites, not least because it was prevalent in Europe and Keynesian ideas held sway in the US.

The debt crisis changed the attitudes of IFIs, lending governments, and commercial lenders. Neoliberal ideas took hold in key US and international agencies and commercial lenders became concerned about the ability of developing nations to repay their loans. In that context, IFIs became the global financial watchdogs and their seal of good housekeeping was necessary to free up new lending – commercial or sovereign. Developing countries looking to renew capital inflows needed to adapt their policies to meet the demands of IFIs and Wall Street.

The argument that the shift to neoliberalism was imposed from abroad takes two forms. One argument is a direct one: in some cases IFIs directly and overtly forced developing country governments to shift to neoliberalism. For example, Mexico's 1982 default on its external debt put the country's economy in a desperate position financially. Both the US Treasury and IFIs pressured the incoming government of President Miguel de la Madrid to embrace market-reforms and the government had no alternative but to shift to neoliberalism. Bolivia in 1985 faced hyper-inflation – inflation rising at such a rapid rate that the currency had effectively lost any value. The World Bank and the IMF had cut off lending to the country – one of the poorest in Latin America. As a result, the government of Victor Paz Estenssoro, the nationalist hero of the 1952 Revolution, had no choice but to turn to neoliberal reforms to gain access to new financing.

The second version of the imposed from abroad argument is an indirect one. In this version, globalization and the decentralization of global finance is the central culprit. IFIs do not have to exert overt pressure to force governments to shift. The need to suit private investors' preferences forces dependent countries to shift their policies. Javier Santiso offers a stark picture of the extent to which foreign leaders, including finance ministers and presidents, learn to present themselves to Wall Street and IFI officials.

For example, the election of Carlos Menem, a left-wing nationalist leader of the Partido Justicialista (Justicialist Party, the Peronist Party) in 1989 in Argentina promised a nationalist, inward looking development program. However, Menem's administration was forced to shift toward neoliberal policies once they understood the gravity and precariousness of the country's financial situation. Desperate to restore inward flows of foreign capital, the Menem administration took drastic and dramatic steps to implement neoliberalism.[25]

Neoliberalism has also weakened democracy by exacerbating the region's tendency towards "delegative democracy." Guillermo O'Donnell defined this concept to refer to a diminished form of democratic governance prevalent in Latin America. In delegative democracies, voters expect their elected leaders to solve their problems without regard for transparency, deliberation or accountability. The basic mechanisms of "horizontal accountability" such as legislative committees either do not exist or do not function the way they do in Western democracies. Instead, presidents and select advisors – often highly trained technically – craft policies behind closed doors away from public scrutiny or legislative negotiation and then pass them on party line votes without deliberation. For example, Gonzalo Sánchez de Lozada, elected president of Bolivia in 1994, was committed to deepening the country's neoliberal reform process. His reform package, labeled the "Plan de Todos" (Plan for Everybody) was developed at the Millennium Foundation, a neoliberal think tank in La Paz. It included privatization of the largest and most important state owned industries in the country as well as the social security system. Critics charged that the program passed with little to no congressional oversight or deliberation. Similarly, neoliberal reforms in Chile or Mexico were developed within policy networks of technical advisors in consultation only with private financial and industrial elites, and then implemented without debate or legislative oversight.[26] For critics, this absence of oversight is central to understanding how policies that often proved regressive and unpopular were destructive of democratic governance.

Yet another concern raised by critics of the neoliberal reform process is that neoliberalism led to the suppression of opposition and indeed undermined the very capacity of civil society to organize. Neoliberal reforms triggered protests and oppositions in a number of countries, particularly to privatization, which has been especially unpopular. Privatization's unpopularity stemmed from widespread perception of corruption,[27] punitive tariff increases for basic needs such as water, as well as the threat of job losses that usually accompanied the sale of state owned assets to private owners. Protests against privatization often triggered violent suppression. The most dramatic instances of this occurred in Bolivia's so-called "Water War" of 2000 and subsequent "Gas War" of 2003. In the latter protest, the death of protestors at the hands of the military led President Sánchez de Lozada to resign from his second term as president and to flee the country to the US, where, as of 2017, he remained as Bolivian authorities sought his extradition for "crimes against humanity."

But, some critics contend that neoliberalism's impact on civil society is even deeper than simple repression of protestors. Marcus Kurtz argues that neoliberalism's destructive impact on important organizations such as labor unions has had the effect of "hollowing out" civil society, leading to a declining capacity to organize and to resist unpopular policies and programs.[28] Carlos Vilas has argued that neoliberalism's emphasis on budget cuts, especially in discretionary areas such as social policy, has diminished the meaning of citizenship.[29] Phillip Oxhorn shares that concern, warning that neoliberalism's focus on markets reduces the meaning of citizen to consumer. All these perspectives share a common perception that neoliberalism is fundamentally incompatible with democratic governance.[30] Kurt Weyland offers a softer diagnosis, arguing that in certain respects neoliberalism stabilizes democracy, but a low quality one.[31]

These fundamental weaknesses all contribute to the need to craft electoral support for neoliberalism in ways that further undermine democracy. For critics, neoliberalism's essentially elitist character and destructive impact on civil society force candidates to use strategies such as concealing their true agenda or adding populist elements to their platform as a way to stitch together a coalition of elite and lower class voters. In the former case, candidates who have implemented neoliberalism "by surprise" are common in the electoral landscape of the region.[32] Carlos Menem in Argentina (1989), Victor Paz Estenssoro in Bolivia (1984), Fernando Collor in Brazil (1989), Alberto Fujimori in Peru (1990) or Carlos Andrés Pérez in Venezuela (1989) are prominent examples of candidates who ran on an anti-free market agenda (or in the case of Collor, a vague platform that did not signal the neoliberal reform agenda his government would subsequently pursue) and then switched to neoliberalism upon taking office. Stokes, who coined the term "neoliberalism by surprise," argues that these candidates may be trying to honestly represent the true needs of their constituents based on assessments of the best way to restore economic growth or shifts upon learning the depth of the crisis. Others however are less sanguine. For critical observers, bait and switch electoral tactics undermine the integrity of democratic representation, weaken political parties and their reputations among voters and contribute to voter cynicism about politics.

Another set of concerns raised about neoliberal politics is the affinity between it and populist tactics.[33] Populism in Latin America has historically been associated with leftist and nationalist politicians. Charismatic leaders such as Juan Peron in Argentina appealed directly to lower class voters, relying on anti-elite rhetoric and redistributive policies to build political support for national development oriented ISI programs. "Neopopulists" used anti-elite rhetoric and small-scale compensatory social programs to mobilize lower class votes in favor of programs that primarily benefited economic elites. While traditional populist programs were associated with profligate unsustainable spending, neopopulists used limited spending to support large budget cuts that affected middle class and unionized workers. Traditional populism supported the development of organized interests in the lower class (although critics charged that it was mobilization for the purpose of control). Neopopulism focused on the informal sector poor and offered no possibilities for organization. Neither form of populism was particularly oriented towards strengthening or deepening democracy.

All told, these various criticisms of neoliberalism paint a picture of an economic program that undermines democratic governance, weakens the institutions of representation, and cheapens the meaning of citizenship. For critics, these political faults are a direct function of neoliberalism's elite character. Since neoliberalism's real constituency is the wealthy and foreign capital interests, politicians who endorse it must conceal their real intentions, implement it without any kind of transparency or accountability, and quash the inevitable opposition to it. Neoliberals have to "manufacture" consent in society to accept an economic program that converts them from citizens to consumers and reduces all societal interactions to market ones. In the critical view, neoliberalism does not have a plausible political base and therefore its implementation must by nature be undemocratic.

Neoliberalism and Democracy: The Positive Case

An alternative set of views offers a more positive view of democratic governance and its relation with market enhancing reforms. Needless to say, neoliberalism's advocates view it as inherently compatible with democracy. Protecting freedom in the market protects freedom politically as well. In the classic liberal market view, as exemplified by the Austrian School of economics, the state is the most serious threat to liberty. The extent to which it asserts its presence in the economy is the extent to which it encroaches on individual liberty. While the strongest forms of this view are associated with intellectuals like Friedrich Hayek or Ayn Rand, this perspective continues to find strong expression in the contemporary Republican Party in the United States as well as through US foreign policy, which tends to associate markets and democracy inextricably. But, this more abstract philosophical view of the relation between economic and political freedom is not the only plausible defense of a positive relationship between neoliberalism and democracy.

First and foremost, one can point to the string of successful re-elections of presidents who had implemented neoliberal reforms. Even those who implemented neoliberalism by surprise count among these political successes. For example, Gonzalo Sánchez de Lozada stood for re-election in Bolivia and succeeded four years after his first term ended.[34] Carlos Menem successfully ran for re-election in Argentina after reforming the constitution to permit re-election. Fernando Henrique Cardoso of Brazil also revised the constitution to permit re-election and successfully ran for a second term after four years of the most aggressive promotion of neoliberal reforms in the country's history. In Mexico, roughly 70 years of continuous rule by the Institutional Revolutionary Party (Partido Revolucionario Institucional, PRI) gave way after 20 years of neoliberal reforms to a party further to the right and more overtly pro-market. The new victorious party, the PAN (Partido Acción Nacional, National Political Action Party) won the subsequent elections in 2006 with the PRI returning in 2012, still supporting a neoliberal orientation. In Peru, the stealth neoliberal Alberto Fujimori successfully ran for re-election after revising the constitution to permit it as well. Fujimori's authoritarian tendencies brought down his effort to run again in 2001, but he was followed by the Stanford University trained, pro-market Alejandro Toledo, who in turn was followed by Alán García, a repentant populist ISI advocate turned moderate pro-market president. In short, neoliberalism was introduced through "bait and switch" tactics on a few occasions. But, many neoliberal presidents were electorally successful, even among the neoliberals by surprise, and neoliberal politicians continued to prosper in places like Mexico and Peru.

There are three important arguments that help to explain the electoral successes of neoliberalism. The first of these is that the critics have overstated the extent to which neoliberalism is an elitist program. At the very least, even the reform critics concede that neoliberalism succeeded in containing inflation. Inflation is a very destructive economic problem, but is particularly a scourge of the poor. As President Fernando Henrique Cardoso observed, "controlling inflation is the linchpin of social policy for the poor."[35] In fact, Cardoso's success with inflation through the 1994 Real Plan led to one of the most rapid reductions in the level of poverty in the history of the country. Voters in Argentina, Bolivia, Chile, Mexico and Peru among others all responded with enthusiasm to the end of inflation. Neoliberals argue that the positive effects were not limited to inflation. Nevertheless, inflation alone provided a powerful impetus for neoliberalism politically.

Neoliberalism's performance with inflation is only part of what in fact has proven to be deeper support for market reforms than the critics have tended to believe. Kurt Weyland has advanced an argument in favor of support for reforms relying on prospect theory. Prospect theory emerged out of the study of psychology and refers to the tendency of individuals to assess risk differently depending on whether they believe they are in "the domain of gains" or the "domain of losses." Individuals who believe that they are generally facing improving prospects tend to be very conservative about potential losses, preferring to hold on to what they have and forego large, but riskier gains. Individuals facing certain losses tend to prefer to wager on potentially large gains even at the risk of terrible losses. For Weyland, voters in countries like Argentina or Peru (and Brazil later) saw themselves in the domain of losses and were willing to back neoliberal candidates because they promised escape from the certainty of losses associated with crippling rates of inflation and unemployment.[36] In that sense, neoliberal candidates actually offered meaningful choices to voters and were genuinely and honestly representing their interests when implementing neoliberal policies.

Public opinion research suggests that voter preferences for market reforms may have extended beyond simply desperation for salvation from crisis. For example, polling by Andy Baker found majorities supporting free trade, correctly perceiving the benefits in lower prices for goods. In general, privatization has proven unpopular in Latin America, though specific privatizations such as telephone service have found more popular support. In broader terms, polling by the *Wall Street Journal* found that voters across Latin America have revealed a complex pattern of support for markets versus states. Contrary to expectations, Latin Americans do not automatically believe that the state should manage the economy.[37]

Finally, a broad swath of policy studies have found that legislatures have been more involved in the policy-making process than the critical literature would suggest. Legislatures have tended to protect important domestic constituencies threatened by neoliberal reforms. They have entered to modify or block reforms that were deeply unpopular. They have pushed presidents to modify policies to better meet the expectations of the public. And they have turned on presidents whose neoliberalism has egregiously violated the preferences of the public. For example, Carlos Menem was able to pass much of his neoliberal reform program through the legislature through executive decree and through congressional votes with limited debate. However, his effort to privatize social security in Argentina was deeply unpopular, highly threatening to senior citizens (as in the US), and strongly opposed by labor unions. Despite enjoying a sizable majority in the legislature and strong executive decree authority, the PJ members of congress held up the legislation in committee, called for extensive hearings, ultimately significantly altering the bill, preserving strong elements of state support for the social security system and placing powerful regulatory constraints on the private sector.[38] Examples of legislative involvement in the reform process abound. Eduardo Silva has documented the legislature's involvement in Chile and the involvement of the business community in policy design.[39] A sizable literature exists on legislative involvement in Brazil and Argentina as well. Manzetti has demonstrated the ways in which the legislature has slowed down the reform process even with arguably quite undemocratic presidents such as Alberto Fujimori of Peru.[40] Moreover, Maria Victoria Murillo has argued that executives tailored policy to take into account partisan preferences and the voting base of the party.[41] Thus, both telecommunications and energy privatizations were adjusted to control the private sector and give greater protection to consumers in countries with leftist or nationalist presidents, such as Carlos Menem in Argentina or under the PRI in Mexico. In short, the democratic system worked as it should, according to theories of democratic governance and representation.

The picture of more effective representation is complemented by more positive views of societal organizing as well. For example, Sylvia Rhodes documents the mobilization of consumers around the privatization and regulation of utilities. Effective regulation of privatized utilities depends on consumers to report service problems and thereby help hold utilities accountable. While union membership may have declined in Latin

America, consumer rights do offer new possibilities for organization.[42] Moreover, it is not clear that labor protest is no longer effective. Labor unions in both Costa Rica and Uruguay were able to prevent the privatization of key utilities, such as electricity. Aubrey, Kingstone and Young identified over one hundred large-scale protests against privatization specifically, with many of them successful in altering the terms of privatization or halting/reversing the process entirely.[43] Labor unions were key participants in most of them and in the most successful protests were able to forge links with other groups in society to work collectively against the privatization. Finally, James Petras – a sharp critic of neoliberalism – charts the mounting mobilization of efforts against neoliberalism amongst NGOs and social movements opposed to the reforms entirely. Petras points to debates among critics, offering pointed criticisms of "pragmatists" who accepted the general neoliberal framework while calling for adjustments like increased social spending. Yet, for Petras, the true revolutionary left that rejected neoliberalism's premises and framework was in revival throughout the 1990s. For example, the Landless Movement in Brazil (Movimento dos Trabalhadores Rurais sem Terra, MST) developed a "counter-hegemonic" national strategy that transformed it from a localized rural protest against landlessness to a national movement with ties to the Catholic Church, labor unions, and the urban poor (*favelados*). As such, the MST, with its land invasions and occupations of government offices, was the vanguard of an anti-neoliberalism political movement. Petras' recounting of the vigor of the resurgent left ironically underscores the room for mobilization against neoliberalism present in society.[44]

Resolving the Debate

The question of neoliberalism's fit with democracy is a vexed one, with compelling evidence on both sides of the ledger. There is no doubt that IFIs and international financial pressure constrained leaders in times of crisis and in some cases involved overt pressure to adopt neoliberal policies. There is also no question, however, that neoliberalism was sometimes implemented or embraced by true believers. Victor Paz Estenssoro of Bolivia may have had no choice but to turn to neoliberalism. But, Gonzalo Sánchez de Lozada, Paz Estenssoro's Finance Minister, was a true believer. Mexico faced tremendous pressure to shift to neoliberal reforms in 1982, but the technocratic wing of the party that assumed control of policy-making and the presidency until the party's defeat in 2000 was sincerely neoliberal in its beliefs. There is no question either that neoliberal reforms led governments to suppress protests. But, it is also true that they gave rise to new opportunities for mobilization. Finally, there are clear instances in which executives crafted policies behind closed doors and passed them through decree or ushered them through passive legislatures. But, there are also ample examples of extended legislative participation.

In short, the neoliberal landscape features both undemocratic and democratic qualities.

The best response may be that neoliberalism is neither a democratic nor an undemocratic system. Instead, the strength of democracy in a given country is a more important factor. It is worth remembering that most Latin American countries were emerging from long periods of authoritarianism when neoliberalism swept the region and those countries were not models of democratic rule prior to their authoritarian periods either. Where democratic governance was particularly weak, neoliberalism manifested in particularly undemocratic ways. In the most democratic settings, neoliberal reforms encountered opposition when they were unpopular and political actors had to negotiate over their policy preferences. Thus, Costa Rica and Uruguay, two of the most democratic countries in the region, implemented neoliberal reforms, but much more gradually, transparently and with much greater levels of debate, negotiation and compromise. By contrast, Bolivia or Ecuador are two countries with nominally democratic governments but that suffer from extraordinary levels of corruption, poorly institutionalized party systems, and systematic discrimination against, and exclusion of, their indigenous majorities. Not surprisingly, neoliberal reforms in these countries triggered violent protests, violent repression, including states of siege in Bolivia, and extra-constitutional changes of government triggered by violent reactions to reforms (multiple coups in Ecuador, and the flight of Sánchez de Lozada from Bolivia). Ultimately, neoliberalism's democratic failings reflect weaknesses in the institutions of representation and deliberation that make possible meaningful participation in decision-making and negotiation over policy. It is not clear that neoliberalism exacerbates the institutional and political shortcomings of Latin American democracy. Arguably, neither does it improve them. Neoliberalism's compatibility with democracy depends on the pre-existing strength and depth of democracy.

In fact, the greatest argument for the plausible compatibility of neoliberalism and democracy is the very resurgence of the left discussed by James Petras. Beginning in 1998 with the election of Hugo Chávez in Venezuela, neoliberalism was tested and defeated repeatedly at the ballot box. Subsequent elections in Argentina, Bolivia, Brazil, Chile, El Salvador, Honduras and Uruguay all saw victories for leftist candidates, most of whom campaigned overtly against neoliberalism. The turn to the left scared a number of Western observers who wondered, for example, if they "had lost Latin America." But, at the same time, there is probably no better indicator of neoliberalism's fit with democracy than if it has to compete in open, fair elections with alternative programs. The string of victories for the left that ran from 1998 through the late 2000s were measures of the extent to which neoliberalism depended on developing a consistent voting base of citizens who believed that it offered a better alternative. The fact that it did not, the reasons for it, and the consequences of the shift to the left are all reviewed in the next chapter. The remaining question is what were the economic, social, and political consequences of neoliberalism? This is reviewed below.

Assessing the Results

Assessing the performance of neoliberalism is not a straightforward task – a problem that helps to fuel the ongoing controversy. There are a number of challenges to sorting out the effects of neoliberal reforms. First, the task is complicated by the fact that neoliberalism was implemented to different degrees and at different times across the region. For example, the Chilean government implemented a deep set of reforms beginning in 1973 shortly after the coup that brought General Pinochet to power, and then again in another set of reforms in the 1980s. The initial reform period was very consistent with Washington Consensus policies. The second set, however, was quite eclectic. It included some very pragmatic constraints on markets on the one hand, and on the other a set of reforms that went much further than anything called for in the Washington Consensus agenda. By contrast with Chile, Brazil – often portrayed in neoliberal circles as a laggard – began a gradual, but continuous process of neoliberal reforms beginning in 1990 with the election of Fernando Collor. Venezuela began implementing neoliberal reforms in 1989 under Carlos Andrés Pérez, then interrupted them with his impeachment in 1992, then began a more limited process under Rafael Caldera in 1995, which in turn ended with the election of Hugo Chávez in 1998. Even Chávez' election, however, did not put an end to market policies initially. Instead, Chávez turned increasingly anti-market (in his policies – his rhetoric was constant) only in the 2000s. Thus, evaluating the impact of neoliberalism in the region is complicated by the fact that under consideration are different time periods, different durations of reforms, and different policies taking effect at different times.

Another problem has to do with the range of policies in the neoliberal program and the risks of making sweeping statements about the full program. For example, labor market reforms have made little progress in Latin America, despite being an important part of the neoliberal agenda. The high costs of hiring and firing workers in the region make the labor market "inflexible" – i.e. they discourage firms from hiring workers when the economy is growing because of the difficulty of firing them when the economy is shrinking. For neoliberal advocates, it is unfair to judge the "Washington Consensus" as a program when few reforms have taken place in a critical area for increasing employment opportunities in the formal labor market. Another area that has seen considerable variation is in privatization. Some countries, such as Bolivia, have privatized a great deal of their state-owned assets. Between 1988 and 1999, Bolivia privatized assets worth roughly 20% of GDP. By contrast, in the same period Uruguay sold state-owned assets worth roughly 1% of GDP. Colombia had privatized assets valued at roughly 5% of GDP. Chile had privatized even less, but that is because most of its privatizations had occurred earlier.[45] The levels of privatization are only one dimension of variation, however. Latin American countries varied in the extent to which they permitted competition in newly privatized sectors such as telecommunications or electricity or whether they granted monopolies to the new private operators. In addition, countries differed in the ways they *regulated* newly privatized utilities. Over the course of the 1990s, leading IFIs came to understand more and more the importance of establishing effective regulatory agencies that both protected consumers from exploitative firms as well as protected firms and the integrity of their contracts from opportunistic governments. But, Latin American countries varied considerably on the performance of those agencies: by the extent to which they actually had regulatory agencies in place prior to privatization, the degree of autonomy from political forces those agencies had, the extent to which government and the legal system protected them from firms' political influence, as well as the extent to which they relied more on market competition to police firms or strict regulatory action.[46] This is just a small sampling of the many ways that countries differed on policies in the Washington Consensus and the difficulty of making aggregate claims about neoliberalism. An honest assessment of neoliberal policies ultimately requires a strict disaggregation of the program into its constituent parts, with each evaluated on its own terms. This, unfortunately, is beyond the scope of this work.

A third difficulty has to do with possible outcomes one may want to explain. Neoliberals promised that following the agenda would restore economic growth, reduce inflation, make public sector debt manageable, and renew investment flows into Latin American countries. Neoliberals also expected that these positive macroeconomic outcomes would restore state capacity to govern effectively and would reduce poverty and possibly inequality. Critics expected neoliberalism to fail at virtually all of these, while in fact sharply worsening poverty, inequality, and state provision of essential services and goods (notably health and education). This is a wide array of outcomes and just as the specific policies need to be separated out, so do the specific outcomes. For example, it is possible to restore growth and reduce inflation while cutting social spending.

A final difficulty in evaluating neoliberalism is that there are other causal factors at work beyond the choice of policies that affect outcomes of interest. Growth is influenced by global growth rates. Investment flows respond to interest rates and stock market valuations in the developed world, regardless of what host countries do.[47] Demographic factors affect social policy. For example, the percentage of senior citizens in the population will influence social policy indicators independent of policy changes. Comparing social policy across two countries with very different demographic profiles must be approached with caution. Countries' economies vary in their connections to other economies and therefore their sensitivity to events beyond their borders and their control. Uruguay is very sensitive to changes in Argentina and Brazil (which are very sensitive to each other in turn). None of the three are as sensitive to the US economy. By contrast, Mexico depends heavily on the US economy and crises in Argentina or Brazil have little effect on its economy.

Finally, all Latin American countries have made policy experiments that do not conform to any conventional program, statist or Washington Consensus. Some of those policies have been great successes, some have been failures, and some produced short-term success, but then failed later. Chile began privatizing its social security system in 1980 and for a long time this appeared a great success and a model for countries considering social security reforms (including in the US). However, over the 1990s and into the 2000s, privatization increasingly became a problem as larger and larger numbers of people not covered by the program became the responsibility of the state. In effect, Chile has witnessed a long, slow, unintended "renationalization" of the system, but one that lacks the contributory financial mechanisms to support it now that the system is private. In response, reforms in 2008 were introduced to strengthen the contributory parts as well as add new non-contributory elements to extend coverage to the poor. Chile, however, also developed "capital controls" – an innovative set of taxes that discouraged investors from rapidly withdrawing their money from the country, thereby stabilizing the country's capital account. In Brazil, the 1994 "real plan" was an innovative, home grown plan for tackling inflation. It was an extraordinary success. The plan was abandoned in 1999 in the face of a new crisis, but inflation had been tamed even without it. In Bolivia, the government of Gonzalo Sánchez de Lozada developed an innovative privatization scheme in which half of the privatized assets from the sale went into the pension system and an old age compensation scheme for all Bolivians 65 and older. The "Bonosol" was an intriguing idea for converting privatization into a form of progressive social policy. But, deep logistical problems and political conflicts killed the program, leaving only cynicism about the privatization process in its wake. A final critical example is the Argentine inflation plan – the "convertibility plan" – that involved setting the value of the Argentine peso to the US dollar and then surrendering monetary policy to a "currency board" that guaranteed that each peso in circulation was backed by a dollar in the banking system. This quasi "dollarization" was enormously successful, rejuvenating a currency that had become worthless in the eyes of Argentines and an economy that was teetering on the brink with mass unemployment and hunger strikes. The IMF did not approve of the plan and only came on board as evidence of its success became clear. Yet, convertibility contained the seeds of its own downfall. In short, the currency was too strong. Over time, its overvaluation undermined the competitiveness of the domestic economy and made debt appear artificially cheap.[48] As growing numbers of observers expressed concern at the unsustainability of the peso

at parity with the US dollar, Argentine officials lacked the political credibility and/or will to end the plan. The final result was the 2001 Peso crisis
that plummeted Argentina into a calamitous economic and political crisis.
In short, governments develop their own policies and these policies can
and do have significant effects. Those policies do not necessarily conform
to any simple description of neoliberalism and may not even be endorsed by
Washington Consensus officials. Assessing the performance of neoliberalism
in the aggregate confronts this challenge as well.

So, how do scholars evaluate neoliberalism? One of the most common
ways is to rely on one of several measures of the extent of reforms. Those
include a structural reform index developed by Eduardo Lora of the Inter-
American Development Bank or a similar one developed by Samuel
Morley et al at CEPAL,[49] and the index of economic freedom developed
by the Heritage Foundation – a conservative Washington think tank. Some,
like Javier Corrales, also look at a narrower set of indicators, such as levels
of privatization, or private investment as a percentage of GDP, as metrics
for measuring the reliance on markets versus states.[50] The index developed
by Eduardo Lora is a particularly useful way of assessing the extent of
neoliberal reforms because it explicitly measures *policies*, not performance.
Lora, recognizing the challenges of separating out the many causal factors
affecting actual outcomes of economic policies, instead sought to evaluate
the *neutrality* of government policies in five different areas: trade, financial
liberalization, privatization, taxes, and labor markets. Neutrality refers to
the extent to which government policy avoids shaping market outcomes
rather than simply supporting basic rules and allowing private markets to
determine outcomes. Table 3.1 below shows the range of values between
1985 and 1999 for the aggregate index (the average score for the five
separate policy areas), with 1 meaning complete policy neutrality and 0
meaning determined completely by government.

The Heritage Foundation's Economic Freedom Index is another widely
cited measure of market reforms.[51] The Heritage Foundation's Index
measures ten areas of "economic freedom" based on a variety of data
mostly from international financial institutions. The ten areas are: business freedom (the ease and cost of starting a business); trade freedom
(tariff and non-tariff barriers to trade); fiscal freedom (an index measure
of the level of taxes); government spending; monetary freedom (a measure of the rate of inflation and the presence of government price controls); investment freedom; financial freedom (largely a measure of
government regulation of financial institutions); free property rights (a
measure of the degree of protection of private property); freedom from
corruption; and free labor markets (a measure of the cost and ease of
hiring and firing workers). The Economic Freedom Index score is an
unweighted aggregate of the ten scores, with 100 being perfectly free and
0 being a perfect command economy. Table 3.2 shows the data for Latin
America over a similar time period.

Table 3.1 Structural Reform Index, 1985–1999

	1985	1990	1991	1992	1993	1994	1995	1996	1997	1998	1999
Argentina	0.338	0.468	0.551	0.574	0.602	0.598	0.595	0.597	0.607	0.604	0.616
Bolivia	0.29	0.466	0.487	0.485	0.474	0.475	0.614	0.711	0.705	0.699	0.69
Brazil	0.259	0.43	0.431	0.449	0.468	0.489	0.515	0.53	0.551	0.58	0.61
Chile	0.488	0.57	0.572	0.564	0.565	0.57	0.577	0.586	0.585	0.585	0.606
Colombia	0.291	0.413	0.477	0.54	0.525	0.534	0.524	0.529	0.555	0.56	0.562
Costa Rica	0.306	0.425	0.42	0.44	0.446	0.453	0.536	0.533	0.542	0.557	0.557
Ecuador	0.309	0.405	0.399	0.456	0.461	0.484	0.536	0.535	0.539	0.536	0.528
El Salvador	0.349	0.399	0.401	0.416	0.494	0.505	0.488	0.497	0.489	0.572	0.566
Guatemala	0.344	0.445	0.444	0.45	0.462	0.475	0.513	0.505	0.509	0.57	0.592
Honduras							0.489	0.5	0.49	0.54	0.511
Mexico	0.29	0.425	0.453	0.479	0.474	0.54	0.531	0.5	0.51	0.501	0.511
Nicaragua						0.574	0.574	0.58	0.623	0.617	0.598
Paraguay	0.355	0.437	0.51	0.542	0.555	0.562	0.563	0.562	0.564	0.563	0.566
Peru	0.279	0.335	0.399	0.459	0.526	0.59	0.598	0.632	0.625	0.643	0.659
Uruguay	0.369	0.372	0.375	0.434	0.437	0.442	0.451	0.452	0.46	0.46	0.477
Venezuela	0.284	0.343	0.37	0.384	0.461	0.48	0.477	0.504	0.501	0.516	0.514
REGIONAL AVERAGE	0.341	0.436	0.455	0.484	0.503	0.522	0.539	0.548	0.554	0.573	0.583

Source: Eduardo Lora, Inter-American Development Bank, Working Paper #346, 2012.

Table 3.2 Heritage Foundation Economic Freedom, 1995–2000

Country	1995	1996	1997	1998	1999	2000
Argentina	68.0	74.7	73.3	70.9	70.6	70.0
Bolivia	56.8	65.2	65.1	68.8	65.6	65.0
Brazil	51.4	48.1	52.6	52.3	61.3	61.1
Chile	71.2	72.6	75.9	74.9	74.1	74.7
Colombia	64.5	64.3	66.4	65.5	65.3	63.3
Costa Rica	68.0	66.4	65.6	65.6	67.4	68.4
Ecuador	57.7	60.1	61.0	62.8	62.9	59.8
El Salvador	69.1	70.1	70.5	70.2	75.1	76.3
Guatemala	62.0	63.7	65.7	65.8	66.2	64.3
Honduras	57.0	56.6	56.0	56.2	56.7	57.6
Mexico	63.1	61.2	57.1	57.9	58.5	59.3
Nicaragua	42.5	54.1	53.3	53.8	54.0	56.9
Panama	71.6	71.8	72.4	72.6	72.6	71.6
Paraguay	65.9	67.1	67.3	65.2	63.7	64.0
Peru	56.9	62.5	63.8	65.0	69.2	68.7
Uruguay	62.5	63.7	67.5	68.6	68.5	69.3
Venezuela	59.8	54.5	52.8	54.0	56.1	57.4

Source: Data from Heritage Foundation, 2010, available at www.heritage.org

One method of trying to evaluate neoliberalism's performance is by classifying countries by the intensity or depth of their reform efforts. For example, Javier Corrales has evaluated the performance of neoliberalism by dividing key cases among aggressive, intermediate and shallow reformers, looking at the outcomes for growth and fiscal deficits.[52] To see the effects of neoliberal policies, Corrales looks at average growth rates for the period 1950–1980, the five years before the onset of major reforms, and the average for 1990–1999. For fiscal deficits, he compares the average for the five years before major reforms, the five years after, and the end point of his study, 1999. The results point to considerable benefits of neoliberalism. The five aggressive reformers (and the beginning year of reforms) are: Argentina (1991), Bolivia (1985), Chile (1985),[53] Mexico (1988), and Peru (1990). The five countries averaged 4.5% GDP growth for the period 1950–1980, but only 1.28% in the five years leading up to their respective neoliberal reform initiation. In the period 1990–1999, the average growth rate for the five countries rose to 4.48%. All but Chile initiated their major reforms in a context of serious economic crisis, marked by inflation, recession and financial imbalances. This is evident from the five year pre-crisis average fiscal deficit, which was -5.98% of GDP (only Chile was running a budget surplus at the time prior to its reforms). In the five years after initiating reforms, the average fiscal deficit for the five countries was down to -0.38% of GDP – a substantial improvement in these countries' macroeconomic balance. By contrast, both the shallow and intermediate reformers initiated more limited reforms and saw either limited gains or in fact significant declines in their macroeconomic performance. For example, the shallow reformers (Ecuador, 1992; Paraguay, 1989; Venezuela, 1992) enjoyed average GDP growth of 5.6% over the period 1950–1980. In the five years leading up to their limited reform efforts, growth had declined to an average among the three of 3.3%. In the 1990–1999 period, following their incomplete reform efforts, growth declined to an average of 2%. None of the three countries ran large fiscal deficits prior to their limited reform periods, averaging a balanced budget over the five year period preceding their reforms. But, all three began to run fiscal deficits in the 1990s with an average of -3% of GDP for the three in 1999. In Corrales' sample, there are only two intermediate reformers (Colombia, 1991, and Brazil, 1994) and their experiences differ in important ways, making their averages less meaningful.[54] Nevertheless, in both cases, the post reform years saw more modest growth rates than in the past (and compared to the aggressive reformers), and less success controlling fiscal deficits. For Corrales, the strongest evidence of the value of neoliberal reforms comes from looking at per capita GDP growth rates, comparing between the "lost decade" years of 1980–1989 and the neoliberal decade of 1990–1999. The shallow reformers appear doubly damned – suffering the consequences of the collapse of the economy and the capacity of the state ("stateness"), while not gaining the benefits of implementing reforms. The data show the stark results. Average per capita GDP over 1980–1990 for the shallow reformers declined roughly 1%. In the 1990s, however, per capita GDP declined roughly a further 0.3%. By contrast, the aggressive reformers saw substantial gains. Per capita GDP for the aggressive reformers declined roughly 1.25% (only Chile saw modest gains) in the 1980s. But, it grew 2.66% for the five countries over the 1990s, with Chile leading the way at a strong 4.4% growth in per capita GDP over the period.

Evelyne Huber and Fred Solt also rely on a classification scheme to discern the effects of neoliberalism. They divide the region's countries into discrete categories based on their levels of neoliberalism and the intensity of reform efforts, but they reach starkly different conclusions than Corrales.[55] The authors use different metrics for scoring neoliberalism and look at a different range of outcomes. To classify the cases, Huber and Solt draw on the widely used Morley, Machado and Pettinato General Reform Index, and separate cases into three categories, with cases differentiated between those above and those below the median. The three categories are: absolute level of the General Reform Index (GRI) as of 1995; the percentage change in score between 1982 and 1995 ("extent of change"); and "magnitude of change," defined as the largest one year change in score, again with cases classified dichotomously between those below the median and those above. Huber and Solt assess the performance of neoliberal reforms by comparing average scores for countries above the median with those below the median in the three categories, looking at GDP growth rates (divided into 1980–1989, 1990–1998, and the volatility of growth rates), poverty and inequality, and democracy scores. The authors find a mixed record of performance for countries with above average GRI scores. Overall, they appear to provide promising environments for economic growth and for democracy. However, growth was considerably more volatile over the 1990–1998 period, and poverty and inequality, and the change in inequality between 1982 and 1995 were inferior to the results for the below median cases.

The case for neoliberalism appears even weaker when looking at the *process* of reform rather than the level – i.e. the extent and magnitude of reform. In these cases, virtually every outcome appears inferior for the above median cases. Growth rates from 1980–1989 and inequality were both worse in the below median cases, but growth and volatility of growth rates from 1990–1998, the change in inequality from 1982 to 1995, and absolute poverty levels were all better in the cases with slower and non-drastic reform processes. Finally, both the rapid/deep reformers appeared less democratic than the slow reformers. Both the absolute level of democracy in 2000 and the rate of improvement since 1982 were better for cases that avoided extensive reforms or drastic episodes of change. In sum, Huber and Solt argue that neoliberalism appears to be consistent with democratic governance and promotes solid economic growth. But, it is also consistent with worsening inequality and higher poverty. More importantly, the reform process entails both political and economic costs that offset the benefits of growth and provide a strong caution about the wisdom of pursuing deep reforms.

Huber and Solt's findings are not stated with the same critical tone as the leftist critiques of scholars such as Petras, Harvey, or Duménil and Levy, but their concerns are consistent with the harsher critiques. As noted earlier, the leftist critiques tend to frame neoliberalism as a political agenda for the redistribution of wealth toward economic elites. In addition to data on income shares of the wealthiest segments of society, leftist critics tend to focus on unemployment and wage levels and in particular poverty levels. For example, Petras, Veltmeyer and Vieux,[56] Green,[57] and Grugel and Riggirozzi[58] all separately report the increasing levels of poverty and indigence over the period 1980 to 1999. For example, Green, drawing on data from CEPAL, acknowledges that the high point for the region was in 1990 when 48% of the population was poor and 23% of the population was indigent. By contrast, only 44% of the population was poor and 19% indigent in 1999. But he points out that both poverty and indigence were higher in 1999 than in 1980 when the rates were 41% and 19% respectively.[59] Alfredo Saad-Filho reports sharp losses to manufacturing and formal employment. In Argentina, Brazil and Mexico, manufacturing's share of GDP fell from 31%, 35% and 26% respectively in the 1980s to 17%, 21% and 19% by 2001. He further notes that open unemployment in the region increased on average in the 1990s from 5.8% to nearly 10% of the workforce. Open unemployment understates the severity of the impact because it does not count *underemployed* workers or the vast army of informal sector workers in Latin America.[60]

Employment is one of the weakest areas of performance for the Washington Consensus and even ostensibly neoliberal advocates report labor market difficulties. Jaime Saavedra, for example, details the changes in the labor market over the 1990s, recording the increases across the region in open unemployment, the increases in the number of workers who lack health or pension benefits, increases in the size of the informal sector, and finally a general trend of low-quality job creation. For example, open unemployment in Argentina, Brazil, Chile, Colombia, Mexico, Peru and Venezuela averaged 7.5% in 1990. In 2000, the average rate of unemployment across the seven countries was 10.6% and only Mexico reported lower rates than in 1990. To some extent, these worsened rates reflect the recession that hit the region in 1998, but in 1996 only Chile and Peru (very modestly) had better unemployment rates than in 1990. Economic growth in the region produced jobs, just not fast enough to keep pace with population growth. In the seven countries, informal sector employment increased markedly in every country but Chile and Mexico, and exceeding 50% of the labor market in Brazil, Colombia, Peru and Venezuela. In an expanded sample including Ecuador and Uruguay, Saavedra observes that the percentage of workers without access to social security increased in four of the nine countries (Argentina, Brazil, Ecuador and Peru) and exceeded 30% of the workforce in all but Uruguay. Thus, there is no question that neoliberalism's most serious indictment resides in its effects on the labor market.

Nevertheless, there are grounds for being cautious about the direct connection to the Washington Consensus policies. First, absolute poverty and indigence levels declined from 1990 to 2000. Considering that many Latin American countries had not yet implemented neoliberal reforms, it is plausible to argue that the high 1990 rates were a function of the debt crisis and its attendant effects (including the often desperate measures governments used to deal with it) rather than neoliberal policies per se. Second, both Saad-Filho and Saavedra identify exchange rate appreciation as a cause of labor market difficulties in addition to Washington Consensus policies such as trade liberalization. Yet, exchange rate appreciation is not a neoliberal policy per se – instead it reflected various efforts to combat inflation and attract foreign capital inflows. Many of these programs were home policies and not even necessarily supported or even approved by the IMF. Argentina's convertibility plan, Brazil's Real Plan or Ecuador's dollarization all led to overvalued currencies, but were not part of the Washington Consensus.[61] That may support the argument that developing countries cannot escape the dilemmas of *dependent development*,[62] but even if that is the case, it is a problem of any development model not just neoliberalism.

In fact, caution linking neoliberalism to specific consequences was the argument offered by the World Bank's Michael Walton in direct response to Huber and Solt.[63] Walton's position on neoliberalism's performance was by 2000 a pervasive view among neoliberal supporters in key institutions such as the World Bank or the Inter-American Development Bank. In Walton's words: "Shifts to a greater dependence on markets were usually beneficial, probably disappointing relative to the expectations of advocates, and certainly incomplete as a development strategy."[64]

Walton notes that by the late 1990s a greater awareness of the interaction of markets, specific contextual factors, political institutions, and inequality had emerged, as had the need to update Washington Consensus policies. Nevertheless, he goes on to argue that the evidence for neoliberalism's failings is weaker than the critical views suggest. Walton makes his case with simple, descriptive statistics using Morley et al.'s General Reform Index and by reviewing the econometric literature on neoliberalism and its impact on growth, volatility, poverty, inequality, and social spending.

The results that Walton reports are, like Huber and Solt, nuanced in their character, but in general point to weak or inconclusive relationships between market reforms and key outcomes. On growth, Walton compares GRI scores with changes in per capita output (a measure of the productivity of the economy) rather than GDP changes which are affected by many non-policy elements. There is no correlation, positive or negative, between the extent or magnitude of index changes and per capita output. Walton also reviews the econometric literature, which offers better estimates of the impact of reform changes because it controls for standard economic variables in calculating growth. Econometric studies find that open trade and deep financial markets are good for growth while inflation, banking crises, and volatility are bad for growth. In general, the econometric literature shows that less government is better for growth, but it still depends on *effective* government spending on important areas such as infrastructure and human capital. The econometric growth studies also show that Latin America's policy changes led to improvement in predicted growth rates absent policy reforms. In other words, the region's growth rates would have been lower if governments had not initiated neoliberal reforms.

On poverty and inequality, Walton reviews a variety of studies, including one conducted by Samuel Morley for CEPAL. Here again, the picture is more nuanced than Huber and Solt or the more radical critics claim. Looking at five separate studies across 20 countries in the 1970s, 1980s, and 1990s, Walton observes that there is no clear trend on inequality. In the 1990s, two separate studies found increasing inequality in six countries, declining inequality in two, and no real change at all for the remaining 12. It is worth noting that of the 20 countries, the two studies of the 1990s both found increasing inequality in two cases: Peru, an aggressive reformer, and Venezuela, a reform laggard. Walton complements this literature review with a bivariate comparison of both the level of and changes in the GRI with changes in inequality and finds no correlation.

This finding also supports separate work by Nancy Birdsall and Miguel Székely that shows that overall neoliberal reforms have neither helped nor worsened poverty and inequality.[65] Birdsall and Székely make the point that poverty and inequality are long-standing problems in Latin America and constitute a drag on economic performance, as well as being a cause themselves of the resilience of poverty and inequality, regardless of whether the state or markets are the primary mechanism of allocation. Poverty and inequality are drags on the economy because at least 50% of the population effectively are not consumers and generate no domestic savings for use in the economy. Unfortunately, this condition tends to reinforce poverty and inequality. In hard times or times of economic adjustment, the poor tend to withdraw whatever productive assets or developing human capital they may have and convert it into immediate cash for survival. So, poor people who may own a little land, or have children in school who may be developing future human capital that may be leveraged into higher wages at some later date, use them instead to get by. Land is sold and converted into cash; children are withdrawn from school and sent to work to raise money for the family. In either event, assets that could at some later point generate greater income lose that potential, reinforcing poverty as a trap.

This quality of poverty as a trap in the highly unequal Latin American context points to the importance of social policy. Drawing on data from CEPAL, Walton reports that social spending actually increased over the 1990s, very much in contrast to the leftist critique of neoliberalism. Social policy spending was not an explicit priority of the Washington Consensus, but the CEPAL data does make clear that budget cutting did not ultimately result in declining social expenditures. A variety of studies examining disaggregated social expenditures – namely in education, health and pension – also point to the compatibility, or at least mixed effects, between neoliberal reforms and social policy expenditure, suggesting that the harshest critiques of the reform program have overstated their case.[66] Data on social sector performance also seems to indicate a greater compatibility between neoliberalism and social policy. For example, education enrollments in primary and secondary schools both saw regional improvements over the period[67] as did key health care indicators such as life expectancy, physician attended births, birth rates, infant mortality rates and per capita consumption.[68]

Studies of privatization also point to mixed consequences for the region. In a widely cited study, Alberto Chong and Florencio López de Silanes find that overall, privatization has led to progressive outcomes in terms of access to key utilities such as telecommunications, electricity, sanitation, or water.[69] It has also led to improvements in efficiency for these vital sectors. On employment, the results have largely been neutral. Although privatized firms have laid off workers, the increases in efficiency and investment have created new jobs that have offset the losses. Prices, by contrast, have had a more mixed performance, with sharp increases in tariffs in some sectors and reductions in others. This variation depends on very specific contexts, not by sector or country. For example, Walton notes that water privatization was a "fiasco" in Cochabamba, Bolivia, but handled very effectively with very positive results at roughly the same time in La Paz–El Alto.[70] Manzetti points out that the privatization of electricity was badly mismanaged in Chile, but very effectively in Argentina, while the opposite was the case with telecommunications.[71] As a result, one has to be careful to avoid blanket statements about privatization and its effects on the region.

In fact, one of the most important conclusions about neoliberalism is the differential effect Washington Consensus policies had across countries, categories of workers, and sectors of the economy. Walton notes this finding and it is echoed across a large number of studies, from CEPAL to the World Bank. In essence, the shift from a state-led protectionist model to a market driven one provoked a transition. Initially, that transition entailed disruptions as agriculture adjusted, domestic manufacturing adjusted or failed, and new foreign investments entered into the economy. The transition both caused losses and created new opportunities. One of the central ways that the effects of reforms varied was in the labor market, where skilled workers and workers in export competitive sectors enjoyed considerable wage gains in comparison to unskilled workers. Neoliberal advocates expected that trade opening would benefit workers generally. But, in practice, workers with high school or university education saw substantial returns on their skills and education, sharpening inequality between the skilled workforce and the unskilled one. In particular, women made up an increasingly large percentage of the workforce, primarily among unskilled workers, sharpening inequality between male and female-headed households. For some, the new opportunities led to possibilities for upward mobility that had not existed earlier. Carol Graham and Pettinato demonstrate that prospects of upward mobility varied across the region and that voters who believed that they had good future prospects of upward mobility tended to support market reforms.[72]

In conclusion, understanding the effects of the Washington Consensus has to take into account variations across countries and the micro level of the economy. Simply stated, the set of market reforms had differential effects across different contexts. In aggregate terms, the relationship between neoliberalism and important outcomes like growth, poverty and inequality, social policy and democracy is not straightforward. Neoliberalism was not the scourge of the region. Neoliberal policies helped to restore growth, tame budget deficits and inflation, and renew investment flows. Contrary to the strongest critiques, it does not appear to have worsened inequality or poverty and it did not lead to reductions in social spending. In fact, Latin Americans' health and education improved considerably over the 1990s and dramatically since the 1970s. But, if neoliberalism has not been the scourge of the region, nor has it been its savior. Employment creation has neither been robust nor of high quality. Poverty and inequality did not worsen, nor did they improve. Growth returned to the region, but Latin America did not become the East Asian Tigers, such as South Korea. By the late 1990s into the early 2000s, neoliberalism's advocates were noting that market oriented policies needed to be complemented with good, social policies to address poverty, inequality and labor market concerns. More importantly, Latin America needed to address institutional deficiencies that weakened economic and social performance, despite the shift to markets. By 2000, there was arguably a consensus emerging about a greater need for balance and a greater attention to the institutional environment in the region. But, by 2000, the debate in the region shifted as the election of Hugo Chávez marked a shift to the left and back to the state as promoter of economic growth. This shift is explored in greater detail in Chapter Four.

Neoliberalism, Scourge or Savior: A Paired Comparison

Is neoliberalism the scourge or the salvation of Latin America? The aggregate picture is ambiguous. It is neither. Examining specific country cases offers another view of the different ways that neoliberal reforms play out with very different consequences. In this section, two deep reformers are compared. Chile and Bolivia are both examples of countries that embraced extensive neoliberal reforms. Chile began the neoliberal wave in 1973 with the coup that brought General Pinochet to power against the democratically elected Socialist Salvador Allende. In 1985, still under dictatorship, Chile embarked on another set of deep reforms. Bolivia initiated reforms in 1985 under the new democratically elected government of Victor Paz Estenssoro, a nationalist hero of the 1952 Revolution. Faced with a profound economic crisis, Paz Estenssoro launched a neoliberal reform program under the guidance of his Finance Minister Gonzlo Sánchez de Lozada. Ten years later, newly elected president himself, Sánchez de Lozada launched another set of reforms. By 2000, Chile was indisputably the most successful economy in Latin America. Bolivia by contrast had achieved little and was on a path to mounting political and economic chaos again.

Chile

As noted earlier, neoliberalism made its first appearance anywhere in the world in Chile, but its beginning was anything but propitious. Neoliberal reforms were put into place between 1973 and 1975 as the "Chicago Boys" assumed control of the economy. But the reform process occurred under the aegis of a brutal dictatorship and a politically motivated effort to restructure society. The election of Socialist Salvador Allende in 1970 was a watershed in Chile and Latin America. It was one of the few occasions where democratic elections brought to power a genuinely leftist president and although Allende himself was more moderate, his coalition of leftist partners in the Unidad Popular (Popular Unity) included much more radical contingents. For three years, Allende oversaw a controversial process of economic restructuring that deepened state ownership and intervention in the economy and redistributed wealth and income to workers, peasants, and the informal sector poor. Critics argue that the Allende government paid little attention to both the macroeconomic instability and the micro-level disorganization caused by their policies. Defenders argued that "capital" strikes and US opposition undermined the economy. There are grounds for believing that both sides of the debate have legitimate concerns. Nevertheless, economic performance declined precipitously by 1973 and society had become increasingly polarized.[73]

On September 11, 1973 General Pinochet launched a coup against President Allende and unleashed a campaign of terror against both members of the governing coalition and beneficiaries of their policies. Thousands were killed, imprisoned, tortured, and driven into exile as part of the dictatorship's effort to destroy its opponents. The Chicago Boys were charged with renewing economic growth, a process that also promised to break the labor unions, peasant organizations and ISI dependent businesses that constituted the ISI coalition. The neoliberal plan they unleashed was radical, drastic and immediate – arguably the most extreme policy shift in the history of the region. It included removal of all price controls previously established by Allende to contend with inflation, immediate commercial liberalization and the privatization of all companies nationalized during the Allende regime's three years in office. It continued through the mid 1970s with drastic cuts in government expenditures and investments, deregulation of financial markets, including lifting all restrictions on interest rates and foreign banks, and deepening of the privatization program. In 1979, the right to strike was curtailed; the health and social security systems were partially privatized, further restrictions on borrowing foreign currency were lifted, fiscal deficits were deemed illegal, and privatization deepened even further, selling off virtually all state owned enterprises by 1982. Pinochet passed a new constitution in 1980 that enshrined the market reforms in order to guarantee their persistence in the eventual return to democracy.[74]

In the 1980s, policy shifted towards "pragmatic neoliberalism" in the wake of the effects of the debt crisis, with its attendant high interest rates and withdrawal of funds from the region. Pinochet's liberalization policies had made debt cheap and easy for banks and the major business groups (the *piranhas*) and the shock left them highly indebted and vulnerable.[75] By 1982, unemployment had surged to 22% with much more severe effects in poor neighborhoods of Santiago, which in turn became the base of the first signs of organized opposition to the regime. The banking system faced collapse as the economy ground to a virtual halt. Demands for a return to a more activist state policy were mostly ignored, but the regime did actively intervene to save the banking system, including assuming private banks' foreign debt, raised tariffs moderately, introduced new controls on the inflow of foreign capital, and devised a targeted welfare program that offered protection to the poorest segments of Chilean society. The pragmatic response, however, did not stop neoliberal reform as in 1985 tariffs were reduced again and a new set of privatizations amounting to nearly 4% of GDP took place, including the previously intervened private banks and at least partial privatizations of all remaining state companies with the exception of CODELCO, the state owned copper company.[76]

By 1988, the year that external pressure forced Pinochet to mount a referendum on the return of democracy (which he lost), the economy was performing well again, growing quickly with solid macroeconomic fundamentals. In the 1989, the Concertación por el No – the coalition led by the Socialists and the Christian Democrats to campaign for the restoration of democracy – transformed itself into an electoral coalition – La Concertación por la Democrácia (the Coalition for Democracy) – and won the presidential election. Patricio Aylwin of the Christian Democrats took office in March 1990, presiding over an economy that was the envy of Latin America.

Between 1990 and 2000, the Concertación government consolidated the economic program inherited from Pinochet. Pinochet had assured that movement away from the model would be hard. The Senate was packed with appointed senators committed to the Pinochet regime. Similarly, the courts and the bureaucracy were staffed with Pinochet appointees. The electoral system was designed to overstate the strength of conservative parties and acted as a limit on the Concertación's legislative control. The Pinochet constitution of 1980 remained in effect, creating legal obstacles to reform. Finally, both the conservative business community, which had strongly supported Pinochet, and the army, which was granted extraordinary autonomy under the constitution, maintained vigilance over the new democratic government.[77]

But constraints aside, the Concertación government had little interest in changing a model that was so successful. Instead, the government deepened two elements. First, the government continued privatization by selling off its remaining shares in state owned enterprises with the exception of the vital copper industry. Even here, however, the Concertación spun out CODELCO's non-mining activities into separate holdings that were then privatized and the company received legal permission to enter into joint, public–private ventures. In addition, Chile aggressively sought new free trade agreements and inclusion in existing regional ones, including with the US and Mexico as well as the Brazil–Argentina led Mercosur. On the social front, the Concertación deepened and broadened Pinochet's limited social spending, making a much greater commitment to progressive and effective social policy.[78] The results were spectacularly successful by Latin American standards. By the election of 2000 and the transition to Socialist leadership under Ricardo Lagos, Chile had achieved social and economic gains beyond any country in the region. In fact, in the early 1990s, Chile was the only country in which the poverty rate was declining (although inequality had risen markedly) and the quality of life on virtually every measure improved over the course of the 1990s.

Real GDP growth averaged 7.5% between 1992 and 1998. Growth declined in the recession beginning in 1998–1999, but by 2000 had already risen back over 4%. Unemployment remained around 5% – among the lowest in the region – until the recession, and then fell again quickly after 2000. Real wages increased by roughly 5% per year and continued to grow at a somewhat slower pace even through the recession. Inflation fell below 10% by 1995 and as low as 3.5% by 1999. Gross domestic investment hovered around 25% for the whole period – among the highest in the region while debt as a percentage of GDP fell from over 20% in 1992 to around 7% by 1996. In addition, the government ran a budget surplus almost continuously with the exception of small deficits during the recession years.[79] Chile's ability to run deficits during recession was unique in Latin America at the time, as the rest of the continent was forced to adopt "pro-cyclical" measures – that is contractionary measures such as high interest rates, tax increases and budget cuts, all measures that deepen a recessionary trend, therefore "pro" as opposed to countermeasures which serve to reverse economic decline. This alone was a measure of Chile's economic success over this period.[80] As John Williamson has argued, any critique of neoliberalism has to consider the considerable successes of Chile.[81] A further measure of its success is the durability of what has emerged as a consensual model: it consolidated further under Socialist rule from 2000 to 2010 and showed no sign of meaningful change even after electing conservative Sebastian Piñera in 2009 or after the return to the left with the election of Socialist Michelle Bachelet in 2014.

Bolivia

If any critic of neoliberalism must contend with Chile's performance, then any defender must contend with Bolivia's. Bolivia pursued neoliberal reforms more extensively than almost any country in Latin America, certainly matching Chile for its profound transformations. But, while Chile is a model for the region, with an enviable economy and stable politics, Bolivia's politics was volatile and generally anemic in its growth, except for brief and unsustainable periods of higher growth due to extraordinary circumstances. The 2005 election of Evo Morales, the anti-capitalist, anti-US former leader of the Coca growers association, reflected the upheaval in the country, the long history of exclusion of the majority indigenous population, and the weakness of political institutions linking the state to society. It is also an indicator of the failure of neoliberalism to make a meaningful positive influence on everyday lives and helped set the stage for Morales' victory.

Bolivia's neoliberal experiment began in extraordinarily difficult circumstances. After roughly a decade of corrupt and incompetent democratic rule, the country returned to democracy in 1981, deeply indebted with uncontrolled patronage spending and capital flight.[82] The new government of Hernan Siles Suazo presided over a fractious coalition incapable of managing the intense internal disputes and warring with the powerful miners' union, the COB (Central Obrera Boliviana). Between 1982 and 1985, COB unleashed 3,500 work stoppages while Bolivia's GDP growth declined drastically and inflation soared to 20,000%.[83] The economy was in free fall and the currency had become completely valueless as at that rate of inflation it does not function as a medium of exchange. Nobody wants to hold currency that is losing value at a rate beyond calculation. Unable to govern, Siles Suazo called for early elections.

Victor Paz Estenssoro of the National Revolutionary Movement (Movimiento Nacionalista Revolucionario, MNR) assumed the presidency after winning the 1985 elections. Paz Estenssoro was the national hero of the Bolivian revolution of 1952. His administration had nationalized the tin industry and given it to the workers to run, armed workers and peasants, and passed a major land reform. In addition, he formed a governing legislative coalition with the left-wing MIR (Movimiento de Izquierda Revolucionaria, Revolutionary Left Movement). As a result, voters did not expect a radical shift to neoliberalism. But, facing catastrophic finances and severe hyperinflation, Paz Estenssoro had no choice. Three weeks after his inauguration, Paz Estenssoro launched the New Economic Plan (NEP) – a full, fledged rapid shift to neoliberalism. It included privatization, trade liberalization, opened the country to foreign investment and allowed the currency to float. He also sharply cut government spending and closed inefficient mines. The decision to close the mines set him against the COB and he twice declared a state of siege to suppress the resistance to NEP policies, forging patronage arrangements with his principal opposition, former dictator Hugo Banzer of the ADN (Acción Democrática Nacionalista, National Democratic Action Party).[84] The immediate effect on inflation was staggering, dropping it to 9% within months. But it also led to sizable job losses in manufacturing, mining and government. While the influential business organization, the CEPB (Confederación de Empresarios Privados de Bolivia, Confederation of Private Businesspeople of Bolivia), supported the NEP, rapid liberalization, as in Chile, led to large numbers of bankruptcies from domestic firms unable to compete with newly available imports. Real wages declined sharply throughout the economy. The World Bank supported Bolivia's shift to neoliberalism with substantially increased social assistance. Unfortunately, Bolivia's political system remained deeply corrupt and patronage dependent and much of the aid money that entered the country was deviated into corruption and patronage. The NEP began an effort to restructure the economy, but in the end it was limited by the preservation of a destructive state presence.[85]

Neoliberal reforms slowed dramatically from 1989 to 1993 under the presidency of leftist Jaime Paz Zamora of the MIR. Growth in Bolivia was moderate, based on improved export performance and management of external debt, coupled with significant increases in social assistance donations. But, Bolivia took another deep turn into neoliberalism with the election of Gonzalo Sánchez de Lozada in 1993. Sánchez de Lozada was a curious figure. He had been Paz Estenssoro's Finance Minister and the chief architect of the NEP, in conjunction with Harvard Economist Jeffrey Sachs. Sánchez de Lozada, a scion of an elite mine owning family, had been raised in Connecticut and returned to Bolivia with sincere neoliberal beliefs based on exposure to US capitalist democracy. On his election in 1993, Sánchez de Lozada and his brain trust in the Millennium Foundation in La Paz, devised another comprehensive reform package called the "Plan for All" (el Plan de Todos).

The Plan de Todos was an ambitious effort to fundamentally alter the character of state, markets and citizenship in the country. It included privatization of the largest and most important sectors of the economy under an unusual form called "capitalization." It also included privatization of the social security system, drastic decentralization of federal revenues and responsibilities to newly empowered municipalities (and indigenous rights), and education reforms, among a host of other laws designed to enhance citizen rights, strengthen markets, and streamline the state. The most innovative part of the plan was the capitalization scheme. The plan partially privatized SOEs in six of the most important sectors of the economy: telecommunications (ENTEL), rails (ENFE), the national airline (LAB), electricity (ENDE), tin (EMV), and hydrocarbons (YPFB). In exchange for the winning bids, firms were granted 50% ownership of the state owned enterprises and administrative and operational control. In exchange for their shares, the winning firms also had contractual obligations to invest in the sector and to expand service in cases like telecommunications and electricity. The Sánchez de Lozada government then used their 50% of the shares to shore up the insolvent pension system, create a stock market in Bolivia, and use dividends from the shares to pay out a non-contributory pension called the *Bonosol* to all Bolivians 65 and over. The plan was very creative and in conjunction with the remaining elements, it was an innovative effort to establish an equitable, market economy.[86]

The initial results were impressive. The privatizations raised over US$ 1.5 billion. The influx of capital and productive investment led to near historic growth rates with declining debt, inflation, and unemployment. Between 1994 and 1998, GDP growth averaged nearly 5% per year. Inflation fell to 2.4% by 1999, while debt as a percent of GDP fell from almost 80% in 1994 to 55% by 2000. Gross domestic investment rose from 14% of GDP in 1994 to almost 24% by 1998.[87]

The downsides, unfortunately, were important as well.[88] After the initial positive results from the privatizations, investment fell again to roughly

18% of GDP. More importantly, the government's revenues fell as well and budget deficits more than doubled from 1996 to 1997. Furthermore, many of the innovative reforms foundered on fundamental developmental problems. Ambitious, progressive education reforms foundered on institutional inadequacies and lack of support for teacher training and supervision. In many cases, decentralization fed clientelistic, corrupt and authoritarian practices instead of empowering communities. Newly privatized firms underperformed. The rails closed operation, LAB was sold to a Brazilian firm and subsequently closed, and the STET (Italian Telecom), the new private operator, openly violated the terms of its contract on service, access and investment requirements. Sánchez de Lozada had created new regulatory institutions to monitor the former SOEs, but a mix of institutional weaknesses hindered effective operation.[89] The new Bolivian stock market attracted little attention from investors abroad and even the *Bonosol* ran into problems as the government encountered difficulties establishing a realistic list of eligible beneficiaries. The next government of Hugo Banzer (1997–2001) suspended it in the face of mounting fiscal deficits. In addition, Sánchez de Lozada, like Paz Estenssoro before him, used state of siege emergency powers to confront and ultimately suppress opposition to reforms.[90]

When the global recession hit, Bolivia's growth averaged little more than 1% between 1999 and 2001 while unemployment nearly doubled and fiscal deficits exceeded 6% of GDP. One crucial lesson of the Plan de Todos and the subsequent recession was that Bolivia had been an economy that turned almost exclusively on the extraction and export of commodities – again always subject to volatile prices – and a vast informal economy engaged in precarious, low wage activities and excluded from most social benefits. Neoliberalism did not alter that basic equation. Under Banzer, and then again under President Gonzalo Sánchez de Lozada in a second term beginning in 2003, conflicts over privatization triggered violent resistance. Banzer's "Water War" in 2000 was a reaction to a poorly thought out, undemocratic imposition of an unwanted privatization. Sánchez de Lozada's "Gas War" turned on his decision to follow market principles and sell gas through Chile – the efficient choice – rather than Peru. However, Bolivians still smart from the 1879–1884 war in which Chile defeated Bolivia and annexed Bolivia's coastal territory, leaving the country landlocked. The unpopular decision was a trigger for deeper resistance to Sánchez de Lozada's economic policies and when protestors were killed in the ensuing violence, the president was forced to flee the country where, as of 2017, he is under indictment for crimes against humanity. The upshot is straightforward: getting prices right, and withdrawing the state in favor of markets is not a panacea.[91] Bolivia's institutional weaknesses and underdeveloped economy needed creative policy-making and a more substantial solution to its development challenges. Sánchez de Lozada's policies were probably the most comprehensive and the most creative in the entire neoliberal period. Even then, their reliance on markets was not enough. Evo Morales campaigned both on issues of identity and exclusion as well as sharp criticism of the US and the model of capitalism that American officials pushed throughout the world. The failings of neoliberalism as an economic model made it possible and credible for Morales to link it to the political shortcomings as well. The Bolivian experience shows the limits of neoliberalism as a model when basic political and economic institutions serve citizens poorly.

Notes

1 Kuczynski, 1987. The data and discussion below draws on Kuczynski, chapters 1 and 3. Both the data and the analysis are representative of neoliberal views about the problem of the Latin American state and the debt crisis. Kuczynski ran unsuccessfully for the presidency in 2011 and then was elected president in 2016, running at the head of a party he had founded called *Peruanos Por el Kambio* (PPK – Peruvians for Change).
2 Kuczynski, 1987: 10.
3 John Williamson, "What Washington Means by Policy Reform." In *Latin American Adjustment: How Much Has Happened?* John Williamson, ed. (Washington DC: Institute for International Economics, 1990).
4 Williamson, 1990: 7.
5 Although in practice, developing countries cannot finance their deficits through domestic savings, which makes them dependent on the preference of foreign investors and lenders. So, while a small deficit is acceptable in theory, in practice, states had to show investors and lenders that they would be able to service their debt and that in turn depended on maintaining budget surpluses. In practice, particularly in the 1980s when lending to the region was limited, it meant that theory and practice diverged in ways that rendered the more permissive attitude to deficits moot.
6 Williamson, 1990: 8.
7 The idea that deficits represent societies living beyond their means and the lack of political courage to make hard choices is very much a part of the current discussion about fiscal stimulus versus deficit reduction in Western Europe, Japan and the US. For example, see Megan McCardle "Deficits Matter," *Atlantic Monthly* 306, no. 1 (June/July 2010).
8 Note that this is not a peculiarly Latin American issue. This was the prevailing diagnosis of Greece's budget and larger economic woes after the 2008 financial crisis and is the justification for the brutal austerity cuts the European Union has forced on the country.
9 For example, see Walter Molano's discussion of one of the best SOEs in Latin America, Brazil's Telebrás, and its decline into the 1980s in *The Logic of Privatization: The Case of Telecommunications in the Southern Cone of Latin America* (Westport, CT: Praeger Publishers, 1997).
10 For the seven largest economies in Latin America, fringe benefits as a percentage of average industrial wages ranged from a low of 50% in Peru to as high as 80% in Argentina and Brazil. Kuczynski, 1987: 57.
11 James Petras, *The Left Strikes Back: Class Conflict in Latin America in the Age of Neoliberalism* (Boulder, CO: Westview Press, 1999); David Harvey, *A Brief History of Neoliberalism* (New York: Oxford University Press, 2005).
12 Note again the relevance of these arguments to contemporary discussions in the United States. Perhaps the most striking example is the discussion in the

Trump administration about rolling back financial regulations and protections for consumers even after the banking system's failure in 2008–2009 plunged the country into a crisis from which it has only partially recovered.

13 The Phillips Curve is a standard view of the relation between inflation and growth in economics. Typically, high inflation is an indication of rapid growth in the economy and therefore low unemployment. High unemployment is an indicator of slack in the economy (recession) and therefore low inflation. Economic policy in mainstream economics treats inflation and unemployment as trade-offs with policy promoting one or the other depending on the circumstances (inflationary/expansionary policies in the face of high unemployment and recession and contractionary policies in the face of rapid growth and high inflation). The challenge of stagflation was that the simultaneous appearance of high unemployment with high inflation made it difficult to determine the appropriate policy response.

14 See for example *Between Power and Plenty: Foreign Economic Policies of Advanced Industrial Democracies* (Ithaca, NY: Cornell University Press, 1978), edited by Peter Katzenstein, for an excellent political economy account of the variations in responses among advanced industrial democracies in Western Europe and the US.

15 Gérard Duménil and Dominique Lévy, "The Neoliberal Counter-Revolution." In *Neoliberalism: A Critical Reader*, Alfredo Saad-Filho and Deborah Johnson, eds. (London: Pluto Press, 2005): 14.

16 Harvey, 2005: 16.

17 For example, the Obama Administration passed the "Fiduciary Rule" requiring brokers to act in their client's best interests rather than seeking the highest possible returns for themselves. Trump signed a memorandum delaying the rule in anticipation of its reversal in February, 2017, allowing brokers to return to the pre-crisis practice of sacrificing clients' interests in favor of their own profits. "Trump Moves to Roll Back Obama-Era Financial Regulations," *New York Times*, February 2, 2017. Available online at http://www.nytimes.com. Accessed on August 1, 2017.

18 Duncan Green, *The Silent Revolution: The Rise and Crisis of Market Economics in Latin America* (New York: Monthly Review Press, 2003): 58.

19 Green, 2003: 59–60.

20 Javier Santiso, *The Political Economy of Emerging Markets: Actors, Institutions and Financial Crises in Latin America* (New York: Palgrave, 2003).

21 Susan Stokes, *Mandates and Democracy: Neoliberalism by Surprise in Latin America* (New York: Cambridge University Press, 2001).

22 Andy Baker, *The Market and the Masses in Latin America: Policy Reform and Consumption in Liberalizing Economies* (New York: Cambridge University Press, 2010).

23 Sebastián Etchemendy, *Models of Economic Liberalization: Business, Workers and Compensation in Latin America, Spain and Portugal* (New York: Cambridge University Press, 2011).

24 Ironically, some of the best accounts of the mobilization of society against neoliberalism come from critics of the reform process. See for example, Petras, 1999; Jean Grugel, "'Basta de Realidades, Queremos Promesas': Democracy after the Washington Consensus." In *Governance After Neoliberalism in Latin America*, Jean Grugel and Pía Riggirozzi, eds. (New York: Palgrave MacMillan, 2009); Eduardo Silva, *Challenging Neoliberalism in Latin America* (New York: Cambridge University Press, 2009).

25 For an excellent discussion of the Menem administration's conversion to pro-market reforms, see Luigi Manzetti, *Privatization South American Style* (New York: Oxford University Press, 2000).

26 Judith Teichman discusses the role of policy networks to explain the reform process in Argentina, Chile and Mexico, focusing on the alliances formed and the cooperation that developed among technocrats and key private sector allies in *The Politics of Freeing Markets in Latin America: Chile, Argentina and Mexico* (Chapel Hill, NC: University of North Carolina Press, 2001).

27 See Eduardo Lora and Ugo Panizza, "The Future of Structural Reform," *Journal of Democracy* 14, no. 2, 2003.

28 Marcus Kurtz, "The Dilemmas of Democracy in the Open Economy: Lessons from Latin America," *World Politics* 56, no. 2, 2004.

29 Carlos Vilas, "Inequality and the Dismantling of Citizenship," *NACLA Report on the Americas*, May/June, 1997.

30 Phillip Oxhorn, "Beyond Neoliberalism? Latin America's New Crossroads." In *Beyond Neoliberalism in Latin America*, John Burdick, Phillip Oxhorn and Kenneth Roberts, eds. (London: Palgrave MacMillan, 2009). Forrest Colburn, 2002 expresses the same concern.

31 Kurt Weyland, "Neoliberalism and Democracy: A Mixed Record," *Latin American Politics and Society* 46, no. 1, 2004.

32 Stokes, 2001.

33 For example, see Kurt Weyland, "Neopopulism and Neoliberalism in Latin America," *Studies in Comparative International Development* 31, no. 3, 1996.

34 Bolivia did not permit direct re-election and therefore Sánchez de Lozada was required to step down at the end of his term and then ran successfully four years later.

35 Cited in Peter Kingstone, *Crafting Coalitions for Reform: Business Strategies, Political Institutions and Neoliberalism in Brazil* (University Park, PA: Penn State Press, 1999).

36 Weyland, *The Politics of Market Reforms in Fragile Democracies*, 2004.

37 Andy Baker, "Who Wants to Globalize? Consumer Tastes and Labor Markets in a Theory of Trade Policy Beliefs," *American Journal of Political Science* 49, no. 4, 2005; *Wall Street Journal* polls documented in Andy Baker, 2010.

38 Javier Corrales, *Presidents without Parties: The Politics of Economic Reform in Argentina and Venezuela in the 1990s* (University Park, PA: Penn State Press, 2002).

39 Eduardo Silva, *The State and Capital in Chile: Business Elites, Technocrats and Market Economics* (Boulder, CO: Westview Press, 1998).

40 Manzetti, 2000.

41 Maria Victoria Murillo, "Political Bias in Policy Convergence. Privatization Choices in Latin America," *World Politics* 54, no.4, 2002.

42 Sylvia Rhodes, *Social Movements and Free Market Capitalism in Latin America* (Albany, NY: State University of New York Press, 2006).

43 Peter Kingstone, Joseph Young and Rebecca Aubrey, "Privatization and Its Discontents: Resistance to the Hegemony of Neoliberalism in Latin America," *Latin American Politics and Society* 55, no. 3, 2013: 93–116.

44 Petras, 1999.

45 Eduardo Lora, "Structural Reforms in Latin America: What Has Been Reformed and How to Measure it?" Washington DC: Inter-American Development Bank, Working Paper #346, 2012.

46 Maria Victoria Murillo, *Political Competition, Partisanship, and Policy Making in Latin American Public Utilities* (New York: Cambridge University Press, 2009); Brian Levy and Pablo Spiller, *Regulations, Institutions and Commitment: Comparative Study of Telecommunications* (New York: Cambridge University Press, 1996); Manzetti, 2000.

47 Sylvia Maxfield, "Understanding the Political Implication of Financial Internationalization in Emerging Market Countries," *World Development* 26, no. 7, 1998.

48 Note that there are strong parallels between Argentina's economic crisis due to the long period of an overvalued currency, and the contemporary crisis in Greece, where membership in the EU and use of the Euro has had the same effects.

49 Eduardo Lora, "A Decade of Structural Reforms in Latin America: What Has Been Reformed and How to Measure it," Working Paper, Inter-American Development Bank, Washington, DC, 1997. Samuel A Morley, Roberto Machado, and Stefano Pettinato, "Indices of Structural Reform in Latin America," *ECLAC Serie Reformas Economicas* 12. Santiago, Chile, 1999. The Morley et al. is more widely used by political scientists, in part because of the greater time range of the index.

50 See Javier Corrales, "Varieties of Market Discontent." In *Constructing Democratic Governance in Latin America*, Jorge Dominguez and Michael Shifter, eds. (Baltimore: Johns Hopkins University Press, 2003).

51 The data is available at http://www.heritage.org. The Index of Economic Freedom generates somewhat more controversy than the Lora index given its overt and partisan commitment to an intensely pro-market philosophy, such as the Austrian School's Friedrich Von Hayek. Critics charge that its method tends to be fuzzier and more prone to bias than Lora's ideologically neutral index (despite the fact that Lora is himself an economist working for a leading IFI associated with the Washington Consensus). For example, the Economic Freedom Index ranks countries on levels of taxation as it sees corporate taxes and taxes on wealth as inherently anti-market, while Lora is more concerned with the productivity and efficiency of taxation, rather than the absolute level.

52 Javier Corrales, "Markets," in *Constructing Democratic Governance in Latin America*, Jorge Dominguez and Michael Shifter, eds. (Baltimore: Johns Hopkins University Press, 2003).

53 Note that Chile's most aggressive reform period began after the 1973 coup and the reforms initiated in the 1980s were more moderate. Eduardo Silva referred to this stage as "pragmatic neoliberalism." Silva, 1998.

54 Brazil's economy historically grew faster than Colombia's and consistently ran high fiscal deficits, while Colombia historically ran moderate deficits or surpluses.

55 Evelyne Huber and Fred Solt, "Successes and Failures of Neoliberalism," *Latin American Research Review* 39, no. 3, 2004.

56 James Petras, Henry Veltmeyer and Steve Vieux, *Neoliberalism and Class Conflict in Latin America* (London: Macmillan, 1997).

57 Duncan Green, 2003: 152.

58 Jean Grugel and Pía Riggirozzi, "The End of the Embrace," in Jean Grugel and Pía Riggirozzi, eds., *Governance After Neoliberalism in Latin America* (New York: Palgrave MacMillan, 2009): 15.

59 Duncan Green, 2003: 152. The CEPAL study defines "poor" as insufficient income to meet basic food and non-food needs while "indigent" indicates insufficient income to meet food needs even if all income is spent on food.

60 Alfredo Saad-Filho, "The Political Economy of Neoliberalism in Latin America." In *Neoliberalism: A Critical Reader*, Alfredo Saad-Filho and Deborah Johnston, eds. (London: Pluto Press, 2005): 226.

61 In fact, John Williamson thought that liberalizing the capital account (i.e. liberalizing flows of capital into and out of the country) was premature and Jagdish Bhagwati, one of the leading champions of free trade, explicitly disagreed with liberalized capital flows as well.

62 James E. Mahon, *Mobile Capital and Latin American Development* (University Park: Penn State University Press, 1996).

63 Michael Walton, "Neoliberalism in Latin America: Good, Bad or Incomplete?" *Latin America Research Review* 39, no. 3, 2004.

64 Walton, 2004: 165.
65 Nancy Birdsall and Miguel Székely, "Bootstraps, not Band-Aids: Poverty, Equity and Social Policy." In *After the Washington Consensus: Restarting Growth and Reform in Latin America*, John Williamson and Pedro Pablo Kuczynski, eds. (Washington DC: Institute for International Economics, 2003).
66 See, for example, Robert Kaufman and Alex Segura-Ubiergo, "Globalization, Domestic Politics, and Social Spending: A Time Series, Cross Section Analysis 1973–1997," *World Politics* 53, no. 4, 2001; Erik Wibbels and Moises Arce, "Globalization, Taxation, and Burden-Shifting in Latin America," *International Organization* 57, 2003.
67 Laurence Wolff and Claudio de Moura Castro, "Education and Training: The Task Ahead." In *After the Washington Consensus: Restarting Growth and Reform in Latin America*, John Williamson and Pedro Pablo Kuczynski, eds. (Washington DC: Institute for International Economics, 2003).
68 James McGuire, *Wealth, Health and Democracy in East Asia and Latin America* (New York: Cambridge University Press, 2010).
69 Alberto Chong and Florencio López de Silanes, "The Truth about Privatization in Latin America," Washington: DC: Inter-American Development Bank, Research Network Working Paper #R-486, 2003.
70 Walton, 2004: 179.
71 Luigi Manzetti, "The Political Economy of Regulatory Policy." In *Regulatory Policy in Latin America: Post-Privatization Realities* (Miami: North-South Center Press, 2000).
72 Carol Graham and Stefano Pettinato, "Hardship and Happiness: Social Mobility and Public Perceptions during Market Reforms." In *Post-Stabilization Politics in Latin America*, Carol Wise and Riordan Roett, eds. (Washington DC: Brookings Institution Press, 2003).
73 Lois Hecht Oppenheim, *Politics in Chile: Socialism, Authoritarianism and Market Democracy* (Boulder, CO: Westview Press, 2007).
74 Judith Teichman, *The Politics of Freeing Markets in Latin America: Chile, Argentina and Mexico* (Chapel Hill, NC: University of North Carolina Press, 2001).
75 Silva, 1998.
76 Teichman, 2001.
77 Silva, 1998.
78 Teichman, 2001.
79 Data from USAID, "Latin America and the Caribbean Selected Economic and Social Data," Washington DC: United States Agency for International Aid and Development, 2002.
80 Ricardo Hausmann, Michael Gavin, Carmen Pages-Serra and Ernesto Stein, "Financial Turmoil and the Choice of Exchange Rate Regime," Working Paper No. 400. Washington DC: Inter-American Development Bank, 1999. Available on the web at http://www.iadb.org.
81 Williamson, 2003.
82 Herbert S. Klein, *A Concise History of Bolivia* (New York: Cambridge University Press, 2003).
83 Benjamin Kohl and Linda Farthing, 2006.
84 Eduardo Gamarra, "The Case of Bolivia." In *Presidentialism and Democracy in Latin America*, Scott Mainwaring and Matthew Shugart, eds. (New York: Cambridge University Press, 1997).
85 Eduardo A. Gamarra, "Crafting Political Support for Stabilization." In *Democracy, Markets, and Structural Reform in Latin America*, William C. Smith, Carlos H. Acuña, and Eduardo A. Gamarra, eds. (Miami: University of Miami, North-South Center Press, 1994).

86 George Gray Molina, Ernesto Pérez de Rada, and Ernesto Yañez, "La economía política de reformas institucionales en Bolivia," Washington DC: Inter-American Development Bank, Working Paper #350, 1999.
87 Data from USAID, 2002, available at http://www.usaid.gov/result-and-data/data-resources.
88 Benjamin Kohl, "Privatization Bolivian Style: A Cautionary Tale," *International Journal of Urban and Regional Research* 28, no. 4: 893–908, 2004.
89 Confidential author interviews, Ministry of Telecommunications and SIRESE (Sistema de Regulación Sectorial, Sectoral Regulatory System), March 2003, La Paz.
90 Kohl and Farthing, 2006.
91 Albert Fishlow makes the crucial point that neoliberal prescriptions run the risk of undermining the capacity to get policies right in the interests of getting prices right. "Some Reflections on Comparative Latin American Economic Performance and Policy." In *Economic Liberalization: No Panacea*, Tariq Banuri, ed. (New York: Oxford University Press, 1991).

4 Democracy, Development and the Pink Tide

The period of neoliberal hegemony – the pervasive mentality of TINA ("There is no alternative") that permeated the region and studies of development[1] lasted roughly from 1985 into the early 2000s. During that time, both scholarly and official discourse really did make it seem as if no alternatives existed. In 1993, Jorge Castañeda, a prominent Mexican scholar, observed, "the United States and capitalism have won, and in few areas of the globe is that victory so clear-cut, sweet and spectacular as in Latin America."[2] Castañeda's observation appeared in *Utopia Unarmed*, a book that quickly emerged as an essential reference on the rise and fall of the left in Latin America. It offered a rich, detailed analysis of the left's history in the region and dissected the errors – political and economic of the apparently vanished progressives and revolutionaries of the past. Perhaps most importantly, it made an impassioned appeal for a renewed left and proposed an agenda for its resurrection. For Castañeda, a robust left was necessary to push to continue to address the ongoing deep inequities in the region – inequities that neoliberalism was not resolving. But, as the opening quote suggests, Castañeda, like virtually all other observers of the region, had little confidence that a resurrection of the left was coming any time soon.

Less than ten years later, the picture in the region had changed dramatically as a wave of electoral victories for the reinvigorated left fundamentally altered the political landscape – a veritable "Pink Tide." The reversal began with the election of Hugo Chávez in Venezuela in 1998. At the time, Venezuela appeared sui generis, responding to its own idiosyncratic conditions, and initially it did not appear that Chávez' economic policies would match his anti-US and anti-capitalism rhetoric. Both were misconceptions. Chávez soon began a much more concerted turn away from market oriented policies and additional leftist victories pointed to a new trend. In the fifteen years after the publication of *Utopia Unarmed*, Latin America went from the region where US-style capitalism had won its greatest victory to a region where observers wondered was "Washington losing Latin America?"[3]

By 2017, fifteen of the seventeen countries covered in this book had elected a leftist president at least once and eight still had leftist presidents as of this writing. Many of the victorious leftists campaigned actively and explicitly against neoliberalism and US style capitalism. Presidents in Bolivia, Ecuador, Nicaragua and Honduras allied with Chávez, the region's most aggressive critic of neoliberalism and the US and joined the Cuban-Venezuelan Bolivarian Alliance for the Americas (Alternativa Bolivariana para los Pueblos de Nuestra América, ALBA) – the anti US-led Free Trade of the Americas (FTAA) pact. The wave of leftist victories alarmed Washington and neoliberalism's advocates and sparked a near industry of evaluation in academia. The shift was stunning and almost completely unexpected.[4]

There are two crucial questions that arise out of this turn to the left. The first is: What happened? How did the period of neoliberal hegemony end so quickly and apparently so completely? On the face of it, the easiest answer would be that the shift confirmed the critics' view of neoliberalism as an undemocratically imposed, elitist economic program that citizens rose up against and rejected – a "backlash" against reforms. The book has not been closed yet on the causes of the turn to the left, but the evidence suggests that neoliberalism, at least as a defined set of policies and a belief in the value of market, is not dead and that voters in general have not rejected it. Indeed, two countries, Colombia and Mexico, never embraced the left, while the right has returned to govern in seven cases. Instead of an explicit rejection of neoliberalism, a mixture of conjunctural and idiosyncratic causes, coupled with some of the weaknesses of neoliberalism, fostered a modest leftward shift in voter preferences, as well as an anti-incumbent wave that brought the left back to power. In many countries, one could argue that the turn to the left is best understood as "normal" democratic politics: voters punished incumbents for weak economic performance and voted for the opposition in their place. In some countries, the dynamic was more revolutionary, but many of these countries had very specific factors that were not necessarily about state versus market. In most countries that experienced a more radical shift, the party system had become, or always had been, de-institutionalized, opening the door to more volatile politics.[5] For example, in Bolivia and Ecuador, long-standing discrimination and exclusion of the indigenous played a crucial role. In these countries, along with Venezuela, the weaknesses of liberal democracy invited broad and direct appeals to the large mass of the poor built on a more participatory form of "popular" democracy.[6] In sum, the story is more complex than a simple voter backlash against the authoritarian and elitist character of neoliberalism.

The second crucial question is what was the consequence of the region's turn to the left? Again, the obvious expectation was a rolling back of market-reforms, a return to state-led development, and a slew of possible, traditional leftist or nationalist policies, including measures to limit foreign investments, redistribute wealth, and promote domestic producers and workers. Again, the answer to the question is more complex. First and foremost, on the aggregate, the region did not turn markedly anti-market. Both public opinion polls and measures of market friendly policies (such as the Inter-American Development Bank's Structural Reform Index, or to a lesser extent the Heritage Foundation's Index of Economic Freedom) do not show significant reversals from 1999 on. One important reason for that is that the turn to the left was not a uniform process. Analysts have argued about the best ways to classify the left and indeed have come up with several plausible ones that capture different aspects of leftist politics and policy in the region. Others have argued that trying to group the left into different types tramples over such big and important differences among the cases that classification ends up obscuring more than illuminating.

This is a very important caveat and the discussion below takes seriously the risk of lumping cases together unfairly. Yet, it is still helpful to offer "ideal types" or modal examples that point to differing tendencies that can be classified and analyzed. One way to avoid over-simplification is to focus on governments and their orientation rather than countries. Governments could and did shift approaches even in the same country and sometimes even the same party.

Among the alternative approaches to thinking about the left, one way focuses on policy and policy-making – that is to say what a government of the left does rather than what it says or who votes for it.[7] This approach identifies two distinct lefts in the region: one more antagonistic towards neoliberalism and the political system that implemented it, what Kurt Weyland, Wendy Hunter and Raúl Madrid call the "contestatory" left;[8] the other a more "moderate" or "pragmatic" left that has retained a strong pro-market orientation, but has sought to condition or qualify neoliberalism – what some have referred to as "neoliberalism with a human face." Of course, some countries remained under right wing governments that have not rejected neoliberalism rhetorically or otherwise, the most important of these being Colombia and Mexico, and Costa Rica until 2014. Moreover, even "contestatory" regimes, such as Ecuador under Rafael Correa, Bolivia under Evo Morales and even Venezuela under Hugo Chávez remain dependent on foreign investment in natural resource extraction and access to global markets. Growth still requires investment and trade. It is possible, then, that leftist government did not alter market orientation that much. So, what difference did the left really make?

This chapter explores these two crucial questions for the region. Several claims are advanced. First, the shift to the left was primarily conjunctural or reflected country specific factors that were not about state versus markets. Reversing massive discrimination against the indigenous, for example, does not mean that improving access to markets could not be an impor-tant part of the solution.[9] Latin American citizens did not turn against the market ideologically. Public opinion on the question of state versus market is relatively moderate. Second, the best way to evaluate the left is by comparing between the right and the two idealized or polar types of the leftist policy and political orientation: one that more aggressively challenged democratic capitalist institutions and policies, and one that has adopted a more pragmatic approach. Country cases do not fall rigidly into these categories and there are similarities in policy and performance among cases that cross categories. As a result, this is an evaluation of differing strategies or orientations rather than fixed classification of countries into types. Third, this pragmatic, moderate left orientation has performed better than either the more "contestatory" approach or than the right. The pragmatic view reflects an understanding of the need for balance between markets and the state and inclusive public policy-making. A healthy mix of market, state and effective social policy make sustainable democratic development likelier. Finally, despite the greater success of this pragmatic approach, the region continues to face serious challenges regarding poverty, inequality, human capital development, and economic growth. This last point is explored in greater depth in Chapter Five.

The Turn to the Left?

How sweeping was the shift to the left? Between 1998 and 2014, leftists won elections and held office in Venezuela (1999–present); Chile (2000–2010; 2014–present); Brazil (2003–2016);[10] Argentina (2003–2016); Panama (2004–2009); Uruguay (2005–present); Bolivia (2006–present); Honduras (2006–2009);[11] Nicaragua (2007–present); Peru (2007–2016);[12] Ecuador (2007–present); Paraguay (2008–2012); El Salvador (2009); and Costa Rica (2014–present). Leftists successfully stood for re-election in most of these countries (or were succeeded by presidents of their own party) in Argentina, Bolivia, Brazil, Chile, Ecuador, El Salvador, Peru, Uruguay and Venezuela. In that time, the right returned to power in Honduras (2009, but through removal of the leftist president), Chile (2010, only to lose power again in 2014), Panama (2012), Argentina (2016), Brazil (2016), and Peru (2016). A brief summary of the wave of leftist victories follows below.

Venezuela: Hugo Chávez' election in 1998 was the first in the region as voters in Venezuela embraced the one-time failed coup leader whose scorn of the decaying "Punto-Fijo" party system helped bolster his credentials as a revolutionary figure. After rewriting the constitution and substantially overhauling the political system, Chávez called new elections in 2000. An aborted coup attempt in 2002 that Chávez blamed on the US only solidified his power. He was easily re-elected in 2006. In 2009, a national referendum eliminated presidential term limits, removing any restrictions on Chávez continuing to run for office, and Chávez remained in office until his death.

Chile: In Chile, the Concertación coalition of Christian Democrats and Socialists were instrumental in restoring democracy to the country in 1989. Since then, the coalition controlled the presidency under Christian Democratic rule through the 1990s. In 2000, however, Socialist Ricardo

Lagos emerged victorious and the Socialists returned to power for the first time since the 1973 coup against President Salvador Allende. The success of Ricardo Lagos' government paved the way for the election of Michelle Bachelet of the Socialist Party in 2005. Bachelet left office with strong approval ratings, but could not stand for re-election under the Chilean constitution. While the right won the 2009 election under Sebastián Piñera, Bachelet successfully stood for election again in 2014.

Brazil: In 2002, Luiz Inácio Lula da Silva, the perennial runner-up in every direct election since Brazil's restoration of democracy in 1985, finally won control of the presidency for his Workers' Party. Lula had presided over a gradual shift towards the center from his early days as first a union leader then an avowedly socialist party leader. His more moderate stance succeeded in a poor economic context and discontent over the incumbent Social Democratic party's neoliberal orientation. Lula was re-elected in 2006 and left office with strong enough public support to be able to effectively hand pick his successor, the far more technocratic Dilma Rousseff. Dilma began office with high public approval, but declining economic conditions combined with growing unrest and a massive corruption scandal eroded her popularity and political support in Congress. She won re-election in 2014, but was subsequently suspended and then removed through a controversial impeachment in 2016.

Argentina: Argentina's economic and political collapse in 2001 was perhaps the most dramatic in the region in modern times. The crisis of December 2001 saw the country declare a default on its debt, freeze the nation's bank account to contend with a collapse of the currency, and led to five presidents in two weeks. In 2003, Néstor Kirchner of the Peronist Party (Partido Justicialista) won the presidency, ironically defeating his Peronist predecessor Carlos Menem. By 2003, Menem was associated both with market reforms and with corruption. Kirchner's fiery, statist rhetoric easily defeated Menem and other market-oriented rivals. In 2006, Kirchner's wife, Cristina Fernández de Kirchner successfully ran for office, benefiting from Argentina's export commodity boom. She was re-elected in 2011, but declining economic performance and growing corruption scandals eroded support for her and her party, and the right under Mauricio Macri defeated the Peronist candidate Daniel Scioli in 2016.

Uruguay: In Uruguay, Socialist Tabaré Vazquez, leader of the Frente Amplio (Broad Front), a coalition of leftist parties including the guerrilla movements that had fought against military rule, defeated the country's two main political parties and claimed the presidency in 2004. In 2009, despite some anger on the left over Vazquez' moderate government and some fear in the center of a move back to the left for the Frente's candidate, former guerilla leader José Mújica, the Frente captured the presidency again. The Frente Amplio's effective governance helped maintain support for the party as Tabaré Vazquez returned to the presidency in 2015.

Bolivia: In Bolivia, Evo Morales, an indigenous leader of the coca growers association, led his young pan-indigenous party Movimiento al Socialismo (MAS, Movement for Socialism) to victory over the traditional political forces in the country in 2005. Morales blended appeals for indigenous justice with hostility to US style capitalism (and the US) with considerable success. Despite early intense conflicts over constitutional reform and growing allegations of corruption, Morales maintained high levels of public approval, winning re-election twice. Nevertheless, he lost a 2016 referendum seeking a constitutional reform to allow him to run for a fourth term in 2019. As of 2017, it is unclear whether he and the MAS will honor the results.

Peru: In 2006, Alán García returned to power in Peru. As a controversial, populist president from 1985–1990, García had presided over one of the least successful economic programs in Latin America in the 1980s. García's return to power featured a substantially moderated program, so much so that many analysts do not count García among the list of leftist presidents. In 2011, Ollanta Humala, a military officer who consciously styled himself and allied with Hugo Chávez, won the presidency suggesting the possibility that Peru would ride indigenous and peasant anger to join the ALBA bloc. Yet, once in office, Humala followed García's example, again raising charges that he should not be counted as a leftist president. Although both presidents increased social spending and made efforts to enhance equity, policy remained oriented towards preferential treatment for the extractive industry, principally mining. In 2016, noted Peruvian neoliberal scholar and banker, Pedro Pablo Kuczynski won election, backed by a newly created party named *Peruanos por el Kambio* (Peruvians for Change) in order to mirror his initials.

Ecuador: Rafael Correa was able to stitch together a coalition with indigenous backing and win the presidency after a sustained period of tremendous political instability in the country. As the candidate of the Alianza PAIS, Correa aligned himself with Hugo Chávez and played to a leftist constituency on the first round of balloting. After securing first place, he moderated somewhat and won the second round with 57% of the vote. Correa built a strong party around him, centered in his authority and abetted by strong commodity revenues due to high oil prices. He was re-elected in 2013. Unable to stand for re-election, he hand picked a successor, Vice President Lenin Moreno, who subsequently won in 2017, although the election was marred by strong accusations of fraud.

Nicaragua: Daniel Ortega returned to power in 2005 in Nicaragua after a sixteen year gap. Ortega was leader of the Sandinista movement that had ousted the dictator Somoza from power in 1979. The Sandinistas faced active US opposition under Ronald Reagan, including explicit support of violent resistance from the "contras," made up primarily of former "*somozistas*." For their part, the Sandinistas allied themselves with Cuba and leftist guerrilla movements in the region while steadily entrenching an authoritarian regime of their own. Ortega's return to the presidency has witnessed a revival of his and the Sandanista's authoritarian tendencies as the party has moved to remove opposition, concentrate authority in the executive and eliminate legal barriers to re-election. With the state cracking down on any opposition, Ortega was re-elected in 2011 and then again in 2016, although the latter occurred under dubious legal circumstances and no actual opposition candidate.

Honduras: In Honduras, Manuel Zelaya of the Partido Liberal (Liberal Party) won election in 2007 and promptly deepened ties with Cuba and joined Hugo Chávez' growing alliance of the overtly anti-US and anti-Market Bolivarian Alternative for the Americas. His efforts to promote a Chávez style restructuring of the political system provoked a controversial extra-constitutional removal returning the right to the presidency.

Paraguay: Former Catholic Bishop, Fernando Lugo entered into national politics on a pro-poor platform, challenging the dominance of the Colorado Party. In 2008, he won the election with 40% of the vote, heading a coalition called the Alliance for Progressive Change – the first election of a leftist president since the 1930s and first defeat for the Colorado Party in over 60 years. Lugo claimed his main concerns were tackling corruption and land reform, both efforts that particularly threaten political and economic elites. In a process reminiscent of the extra-constitutional removal of Manuel Zelaya in Honduras, the Chamber of Deputies and Senate brought impeachment charges and convicted Lugo over June 21 and 22, 2012. Although Paraguay's Supreme Court validated the impeachment, Paraguay's neighboring governments of both the left and the right denounced it.

El Salvador: The FMLN (Frente Maribundo Marti por la Liberarción Nacional), former guerilla movement turned political party, captured the presidency of El Salvador for the first time in 2009. Mauricio Funes claimed to want to model his regime on the moderate left, not Chávez. Despite serious concerns about rising crime and allegations of fraud and irregularities, Vice President Salvador Sánchez Cerén won election in a two round presidential election in 2014.

Costa Rica: Costa Rica elected its first leftist president in 2014, bucking the trend in the rest of the region. Luis Guillermo Solís of the *Partido Acción Ciudadana* (Citizens' Action Party) won in an uncontested second round as polls showed his candidate Johnny Araya Monge of the National Liberation Party (Partido Liberación Nacional, PLN) trailing badly. Solís benefited from Costa Rica's deteriorating economic situation and rising crime and the unpopularity of the incumbent PLN President, Laura Chinchilla.

The Politics of Rejecting Neoliberalism

Over the 1990s, Latin America traveled from "there is no alternative" to the Pink Tide of the 2000s during which leftists regularly won election and re-election. How did the region shift so dramatically? As the evidence in the previous chapter demonstrates, neoliberalism's economic, political and social record was mixed. Neoliberalism helped to restore economic growth in the region, eliminated inflation, helped curtail debt and deficits, and created new economic opportunities for many citizens. The evidence suggests that neoliberalism neither hurt nor helped inequality and poverty. Social spending appears to have been neutral as well with respect to neoliberalism. Free trade helped to reduce prices on basic consumer goods, while privatization improved access to a range of vital utilities – in particular telephones and electricity.

But, neoliberalism suffered from significant performance issues that affected voters' programmatic preferences. Most importantly, neoliberalism did not live up to its own promises. By the late 1990s into the 2000s, even advocates in formal positions in institutions like the World Bank or the Inter-American Development Bank acknowledged that market policies were insufficient. Neoliberalism had inflicted transition costs as the state cut back on employment, altered spending priorities, removed protection from domestic industries, and privatized SOEs. The explicit promise was short-term pain for long-term gain. But, by the late 1990s, the long-term gains were not as strong as promised and the short-term pain more enduring and more painful than expected.

As discussed in Chapter Three, this was particularly evident in the labor market where neoliberalism seemed to have hit formal employment in government, SOEs, and private manufacturing particularly hard. In its place, neoliberal reforms created new jobs, but without the pay, benefits or security of the ones they were replacing. Saavedra points out that the mistaken estimates of the employment consequences derived from the Heckscher–Olin theory of trade. The Heckscher–Olin theory states that factors that are relatively abundant in a protected economy stand to gain from increasing exposure to trade. In Latin America, labor is abundant while capital is scarce. In a closed economy, scarce factors can leverage their scarcity to extract higher prices, while abundant ones lose out because of their relative over-supply. However, an open economy changes the relative supply of both capital and labor. In a simple Heckscher–Olin framework, the demand for unskilled labor should have risen, driving up wages and employment. Instead, the returns from free trade went to "skilled" labor rather than labor as a whole, driving up the return on education, but penalizing the large number of workers in insecure, low wage, low to no benefit jobs. Although the aggregate unemployment rate did not indicate a definite neoliberalism effect, the more micro level data points to tangible reasons for voter disappointment in neoliberalism.[13]

For neoliberals, the answer to the micro level problems is labor market reforms that would lower the cost to employers of hiring and firing workers. Latin American labor contracts add substantial costs to hiring and/or firing workers, including a large number of taxes (payroll, health, pension, etc.)

and other non-tax costs (such as vacation pay or legally mandated annual bonuses) disproportionate to the wealth and productivity of Latin American economies. Dismissal entails high severance payments and onerous bureaucratic obstacles. Greater labor market flexibility would remove the strong incentives that exist for employers to avoid hiring additional workers or to rely on temporary contracts or to move their businesses into the informal sector. Labor market reforms, however, are the set of reforms that have uniformly and consistently made the least inroad in Latin America. Neoliberal advocates have a strong case that labor market reforms *could* improve employment and judging the program on an uncompleted agenda is unfair. That may be true. It is, nevertheless, little consolation to voters.

Job market uncertainties have important consequences. Job duration and turnover rates increased substantially over the 1990s, leading to greater concern about holding on to jobs and higher movement in and out of the formal labor market. Matthew Singer argues that informal sector voters, lacking the various protections offered by social policy, were particularly sensitive to socio-economic conditions and likely to punish incumbents for weak performance. Singer's data shows that over the period 1996 to 2005, over 70% of Latin Americans on average across the region were concerned or very concerned about losing their jobs. By contrast, similar polling in 1999 in EU member states found that for most countries fewer than 30% of workers felt similar concerns.[14] In a related vein, Javier Corrales notes that the movement into informality came mainly among women and unskilled workers. Young men finding work, but at low pay and with limited security or young men who frequently failed to find employment gravitated towards crime instead. Thus, one consequence of the failure of the job market has been skyrocketing crime rates in many Latin American countries,[15] which in turn has been a prominent concern for Latin American voters. Homicide rates averaged over 22 per 100,000 people in 2008, with a range from lows in Peru (3.2), Argentina (5.2) or Uruguay (5.8) and highs in Honduras (60.9), Venezuela (52), and El Salvador (51.8). The United States, which has one of the highest rates in the OECD, had a rate of 5.4 in 2008. Surveys showed very high levels of public concern, with almost half the countries in the region recording higher than 90% of the population concerned or very concerned about it.[16]

Another weakness of neoliberalism is that liberalizing the capital account – permitting the free flow of capital in and out of the country – exposed Latin American economies to the risks of rapid outflows of capital and the devastating consequences that could result from this. Capital account liberalization was not a central tenet of the "Washington Consensus" and in fact is one the key critiques of former World Bank Chief Economist Joseph Stiglitz.[17] Stiglitz and others within the Washington Consensus institutions,[18] worried about the dangers of rapid outflows of highly mobile investments, such as in developing country stock markets (portfolio investment) for countries with weak financial profiles. Instead, capital account liberalization should have been the last step in the establishment of a market economy once deep financial markets and ample trade generated sufficient reserves to withstand large outflows of capital. However, for the neoliberal reformist governments, desperate to attract foreign investment and to help offset deep budget cuts, capital account liberalization also was an element in attracting foreign capital. Portfolio investment, along with privatization proceeds, was a significant source of foreign capital in the 1990s.

The problem with this "hot money" was that it was highly sensitive to changes in key macro-economic indicators such as inflation or government budget deficits. The rapid movement of capital out of the country has a number of perverse effects: it undermines the local currency as holders of domestic currency dump it in favor of secure foreign ones; the often sharp devaluation that follows increases the cost of imports and by extension lowers the standard of living for most consumers; the flight of capital increases the difficulty of servicing external debt; finally, rapid outflows of capital drain government resources that could be used for productive investments, such as for social policies or for infrastructure. The fear of capital outflows forces governments to pay careful attention to inflation, budget deficits, and national accounts. Governments that did not appear to be adhering to "sound" macro-economic principles ran the risk of trig-gering the exit of capital. Unfortunately, the fear of capital flight can be self-fulfilling. No investor (domestic or foreign) wants to be holding currency that is about to devalue sharply and the early signs of exit can spark a rapid outflow. In developing countries, currency crises are also dangerous because foreign investors can make, and indeed have made herd-like deci-sions that if one Latin American market is unsafe, then so are the others. In fact, currency crises in one regional market can trigger outflows or a halt in foreign investment in other regional markets.

This in fact is what occurred in "emerging markets" including Latin America throughout the period of neoliberal hegemony. The 1990s witnessed repeated currency crises: the 1994 Mexican Peso crisis and resulting "Tequila Effect" in the rest of Latin America; the 1997 "Asian Flu" that crippled East Asian economies and reverberated in Latin America as well; the 1998 Russian Ruble crisis; the 1999 Brazilian Real crisis; and the 2001 Argentine Peso crisis that led to a political breakdown and five presidents in four weeks. In each instance, rapid outflows of capital drained the country's reserves of foreign currency, forcing immediate, sharp devaluations, and a host of "pro-cyclical" measures to stem the tide. Those included measures such as significant increases in interest rates to attract capital back to the country and new budget cuts to heighten the government's credibility to protect the value of the currency. Pro-cyclical measures deepen whatever economic trend is taking place, so these pro-cyclical measures designed to preserve the stability of the currency tended to deepen the accompanying recessions.

The immediate aftermath of a currency crisis can be devastating. Luigi Manzetti notes that currency crises are usually associated with sharp increases in poverty and can destroy incipient human capital building policies by undermining social policy outlays in education and health. For example, the currency crisis in Russia in 1998 pushed 20% of the population into poverty. In Mexico, per capita consumption in 1995 fell 11% and infant mortality rose 21%. Argentina's brutal currency crisis in 2001 drove GDP down by 10%. Per capita income fell from over US$ 8,000 in 1998 to US$ 2,500 in 2002.[19]

Both of these problems are functions of market reforms. But neoliberal presidents and candidates faced an additional economic problem that contributed to weak performance. Opening the economy and increasing the dependence on foreign trade depends on the strength of the global economy. In the early to mid 1990s, the global economy grew at a moderate pace, but by the late 1990s the global economy had sunk into recession. Slow growth reduced demand for Latin America's commodity exports. GDP growth slowed in Latin America and unemployment rose, sometimes markedly, as a consequence. Thus, candidates promoting neoliberal economic programs faced concerns about employment, the exhaustion and anger over currency shocks, and slowed growth in the face of global recession. Global growth rates did not pick up again until 2003, by which point neoliberalism was on the defensive throughout the region.

Neoliberal candidates faced another series of challenges that varied across countries. Taming inflation was a major achievement and several presidents secured re-election based at least on part because of that success. Carlos Menem in Argentina, Fernando Henrique Cardoso in Brazil (who was elected president on the basis of his success as the finance minister who tamed inflation) or Alberto Fujimori all benefited politically from their success with inflation. But, with inflation tamed, other issues became important. Employment, as mentioned earlier, joined concerns over rapidly rising crime rates, anger over corruption, and concerns with issues like health, education, and landlessness. Performance on all these issues was less effective and Latin American voters understandably sought candidates who could offer meaningful responses to these issues.

To be fair, not all these problems emerged *because of* neoliberalism. Unequal distribution of land is as old as the Spanish and Portuguese presence in the region. Social policies under the old ISI regimes were highly regressive and largely ineffective for much of the population. Corruption is an ingrained feature of Latin American politics. Yet, while neoliberals argued that the withdrawal of the state would decrease the opportunities for corruption, the reality is that it created new, different opportunities.[20] In particular, the privatization process was riddled with both real corruption and the perception of corruption that fueled public hostility to the privatization program.[21] In fact, Eduardo Lora and Ugo Panizza noted that opposition to privatization was stronger the greater the perception of corruption in the process.[22] Anger over corruption was a crucial factor in both Alberto Fujimori's and Carlos Menem's failed third presidential term bids. Finally, increased foreign investment and market competition in the rural sector did contribute to greater concentrations of land and some loss of land by small farmers.[23] For example, this redistributive process was an important factor in the rise of the Zapatista rebellion in Southern Mexico.

One thing that did not drive the victory of the left was a "backlash" against an imposed elitist program or an ideological shift of Latin Americans to the left. A number of public opinion studies demonstrate that Latin Americans could and did differentiate among different elements of the Washington Consensus, approving of some and disapproving of others. For example, Andy Baker demonstrates that Latin Americans actively disliked privatization, but were enthusiastic about free trade, regional integration, and foreign investment in their countries. Even with privatization, Latin Americans discriminated by sector. Large majorities approved of private ownership of television and airlines and roughly half supported private ownership of telephones. By contrast, most Latin Americans believed social policy – schools, health and pensions – should remain the domain of the state.[24] Tracking public opinion through the wave of leftist victories, Marco Morales shows that the left grew stronger in the 2000s, but only marginally. For the most part, leftist candidates won by forging broad ideological coalitions that were centrist in their voter ideological profile.[25] Andy Baker and Kenneth Greene also found that Latin American voters shifted to the left only modestly.[26] Latin American voters did register declining enthusiasm for market policies, but by 2007, large majorities still approved of free trade, globalization, market dominance of productive activity, and foreign investment. However, declining satisfaction with privatization and utility prices (such as phones, electricity or water) coupled with stagnation in the benefits from market reforms led to a move *toward* the left from slightly right of center to a more centrist position. In their view, leftist candidates have won mandates to modify neoliberalism, but not jettison it. Thus, leftist presidents' rhetoric and the reaction of observers (thrilled leftists and panicked neo-liberals) is out of synch with the considered and moderate behavior of voters.

In sum, uncertainty about employment, anger about corruption and crime, disappointment over the unevenness of neoliberalism's benefits all helped shift the Latin American political landscape leftwards. The question is, what difference did the wave of leftist electoral victories have on policy outputs and performance? Before we can address that question, we need to first consider what the left is in Latin America and acknowledge the alternative strands that have taken power in the region.

The Two Lefts in Latin America

The left in Latin America has never been monolithic or united – not now nor at any time in the past. The various expressions of the left have varied by internal organization, tactics, bases of support, as well as economic and political goals. Parts of the left have been revolutionary and embraced or tolerated violence as a means to an end. Parts of the left have been undemocratic. Some left wing parties have been more nationalist in their orientation, willing to work with segments of domestic capitalists to promote national development. Others have been oriented to international movements. In some countries, the left was violently suppressed and routinely excluded. In others, the left moderated and held or shared political power. These many manifestations have led to considerable debates and disagreements on how to define the left and which movements were really leftist and which were not. For example, figures like Juan Perón of Argentina or Lázaro Cárdenas of Mexico have provoked considerable debates about whether they were really leftists or agents of capitalist development who tamed the working classes. Robert Kaufman and Segura-Ubiergo avoid the term "left" and label these parties "popular" for their bases in organized working classes and their national development orientation.[27] For many analysts, the populism of key national development oriented presidents calls into question whether they were genuinely leftists. For others, populism was merely one manifestation of leftist politics.

The contemporary left has also generated a considerable debate that, like the earlier one, has not achieved any consensus. Scholars again have argued over proper labels, such as whether specific presidents should be labeled "populist" or "social democrats" and have differed over how these terms should be defined. Some scholars, like James Petras, have identified multiple strands of the left, from self-help and communitarian groups, to the various strands of revolutionary leftists who reject liberal democracy and capitalism to "adapters" and "pragmatic reformers" who offer different forms of accommodation to capitalism and neoliberalism specifically.[28] Javier Corrales identifies a wide range of groups that constituted a very diffuse voting base of the left.[29] Steven Levitsky and Kenneth Roberts focus on the organizational character of the governing party.[30]

The most common approach to understanding the left in Latin America during the Pink Tide was to divide leftist governments into two groups: one more moderate,[31] including at least Brazil, Chile, and Uruguay; and another more radical,[32] including Bolivia, Ecuador, and Venezuela. Even this simple classification is not straightforward. For example, cases like Argentina and Nicaragua do not obviously belong to one or the other grouping, while plausible arguments classify Peru as right wing rather than leftist of either variant. Similarly, Bolivia's leftist experiment has had more institutionalizing and moderating elements than Venezuela, while Brazil's leftist government became more statist, particularly after finding massive oil deposits offshore. Thus, it is important to look carefully at specific cases rather than relying on simple classificatory schemes for shorthand judgments. Nevertheless, these "ideal types" do point to some differences. All leftist governments are united by a commitment to equitable development, social justice, and a belief in the state as an effective agent of these aims. But, how they approach these goals can differ considerably.

This chapter draws on the work of Kurt Weyland, Wendy Hunter and Raúl Madrid to frame the comparison within the left and between the left and right.[33] Weyland et al. differentiate between a "moderate" left, which accepts the constraints of democratic capitalism and works within it to advance its goals, and the "contestatory" left. Weyland et al. call this latter left "contestatory" because they are clearly contesting the institutions and rules of global capitalism and liberal democracy, but they are not truly revolutionary, like Fidel Castro or Ché Guevara. The more moderate left – regardless of differences among the governments – share certain common elements. First, the overall policy orientation has been much more accepting of neoliberalism than the more radical version. For example, President Lula of Brazil, despite a long history of hostility to neoliberalism and overt criticism of privatization while on the campaign trail in 2002, maintained a strong commitment to Washington Consensus budget principles and extended privatization in the electricity sector. In Chile, the Socialist president Michelle Bachelet considered labor market reforms to "flexibilize" hiring and firing practices – a Washington Consensus priority – although she did not in the end introduce them.

The moderate cases also stand out for the leftist presidents' willingness to work within the existing political system rather than seek substantial reforms or restructuring of the basic institutions of politics. Working within the system, however, entails compromise, negotiation, and acceptance of the limits of public opinion. All four cases stand out for the willingness of their presidents to bridge the ideological space that spans from their narrower bases into the broad middle of the ideological spectrum. That broad middle, as noted earlier, is not revolutionary or hostile to the market. One consequence is that "true believers" have not always been happy with the performance of their own parties. In the moderate cases, leftist leaders have had to withstand accusations of betrayal of the goals and methods of the left. For example, in Brazil, President Lula faced a revolt within his own party, and ultimately expelled four members further to the left of his party, over disagreements about the administration's rightward tilt. In Uruguay, Tabaré Vazquez angered elements of the left of his coalition for the moderation of his program and although his successor José Mújica advocated a sharper turn to the left in 2009, his administration also maintained a bridge to the country's centrist voters.

By contrast, in what Weyland et al. have called "contestatory" cases, leftist presidents have called into question substantial aspects of the pre-existing economic and political bases of their countries. Unlike their moderate leftist peers, contestatory leftists have openly attacked their opponents, questioning their legitimacy and their right to participate in politics. The left in these cases have been very comfortable with extra-institutional tactics, such as mobilizing protest marches, and even violent confrontation as a means to their reform ends. The contestatory left has been openly and aggressively critical of the US, describing neoliberal reforms as an American imposition.

The aggressive, uncompromising nature of the left's position in these countries is matched by an aggressive stance on political reforms. Hugo Chávez engineered a complete overhaul of Venezuela's political system, including writing and ratifying a new constitution. Under Chávez' auspices, and with his financial support as well, both Rafael Correa of Ecuador and Evo Morales of Bolivia followed similar strategies of dramatic constitutional revisions. Manuel Zelaya of Honduras was ousted in a controversial coup over his efforts, also supported and financed by Chávez, to revise the constitution. The constitutional reforms were more than mere tinkering at the edges. They entailed fundamental alterations of the basic structure and rights of the country's political and legal system. In Venezuela, the constitution granted sweeping new powers to the presidency and created a new branch of government based on citizen participation. Bolivia's new constitution redressed the country's long and disgraceful history of discrimination against the indigenous majority. In Ecuador, anger over multinational corporations' exploitation of natural resources led to a new constitution that, among other things, granted rights to nature. More importantly, it altered rules to concentrate more power in the hands of the presidency.

Finally, the contestatory regimes were more comfortable making larger changes in the economy and in particular were less protective of property rights. One may argue about whether or not they introduced new forms of economic management. Hugo Chávez, for example, claimed that his model of economic development was a novel approach called "endogenous" development. Critics, however, suggested that it was simply a return to the nationalist, ISI past.[34] Evo Morales renationalized the oil and gas sectors and forced the renegotiation of contracts with multinational corporations. A case certainly can be made that the original contracts did not grant sufficient benefit to the host country. But, as George Gray-Molina has argued, using state power to obtain more of the benefit of oil and gas extraction did not fundamentally address Bolivia's historic problem of slow growth, underdevelopment and dependence on a small number of commodities (mainly oil and gas).[35] Ecuador's new constitution proclaimed the rights of nature against exploitation, but at the same the government engaged in a public relations campaign in developed countries to encourage more direct foreign investment in its extraction industries.[36] The question then is between the left and the right, and between the moderate and the contestatory left, what difference does it make for policy and performance?

Neoliberalism in Retreat? The Aggregate Picture

The wave of leftist victories beginning in 1998 signaled the beginning of a Pink Tide. The Pink Tide then coincided with the start of the commodity boom. As noted in Chapter One, a lot did change in the region over the 2000s, enough that many felt Latin America had entered a "Golden Era." The fact that the Pink Tide coincided with the commodity boom, however, makes it much harder to make definitive pronouncements about the left and market reforms. The problem is compounded by arguments over how to classify regimes and how to define the left. That presents a problem because the limited sample of Latin American countries – no more than 17–20 in most analyses – means that a shift of one or two countries from one category to another can significantly change the conclusions.

Do partisan differences matter? To answer this question, this section considers the differences among the contestatory and moderate lefts and the right. It looks at five criteria: democracy, market orientation, growth, social policy, and the role of the state. Overall, the data suggest that the Pink Tide did not lead to dramatic changes in Latin America in terms of the development model. Instead, they suggest that all Latin American countries benefited from the commodity boom, regardless of partisan identity. But, there was some evidence of two distinct tendencies. On one side, the contestatory left was more likely to support a retreat from neo-liberal reforms and less committed to liberal democratic rules. On the other is the emergence of a stable politics that we might call "neoliberalism with a human face," but that appeared on both the left and the right. In brief, the evidence suggested that well institutionalized political systems were likelier to support a moderate, pragmatic approach.[37]

Democracy

For Weyland et al., the contestatory left challenged the politics of market-oriented democracy. Presidents Chávez, Morales, Correa, Zelaya and the Kirchners in Argentina, all rhetorically at least, explicitly criticized neo-liberal economics and to some extent overhauled, (or attempted to), the political structure of the country in support of their larger economic and political goals. By contrast, the moderate left of Presidents Lula and Dilma in Brazil, Lagos and Bachelet in Chile, Vazquez and Mújica in Uruguay, and García and Humala in Peru may have criticized neoliberal economics, but supported more moderate and modest adjustments to the model. (Note, however, that Levtisky and Roberts argue that Bolivia under Morales fits more closely with the moderate cases due to the dispersion of authority within what became a strong, established political party under the MAS). Furthermore, they did so without challenging the political structure of the country. The need to work within existing institutions led them to make compromises and seek out agreement that moderated stronger leftist tendencies that existed within their parties. In the con-testatory cases, leftist presidents overthrew existing institutions and forged new electoral bases by playing to deeply ingrained anger and divisions in society. In the moderate cases, presidents moved their parties to the center to forge electoral coalitions built on pragmatic, centrist votes. Right wing governments during this period also forged centrist coalitions and also moderated neoliberal reforms (though right wing governments in the 1990s frequently did not with Peru under Alberto Fujimori a particularly clear example).

The data from Freedom House supports the argument made by Weyland et al. Democratic governance improved slightly over the period, continuing the general trend since the 1980s (see Table 4.1). Average Freedom House scores for the region declined roughly 10% (with lower scores better) between 1999 and 2009. Only Bolivia, Ecuador and Nicaragua saw their scores worsen, while ten of the eighteen countries improved their ratings. As of 2009, Freedom House classified nine countries as "Free." Chile,

Table 4.1 Freedom House Scores, Civil and Political Liberties Combined, 1999–2014

Year		1999	2002	2004	2006	2008	2010	2012	2014
	Combined Score								
Argentina		5	6	4	4	4	4	4	4
Bolivia		4	5	6	6	6	6	6	6
Brazil		7	5	5	4	4	4	4	4
Chile		4	3	2	2	2	2	2	2
Colombia		8	8	8	6	7	7	7	7
Costa Rica		3	3	2	2	2	2	2	2
Ecuador		5	6	6	6	6	6	6	6
El Salvador		5	5	5	5	5	5	5	5
Guatemala		7	8	8	7	7	8	7	7
Honduras		6	6	6	6	6	8	8	8
Mexico		7	4	4	5	5	6	6	6
Nicaragua		6	6	6	6	7	8	9	7
Panama		3	3	3	3	3	3	3	4
Paraguay		7	7	6	6	6	6	6	6
Peru		9	5	5	5	5	5	5	5
Uruguay		3	2	2	2	2	2	2	2
Venezuela		8	7	7	8	8	10	10	10

Source: Data from Freedom House, available at www.freedomhouse.org

Costa Rica and Uruguay remained the region's leaders receiving the best possible scores (1 on political liberties and 1 on civil liberties), with Panama not far behind. By contrast, Bolivia, Colombia, Ecuador, Guatemala, Nicaragua, Paraguay and Venezuela were classified as only "Partially Free" with Bolivia, Ecuador and Nicaragua's scores worsening over the period. Venezuela's score remained constant, but had worsened considerably from the 1990s into the 2000s. On the positive ledger, ten countries' scores improved over the period with marked changes in Brazil, Chile and Peru.

Again, the evidence seems to support Weyland et al.'s characterization of the contestatory left. Most of the weakest democracy scores were for Bolivia, Ecuador, Nicaragua, and Venezuela. Colombian democracy contended with a serious armed insurrection throughout the 1990s and 2000s and the violence and abuses associated with what is in effect a civil war accounts for Colombia's democratic deficiencies rather than neoliberal economic policies. Mexico's scores have worsened since 2010, largely due to drug related violence and efforts to crack down on it. Guatemala's long civil war ended formally in 1996, but the legacy of violence and discrimination against the majority indigenous population continues to limit the quality of democracy. Overall, however, the data suggest that the contestatory left's aggressive politics have some link to the weakening of democracy.

The counter argument is that the term "democracy" itself is open to debate and measures like the ones from Freedom House are measuring liberal democracy with its emphasis on laws and procedures, as opposed to participatory or popular forms of democracy. Contestatory regimes specifically and explicitly critique liberal rules as discriminatory and exclusionary and serving the interests of the most powerful, and that justifies efforts to re-write constitutions and use the mobilization of the poor to alter the balance of power in society. This is not a frivolous argument. Democratic rules did in fact exclude large portions of the population, for example through explicit rules against indigenous parties competing in politics. What the Freedom House data do help reveal is that the contestatory regimes did in fact seek to alter the rules, sometimes accepting or even mobilizing intense conflict. Whether it was justified is a normative debate that cannot be resolved using measures such as those of Freedom House. It is also important to note that the right was also prepared to violate rules in order to bring down leftist presidents.[38] This occurred in Honduras and Paraguay and critics argue that it was the case in Brazil in 2015–2016 as well.

Market Orientation

In the aggregate, the "retreat from globalization" or reversal of market reforms has not been that pronounced as one might expect from the rise of the left, although the "contestatory" left did move away from the market orientation more assertively. More importantly, partisan identity is not the strongest predictor of market orientation. Eduardo Lora's structural reform index continues up to 2009 and so we can look at how policy shifted over a good portion of the Pink Tide, though it misses some of the reforms after the rise to power of Evo Morales, Rafael Correa, and Cristina Fernández de Kirchner. What is striking about the structural reform index is in fact how little changed from 2000 to 2009. In fact, the average score for 2009 is 5.5% higher than in 2000 and the score increased for every country, even though only Chile and Venezuela had leftist governments in 2000 while twelve countries had leftist governments in 2000. The largest increases came in Paraguay and Brazil under leftist governments and then Peru under neoliberal Alberto Toledo. The lowest absolute score on the index, 0.53, belonged to Mexico under right wing government as well (and the least change over the period). It is important to recall that Lora's index measures the *neutrality* of policies, not the economic outcomes. Neutrality captures the extent to which policies distort prices in the market. Since neoliberals argue for the need to "get prices right," neutrality is their goal. Lora, however, notes that the index measures the effects of policies and not the *quality* of policies, recognizing that there may in fact be good reasons for the state to intervene in ways that alter prices, such as for industrial policy or to promote equitable outcomes. The main conclusion, however, is that for the most part, Latin American governments did not move away from market economies or undo the substantial shift since the late 1980s and early 1990s.

However, some Latin American countries took steps to alter the presence of the state in ways that did affect the private sector, foreign and domestic. The Heritage Foundation Economic Freedom Index provides a different indication of market reform trends that looks at a range of "freedoms" that have stronger normative and therefore more subjective biases built in, including protection of private property rights, freedom from corruption, ease of business regulation, and government spending. In that sense, the Heritage Foundation index is a good measure of how neoliberal advocates see a government's behaviour (see Table 4.2). The results here point to somewhat different conclusions. If we compare average scores over 2000–2009 (the same period as the structural reform index), the average economic freedom score declined by roughly 6.5% from 65.2 to 60.9%. If we exclude Argentina and Venezuela from the sample as the two largest outliers, the average score only declines about 3%, but it still declines in almost every country in the region except Chile and Mexico under right wing governments, and Honduras and Nicaragua under leftist presidents.[39] Extending the data to 2015, after the end of the commodity boom, does not alter the story much. The trend was still downward, though much less, averaging only a 1% decrease even with the market reversal leaders of Argentina and Venezuela. To the extent that reversals happened, they mostly occurred during the "super cycle." The other interesting note is that seven of the scores did move towards "freer" with right wing governments in Colombia, Costa Rica, Guatemala, Mexico and the controversial Peruvian case making up five of the seven.

Table 4.2 Heritage Foundation, Economic Freedom Index, 2000–2014

Country	2000–2014	Leftist Change	2000	2002	2004	2006	2008	2010	2012	2014
Argentina	−36.00%	−32.00%	70	65.7	**53.9**	**54.6**	**55.1**	**51.2**	**48**	**44.6**
Bolivia	−25.00%	−24.00%	65	65.1	64.5	**58.7**	**53.2**	**49.4**	**50.2**	**48.4**
Brazil	−6.00%	−8.00%	61.1	**61.5**	62	**60.9**	**55.9**	**55.6**	**57.9**	**56.9**
Chile	5.00%	10.00%	**74.7**	**77.8**	**76.9**	**79.3**	**79.8**	77.2	**78.3**	**78.7**
Colombia	11.00%		63.3	64.2	61.2	60.1	61.9	65.5	68	70.7
Costa Rica	−2.00%	−1.00%	68.4	67.5	66.4	66.4	64.8	65.9	68	**66.9**
Ecuador	−19.00%	−9.00%	59.8	53.1	**54.4**	**54.8**	**55.4**	**49.3**	**48.3**	**48**
El Salvador	−13.00%	−4.00%	76.3	73	71.2	70.5	69.2	**69.9**	**68.7**	**66.2**
Guatemala	−4.00%	−4.00%	64.3	62.3	59.6	60.1	60.5	**61**	**60.9**	61.2
Honduras	0.00%	0.03%	57.6	58.7	55.3	58.7	**60.2**	58.3	58.8	57.1
Mexico	12.00%		59.3	63	66	64.9	66.4	68.3	65.3	66.8
Nicaragua	2.00%	−4.00%	56.9	61.1	61.4	**63.1**	**60**	**58.3**	**57.9**	**58.4**
Panama	−11.00%		71.6	68.5	65.3	65.5	64.7	64.8	65.2	63.4
Paraguay	−3.00%	2.00%	64	59.6	56.7	56.3	60.5	**61.3**	**61.8**	62
Peru	−1.00%	4.00%	68.7	64.8	64.7	**60.3**	**63.5**	**67.6**	**68.7**	**67.4**
Uruguay	0.00%	0.00%	69.3	68.7	**66.7**	**65.8**	**68.1**	**69.8**	**69.9**	**69.3**
Venezuela	−36.00%	−36.00%	**57.4**	**54.7**	**46.7**	**45**	**45**	**37.1**	**38.1**	**36.3**

Source: Data from Heritage Foundation, available online at www.heritage.org

Note: Years under leftist government are in bold.

On average, neither index tells a story of major change in the region although the four cases that moved farther away from the market according to the Heritage Foundation are the three "typical" cases of the contestatory left, Bolivia, Ecuador and Venezuela, along with Argentina. A closer look at the index components shows where the changes occurred. In three of the four cases, large increases in government spending, "macroeconomic populism" as neoliberal observers would label it,[40] helped drive the changes in scores. Bolivia under Evo Morales used commodity revenues to increase spending, but with more restraint and with much more attention to future risks to macroeconomic stability. Both Argentina and Venezuela tolerated higher levels of inflation and along with Ecuador increased government spending with less concern for the risks when the boom ended. But, the biggest driver of "less free" scores shared by all four cases were the measures for protecting property rights as well as investment and financial freedom. Where these four cases differed the most was in re-nationalization (or in the case of Ecuador, overt attacks against business groups that had long dominated Ecuadorean politics). In all four cases, leftist governments re-nationalized high profile companies in key sectors or asserted the privi-leges of state owned energy companies against multinational corporations (MNCs). In addition, all four cases promoted regulatory changes to con-strain foreign capital. None of these changes were inherently bad policy or bad ideas and as the structural reform index suggests they were not necessarily anti-market either. They were, however, directed against busi-ness and/or MNCs. This may represent an important shift politically, but it is hard to claim that any of the four were inventing new economic development paradigms.

Economic Performance

One critical factor is that Latin America in general benefited enormously from the expansion of the global economy between 2003 and 2012, even after the spread of the global economic crisis. Several leftist governments came to power on the back of the global recession beginning in 1998 that drove down commodity prices and drove unemployment up in Latin America. However, as of 2003, global growth renewed, expanding at a rate of roughly 5% per year until the crisis of 2009. The downturn in 2009 led to sharp declines in exports, investments, GDP growth and per capita income in 2009 (and to a much lesser extent in 2008). But global growth then returned to roughly 4% as of 2010 with the region returning as well to robust increases in GDP growth, exports, investments, and per capita income. Global expansion occurred because China, and to a lesser extent India, drove it through their voracious consumption of commodities. With Chinese average growth rates around 9% per year even through the 2008–2009 crisis, Latin America boomed as a commodity exporter. Countries like Brazil saw trade surpluses for the first time in modern history. China quickly became the largest or second largest export market for Argentina, Brazil, Chile, Costa Rica and Peru, among others. China's appetite for Latin American primary goods pushed regional growth rates and China's continued role as a consumer of commodities shielded Latin America from its worst effects.

Table 4.3 looks at growth rates from 2000 to 2014 and shows that leftist government had little effect on growth rates, negatively or positively. In general, growth under leftist government tended to reflect growth rates of the period – low during the recessionary years of 2000–2002 and increasing from 2003–2012. Countries with strong growth rates during the period grew regardless of moderate left, contestatory left or rightist government. For example, both Peru and Uruguay enjoyed rapid growth well above the regional average once they emerged from the global recession. High growth began before the election of leftist presidents and continued after. Hugo Chávez was president the whole period. During the recession, low oil prices led to sharp declines in the GDP growth rate. The rapid increase

Table 4.3 Latin American Growth Rates, 2000–2014, Averages, and Left Governments

Dates	2000–2014	2003–2012	Left Govt
Argentina	3.49	6.51	5.71
Bolivia	4.23	4.46	5.05
Brazil	3.31	3.8	3.41
Chile	4.03	4.44	3.92
Colombia	4.36	4.73	
Costa Rica	4.15	4.96	
Ecuador	4.26	4.63	4.27
El Salvador	1.92	1.9	1
Guatemala	3.47	3.44	2.76
Honduras	3.61	3.59	3.63
Mexico	2.34	2.67	
Nicaragua	3.54	3.62	3.64
Panama	6.63	7.95	8.07
Paraguay	5.29	6.25	5.13
Peru	3.64	3.93	3.71
Uruguay	3.11	5.16	5.44
Venezuela	3.02	4.98	3.02
Latin America	3.79	4.53	4.2

Source: Data available at World Bank, www.worldbank.org

in oil prices after 2003 spurred GDP growth rates well above the regional average.

The region's export boom contributed to another crucial improvement in circumstances. Just as the 1980s debt crisis emerged, in part because of the appreciation of the dollar, so too the region's net external debt has declined as booming export economies led to a relative weakening of the dollar against Latin American currencies. Rising export revenues coupled with appreciating currencies have allowed many Latin American countries to pay down significant portions of their external, dollar denominated debt. For example, as of 2010, Brazil – the largest external debtor of the region through the debt crisis and into the 1990s, had completely paid off its external, dollar denominated debt. Debt servicing, the cost to society of paying interest on the debt, fell from 22.7% to 15.95% of total exports between 2005 and 2007 alone, indicating a dramatic improvement for the region's financial strength.[41] Over a thirty-year stretch, Latin America went from the "lost decade" of the most deeply indebted region in the world to a region flush with surpluses.

Latin American nations on average also benefited from their years of neoliberal reforms. Greater attention to reducing budget deficits, increasing tax revenues, shifting spending priorities, strengthening financial systems and regulation of banks, and promoting exports meant that many Latin American nations were in strong positions to protect their economies through stimulus spending – more so than even the European Union. Some of the leading economies of the region injected between 2% and 9% of GDP to stimulate their economies through a mix of government programs and tax cuts. Roughly half the countries in the region implemented personal and/or corporate tax cuts (Chile, Colombia, Guatemala, and Mexico implemented both). Virtually every country in the region initiated spending programs in infrastructure, housing, agriculture, and support for small and medium enterprises.[42] Several countries invested in supporting strategic sectors of the economy to promote long-term development. Two of the weaker responses, however, were from the contestatory left as Ecuador and Venezuela offered fewer fiscal incentives to spur economic growth than almost every other Latin American nation.

Data on other aspects of economic performance are also ambiguous as they reflect significant differences in the way the commodity boom and the US originated financial crisis of 2008–2009 affected the region. For example, Argentina and Venezuela maintained very loose fiscal policies, spending freely in the period leading up to the crisis, consistent with a return to a statist model. But, strong commodity exports left their respective governments with fiscal surpluses. Bolivia actually maintained fiscal control and saved high export revenues in a stabilization fund that shielded the country from the drop in commodity prices while keeping inflation low. Brazil maintained strong fiscal controls, using inflation targeting as the government's guide for fiscal policy. Over the 2000s, however, fiscal policy loosened in response to commodity export strength and the prospect of electoral competition in 2010. By contrast, Chile, Peru and Uruguay have maintained stronger fiscal controls.

Although fiscal positions do not offer clear evidence, inflation appears more suggestive. The average inflation rate for the period 2000 to 2009 was 7.13%, excluding Venezuela, which averaged over 20% inflation for the period. Eight countries have had average inflation rates above the regional median, five of which have been among those that could be classified as contestatory, including Argentina, Ecuador, Honduras, Nicaragua and Venezuela. Only Bolivia's average inflation has been below the median. Four countries have had average inflation below 4% for the period: Chile, El Salvador, Panama and Peru. In short, growth and government accounts are shaped by factors beyond government decisions and the boom of the 2000s has made it difficult to sort out direct effects of policy decisions.

Social Policy, Poverty and Inequality

Perhaps the most striking trend of the 2000s is the increase in social spending throughout the region accompanied by (and at least partially causing) marked decreases in poverty and inequality. While the trend in the 2000s was striking, the root of the changes lie in the reform period of the 1980s and 1990s. Careful attention to debt, deficits, and oversized state sectors helped restore Latin America to fiscal health and left the countries in stronger positions to engage in vigorous social spending throughout the region once the boom began. Moreover, banking reforms helped establish stronger, better regulated financial sectors that shielded Latin America from the worst effects of the global financial crisis.[43] The data are clear on education, health, pensions and housing where the secular trend in the region was to increase expenditures, regardless of the partisan identity of the government. Poverty and inequality had become prominent concerns of key IFIs such as the World Bank and the Inter-American Development Bank by the late 1990s, so even the external forces of neoliberalism were pushing in that direction.

The commodity boom created new opportunities to expand social policy. Did partisan identity affect the level of spending? Here, the record is less clear and scholarly analyses arrive at different conclusions. Some studies find no difference between the left and the right on social spending.[44] Others find that leftist governments do increase social spending.[45] By contrast, José Merino argues that there is no advantage of the left over the right. In fact, the right and the moderate left both outperform the contestatory left.[46] One possible explanation for the lack of difference between the right and left is the Meltzer-Richard median voter theorem. Meltzer-Richard posits that high levels of inequality lead to higher levels of redistribution because democracy forces politicians to compete for the median voter to win elections. The greater the distance between the median voter's income and society's mean income, the more the median voter will demand redistribution to narrow the gap.

Evelyne Huber and John D. Stephens[47] argue, by contrast, that the median voter model does not explain redistribution. While they acknowledge the important role of democracy in creating the base conditions for expanding redistributive policy, they argue instead that the expansion of social policy in the 2000s is due to the rise of the left. Economic inequality may create strong demands for redistribution, but it also leads to highly skewed distributions of political power and therefore more resistance to it. Left party power, particularly with its base in the organized working class, reduces the unequal distribution of political power and resources and opens the policy-making arena to alternative policy options. Without the rise of a left capable of competing in and winning elections, the likelihood of redistributive policy is small.

Huber and Stephens' critique of the median voter theorem is an important one and a reminder that political processes and institutions shape outcomes and that societal demands or needs do not simply translate into policy. But, their argument confronts two limitations: first, redistributive policy efforts expanded in the region before the rise of the left in the 2000s; and second, governments of the right in countries like Colombia or Mexico (or Peru) also expanded redistributive efforts. Candelaria Garay[48] confronts this dilemma by arguing that partisanship does not explain the expansion of social policy, but it does help account for its form. Garay accepts that politicians may offer redistribution as a way to capture the votes of "outsiders" – i.e. informal sector workers who do not enjoy formal welfare state protections. But only if there is competition for their votes. Thus, a right wing party will develop redistributive policies to appeal to poor median voters if it faces an electoral threat. Alternatively, parties may be forced to expand redistributive policy in response to pressure from below, such as from protests, social movements, or organized interests allied with the governing party, such as labor unions. Without either source of pressure, governments do not expand social policy for outsiders. But, the two different sources of pressure lead to very different kinds of policies that do tend to reflect partisan differences. Left parties, with their stronger connection to social mobilization from below, offer more expansive and more participatory policies that cover more people with fewer conditions. By contrast, conservative parties holding off electoral competition only have to negotiate policy in legislatures with less pressure to make concessions. The result is more restrictive policies that cover fewer people.

Garay's explanation of the way differences in political parties affect policy outcomes resonates with other studies that show how linkages with social movements and/or organized interests shape policy. For example, Jennifer Pribble traces how party organization, linkages to allied movements/interests, and policy legacies lead to varying outcomes in the design of health care reforms.[49] Jessica Rich shows how state officials and social movements interacted, irrespective of partisan identity of the government, to develop AIDS policy in Brazil.[50] Maureen Donaghy makes a similar argument regarding social movements and the state in housing policy in Brazil.[51] By contrast, John Crabtree and Francisco Durand discuss the development of expansionary social policy in Peru due to electoral pressures, but without the participation of social groups and leading to smaller, more restrictive, and state directed policy.[52] Similarly, Sara Niedzwiecki and Jennifer Pribble analyze what happens to social policy when the right regains power, looking at Sebastián Piñera in Chile and Mauricio Macri in Argentina, and find that social policy did not expand, but electoral pressures kept them from cutting expenditures.[53] In sum, partisan differences help explain variations in policies, but electoral competition and the linkages between parties and society are the critical factors. On this point, it is not clear that the left always has an advantage. What matters most is how governments use money to develop human capital.

This becomes understandable once we look more carefully at the character of social spending. Nancy Birdsall and Miguel Székely note[54] that social policy is an important element of poverty and inequality reduction, but it depends on the type. Social policies that genuinely build human capital (education and health in particular) develop the capacity of the poor to lift themselves out of poverty. Human capital builds sustainable poverty reduction – a propos of the aphorism, "Give a man a fish and you feed him for a day. Teach a man to fish and you feed him for a lifetime." Clientelistic social policies, however, simply offer cash or some other good that does not build lasting individual capacity and often is offered explicitly as part of a political exchange in return for support. Such policies do not construct lasting, sustainable poverty reduction and undermine the quality of democratic governance. If the cash is dependent on commodity revenues, it presents even greater concerns as it does not build human capital and its sustainability rests on commodity prices.

Venezuela and Brazil offer striking contrasts on this score. Social spending in Venezuela suffered from clientelistic practices, vulnerable to economic downturns as it was funded by extraordinary commodity export revenues (oil). Hugo Chávez' *misiones Bolivares* (Bolivarian missions) provided a wide array of benefits for the poor, including education and literacy training programs, health care, subsidized food and housing, environmental protection, university education, indigenous rights, and land reform among others. The Chávez government broadly advertised these missions and claims strong results for them. Critics, however, argue that real expenditures were lower than advertised and the real results considerably worse. In addition, some of the missions increased access, such as to university education or health care, but only by offering very low quality services. For example, the Barrio Adentro Mission relied on Cuban doctors in an "oil for services swap,"[55] who operate in free clinics in poor neighborhoods. But, the personnel working in such clinics often have inadequate training and provided sub-standard care. The Mercal Mission provided subsidized groceries in supermarkets for poor neighborhoods, but price controls to curb rising inflation led to severe shortages of basic items. The Robinson Mission to eradicate illiteracy appears to have been a costly program that had virtually no measurable effect on the actual level of illiteracy.[56] In fact, Francisco Rodriguéz, an economist and one time Chief Economist of the National Assembly under Chávez, was one of the most vocal critics of Chávez, relying on both inside information and technical analysis. Rodriguéz concluded that Chávez' many social programs had no discernible effect on poverty and many indicators of health, education and access to basic services such as running water have deteriorated. Ultimately, poverty fell during the Chávez years, but at a lower rate than under previous oil booms.[57] This is especially the case because Chávez' disregard for neoliberal concerns, such as careful fiscal management, led to the region's highest rate of inflation, which in turn eroded the value of social expenditure and payments to the poor. In fact, Nora Lustig has argued that the reduction in poverty in Venezuela was entirely a product of the commodity boom and, once controlled for, social spending had no effect.[58]

The contrast with social policy in the cases where governments sought to build human capital, not forge clientelistic ties, could not be starker. In Brazil, for example, policy makers were concerned about the performance of poor children in school due to low attendance and frequent repetition of grades. Poor families in Latin America routinely withdraw their children from school for a variety of reasons, including the need to help bring income into the household. The response in Brazil was a program that began as a municipal experiment in 1995 and was then made national policy in 2001.[59] The initial policy, *Bolsa Escola*, was a conditional cash transfer program that paid a monthly cash allowance to poor families on condition that their children enroll in school and maintain good attendance records. Nationalizing the program removed the transfer from municipal politicians and eliminated local level politicians' ability to use the funds in a clientelistic fashion.[60] The program won international awards for its innovation and had enormous success in improving enrollments and attendance while virtually eliminating hunger for the 11 million families that received the stipend as of 2010. The program was also relatively inexpensive – at roughly US\$ 50 per month it doubled household income for the poor while costing about 0.5% of GDP. In that sense, it was a remarkably cost effective program. Mexico's *Oportunidades* program, launched in 1997 as *Progresa* and renamed in 2002 (and subsequently rebranded as *Prospera*), is very similar to *Bolsa Escola*, with approximately 25% of Mexicans receiving benefits. Chile's *Chile Solidario* is similar as well, adding additional conditions such as social and psychological counseling and health care visits. Note, however, that both *Bolsa Família* and *Progresa/Oportunidades* began under right or center governments. In Brazil, President Lula rapidly expanded the new federal program and successfully claimed credit for it. But, these programs reflect changing approaches in the region more than a distinctly leftist view.[61]

In sum, Latin American countries increased expenditures on social policy throughout the 2000s. Poverty and inequality both declined over the period, particularly in countries governed by leftist parties. But, the key is sustainable policies that build human capital, not simply clientelistic payments funded by the commodity boom. It is not clear that partisan differences matter as much as the institutional linkages between governing parties and society. Strong institutional connections to organized interest groups and social movements, electoral competition, and policy legacies arguably are the most important factors affecting social policy outcomes and their sustainability beyond the commodity boom.

The Role of the State[62]

One other area reveals important qualitative differences among the right, moderate left and contestatory left. The neoliberal program entailed reductions in the size of the state and a strong philosophical suspicion of state involvement in the economy. Much of the early period of neoliberalism followed that model as privatizations, spending cuts, and layoffs of state employees reduced the size of the state in an effort to stabilize the economy. But, the state did not wither away and in a number of countries it maintained an important role.[63] As macroeconomic stability improved, Latin American countries looked again to ways to promote economic development.

As with social policy, two models appeared to be emerging in Latin America. In the contestatory left, the state's resurgent role appears in large measure to be more of a return to the past than a novel approach. In Argentina, Bolivia and Venezuela, leftist governments renationalized vital sectors of the economy and reintroduced significant elements of state intervention in markets. In Argentina, the government of Cristina Fernández de Kirchner re-nationalized the pension system in 2008 and then in 2009 Aérolineas Argentinas, the national airline. A wave of renationalizations occurred as well in water and sanitation.[64] Perhaps the biggest impact and most controversial one was the renationalization of the oil company, YPF, in 2012. In addition to these nationalizations, the Kirchners actively intervened in the market, including establishing price controls on select goods and export controls on beef, corn and wheat. Many of these measures were introduced to combat rising inflation, which led to a new round of struggles under Fernández de Kirchner. In particular, the president intervened in the non-partisan National Institute for Statistics and the Census (Instituto Nacional de Estadística e Censos, INDEC) to force it to publish artificially low inflation numbers and in 2010 fired the President of the legally independent Central Bank for his resistance to her efforts to use foreign currency reserves to finance government operations.

In Bolivia, the reinsertion of the state has also been conflictual. Evo Morales re-established a strong state presence in the previously privatized hydrocarbons sector in 2006. Morales argued that the terms of privatization under Gonzalo Sánchez de Lozada had been excessively generous and required the foreign, private operators to renegotiate the contracts. Under the terms of the new contracts, the Bolivian state substantially increased its take – in the order of 70% of gross production values. The move had a big impact on government revenues (almost US$1 billion in 2007) and helped finance Morales' social policy transfers.[65] It opened the door to further re-nationalizations in oil and gas, electricity, telecoms and ultimately the pension system which had been privatized under Sánchez de Lozada. As noted in Chapter Three, privatization had not yielded particularly impressive results in Bolivia so the arguments for renationalization were reasonable and the increased government revenues not only expanded social policy spending, but allowed Morales to maintain safe budget balances. The downside is that the Morales government's aggressive stance towards the market discouraged further private investment as FDI fell from 7.5% from 1995–2004 to 2.7% from 2005–2013 while domestic investment barely increased to compensate. As George Gray-Molina points out, Bolivia's improved revenues were driven largely by hydrocarbon's price increases and not by expanded capacity. This presents increasing risks as oil prices have fallen since their high during the commodity boom.

In Ecuador, Rafael Correa's election in 2007 profoundly altered the character of the country's politics. Ecuador was an extreme case of poorly institutionalized parties, polarized politics, and an inability of any president to form stable governing coalitions. Presidents operated through "ghost coalitions" involving a wide array of side payments and concessions to parties and politicians reluctant to openly cooperate due to the deep public skepticism about politicians and the system.[66] The lack of authority and the weak connections between parties and society led to repeated ousters of presidents, including in 1997, 2000 and 2005. Correa oversaw the writing of a new constitution in 2008 and new elections in 2009 in which his newly formed party, Alianza PAIS won roughly half the seats in Congress. Armed with strong legislative backing, new executive authority, and revenues streaming in from high oil prices, Correa launched his economic program including re-nationalizations in the oil and hydro-electric sectors, new taxes on foreign investment, and a host of new regulations enhancing state controls on prices and investment. He also removed Central Bank independence and centralized the execution of monetary and exchange rate policies in the office of the presidency. Under Correa, FDI fell from an average of 2% of GDP from 1995 to 2006 to less than 1% from 2007 to 2013, but gross capital formation did increase. While Correa's rhetoric was virulently anti-private capital and he did target some of the traditionally powerful domestic business groups, he also cooperated with other business groups and supported the formation of new ones which expanded dramatically under his presidency.[67] By contrast with Morales, however, Correa's control of his budget was much less careful and left Ecuador in a hazardous position as oil prices began to fall.

Finally, as with social policy, the most extreme approach was that of Hugo Chávez. The Chávez administration began a wave of nationalizations in 2006–2007, beginning with oil and moving into cement, steel, rice processing and packaging and even retail supermarkets, and with plans for further nationalizations in telecommunications and banking. Chávez' control over the national oil company, PDVSA, in addition to virtually the entire oil sector, granted him direct, centralized control of the country's oil revenues which represented in excess of 90% of Venezuela's export revenues. Javier Corrales has described the Chávez administration's aggressive stance toward markets and private capital as essentially a return to the ISI, populist approach that prevailed earlier in Venezuelan history and each time collapsed under the weight of its inability to sustain itself financially as oil prices decline. He has called this pattern "ax-relax-collapse" to describe the destructive pattern of massive, unsustainable spending followed by drastic cuts.[68]

The contestatory left's weaker commitment to macroeconomic restraint is evident in the data. Government expenditure as a percentage of GDP has risen sharply in the contestatory left, as has inflation. Not surprisingly, foreign direct investment – vital in all developing countries to overcome limits to domestic savings and technological capacity – has been weak. There are important variations. Venezuela's economy into the 2010s moved into severe imbalances with the highest inflation level in the region by a sizable margin. The model was falling apart while Chávez was alive, but under Maduro it has descended into chaos with severe shortages of essential goods, widespread hunger, and the oil industry in serious decline, even as the country has become more dependent on it. Argentina also wrestled with the consequences of much less fiscal restraint. The Kirchners benefited from high commodity prices during the boom and invested significant amounts in poverty reduction, achieving considerable results. But, the fall of prices hit the country hard, beset by inflation and facing deep resource constraints. By the 2016 elections, both Fernández de Kirchner and the Peronists had lost broad support. Ecuador faced similar problems as dependency on oil forced Correa to attempt to solve growing fiscal problems by raising taxes and adjusting benefits. By contrast, Bolivia under Morales made efforts to protect the country from downturns, establishing a stabilization fund to shield the economy from the effects of declining revenues.[69] Further, solid fiscal management has helped the country continue to grow and it has remained one of the fastest growing countries in the region by 2014.

Both the moderate left and the right suggest a different profile, although with variations. Chile and Uruguay maintained tight control on fiscal deficits and maintained low inflation despite high social spending. The results are evident from the data. Government expenditures as a percentage of GDP have risen only moderately and inflation in the principal moderate left cases has remained low. Foreign direct investment has risen throughout the period.

Brazil is an important deviation from the moderate left story. Brazil tends to run higher fiscal deficits – in part a function of its cumbersome pension system and federal system – but the Lula administration committed itself to transparent fiscal targets as a way to keep control of inflation and reassure foreign investors of its commitment to macroeconomic stability. This "inflation targeting" model, introduced in 1999, appeared to have solved inflation in the country while forcing the government to adhere to strict budgetary controls as a way to keep inflation within acceptable targets. The situation changed in Brazil after 2009–2010. Falling commodity prices hit Brazil even though the country is far less dependent on commodity revenues than any of the contestatory regimes. But, inflation targeting as a model tended to lead to overvaluation of the currency, which in turn hurt domestic manufacturing. The situation grew worse during the global financial crisis as capital flowed into emerging markets looking for better returns. As commodity export revenues fell and domestic manufacturing and employment weakened, the Brazilian economy suffered as well. In response, the Dilma Rousseff administration relaxed the fiscal controls, but at the expense of rising inflation as well. Dilma won the 2014 election, riding on popular support from the poor who had benefited most directly from the PT's expansive social policy innovations such as *Bolsa Família*. But, the country had become deeply polarized over the tension between inflation and redistribution. With the emergence of a massive corruption scandal centered around Petrobras, the jewel in the crown of state-owned enterprises, Dilma's popularity fell even further. Finally, in August 2015, Dilma's coalition allies in Congress turned on her and leveled accusations of violations of the Fiscal Responsibility Law and impeached her a year later. The new interim president, Michel Temer, instantly became engulfed in serious corruption accusations as well, but has moved forward to try to effect brutal cuts to government spending to address the imbalances that emerged in Dilma's last years. As of 2017, it is not clear if his reforms will pass or if he will survive in office. But, Brazil has fallen into deep economic disarray that exaggerates the depth of its problems. While structural reforms of the economy are needed (as in all of Latin America), the basic model still shares more in common with the rest of the moderate left and the right than the contestatory left.

And that model is not wholly neoliberal. The state has not disappeared in the moderate left or for that matter the moderate right. Instead, it follows what Eduardo Silva has called "pragmatic neoliberalism."[70] State policy in the moderate countries has been to complement markets in order to promote economic development. Thus, state development agencies such as Chile's CORFO (Corporación de Fomento de la Producción, Economic

Development Agency) worked to attract foreign investment to the country. Brazil's National Development Bank, the BNDES (Banco Nacional de Desenvolvimento Econômico e Social), similarly helped to bring new investments by acting as a key financier of new development projects in key sectors.[71] For example, the Program for Accelerating Growth set aside some US$ 500 million dollars to finance infrastructure projects. Public credit to finance strategic investments through national development banks have been important spurs to growth in Brazil, Colombia, Costa Rica, Mexico and Peru, ranging from 1% of GDP to as high as 6.5% of GDP.[72] In addition to loans, Latin American governments have extended tax credits to attract foreign investment in diverse sectors from forestry in Chile to mining in Peru to transport in Mexico or to environmental tourism in Costa Rica. Countries like Brazil and Chile have been particularly active as well in promoting state policies to develop and diffuse technology to the private sector. Technology diffusion strategies since the 1990s have focused on stimulating and subsidizing the demand for technological innovation and diffusion and thus are a much more "market driven" process than older approaches in Latin America that were more state led. The key in these emerging policies and institutions is that they are guided by a desire to foster public–private cooperation. They present a sharp contrast with the contestatory left and its hostile attitude towards the private sector. As such this new balanced and pragmatic model of state–market interaction offers a much stronger promise of sustained development over time.

Conclusion

Beginning in 1998, Latin Americans voted for a shift in policy direction. Most of these voters did not reject the market and did not seek a complete reversal of neoliberal reforms. But, performance weaknesses, due more or less directly to neoliberal reforms, led voters to prefer adjustments to the model. The result was "neoliberalism with a human face", or "pragmatic neoliberalism" in the moderate left and in countries governed by the right. In some countries, historic legacies of injustice and exclusion helped foster a more extreme response – the contestatory left. Regardless of partisan identity, the 2000s were a period of growth, increased social spending, declining poverty and inequality and a return of state involvement in the economy. But, the end of the commodity boom created risks to the durability of the social and economic gains over the period, regardless of left or right, contestatory or moderate. The durability of those gains is the subject of the next chapter.

Notes

1 Ronaldo Munck, "Neoliberalism, Necessitarianism and Alternatives in Latin America: There is no alternative (TINA)," *Third World Quarterly* 24, no. 3, 2003.

2 Castañeda, 1993: 3.
3 Peter Hakim, "Is Washington Losing Latin America?" *Foreign Affairs* 85, no. 1, 2006.
4 James Petras' *The Left Strikes Back* is an exception to that trend. Published in 1999, Petras documented the variety of "lefts" in the region and the ways the left was reorganizing and renewing.
5 Gustavo A. Flores-Macías, *After Neoliberalism? The Left and Economic Reforms in Latin America* (Oxford: Oxford University Press, 2012).
6 Gerardo L. Munck, "Liberal vs. Popular Models of Democracy." In *Democracy and its Discontents in Latin America* (Boulder, CO: Lynne Rienner, 2016).
7 For example, see Jorge Castañeda and Marco A. Morales, eds., *Leftovers* (New York: Routledge, 2008); Javier Corrales, "The Many Lefts in Latin America," *Foreign Policy* November/December 2006; or Kurt Weyland, Wendy Hunter and Raúl Madrid, eds., *Leftist Governments in Latin America* (New York: Cambridge University Press, 2010). As an alternative Gerardo Munck, 2016, differentiates among left, center-left, center-right and right and liberal versus popular democracy. Steven Levitsky and Kenneth M. Roberts offer four types of left governing parties based on the concentration of authority and the institutionalization of the party. *The Resurgence of the Latin American Left* (Baltimore: Johns Hopkins University Press, 2011).
8 Weyland, Hunter and Madrid, 2010.
9 In fact, Amartya Sen makes the argument that helping the rural poor gain access to markets is an important advance in freedom. Amartya Sen, 1999.
10 Dilma Rousseff of the Workers Party (Partido dos Trabalhadores, PT) won re-election in 2013, but was suspended on charges of budgetary manipulation in violation of the Fiscal Responsibility Law and subsequently was impeached on April 17, 2016 and then convicted in the Senate and removed from office on August 31, 2016. For a fuller discussion, see Peter Kingstone and Timothy J. Power, "A Fourth Decade of Brazilian Democracy: Challenges, Achievements and Polarization." In *Democratic Brazil Divided*, Peter Kingstone and Timothy J. Power, eds. (Pittsburgh: University of Pittsburgh Press, 2017).
11 Manuel Zelaya was removed from office extra-constitutionally in one of the most controversial crises of presidential politics in the region over the 2000s.
12 Peru is a particularly controversial case as the victor of the 2007 election, Alán García, had been a leftist and the winner of the 2011 election, Ollanta Humala, modeled himself on Hugo Chávez. Yet, both relied on right wing officials and cooperative relations with foreign extractive firms and the private sector. As a result, some observers do not believe the left has held power in Peru. For example, see John Crabtree and Francisco Durand, *Peru: Elite Power and Political Capture* (London: Zed Books, 2017).
13 Jaime Saavedra, "Labor Markets During the 1990s." In *After the Washington Consensus: Restarting Growth and Reform in Latin America*, John Williamson and Pedro Pablo Kuczynski, eds. (Washington DC: Institute for International Economics, 2003).
14 Matthew Singer, "The Electoral Politics of Vulnerability and the Incentive to Cast an Economic Vote," Ph.D. Dissertation, Duke University, 2007: 246–248.
15 Javier Corrales, "The Backlash against Market Reforms in Latin America." In Jorge Dominguez and Michael Shifter, eds., *Constructing Democratic Governance*, 3rd edition (Baltimore, MA: Johns Hopkins University Press, 2008).
16 Daniel Brinks, "A Tale of Two Cities." In *The Handbook of Latin American Politics*, Peter Kingstone and Deborah Yashar, eds. (New York: Routledge Press, 2011).
17 Joseph Stiglitz, *Globalization and its Discontents* (New York: W.W. Norton, 2003).

18 Walton, 2004 for example, cites it as one of the principal errors of the neo-liberal period.
19 Luigi Manzetti, "Political Manipulations and Market Reform Failures," *World Politics* 55, no. 3, 2003.
20 Hector Schamis, "Distributional Coalitions and the Politics of Economic Reform in Latin America," *World Politics* 51, no. 2, 1999.
21 Manzetti, *Privatization South American Style*, 2000.
22 Lora and Panizza, 2003.
23 Kurtz, 2004.
24 Baker, 2010: chapter 3.
25 Marco Morales, "Have Latin Americans Turned Left?" In *Leftovers*, Jorge Castañeda and Marco A. Morales, eds. (New York: Routledge, 2008).
26 Andy Baker and Kenneth F. Greene, "Latin America's Left Mandate: Free-Market Policies and Issue Voting in New Democracies," *World Politics* 63, no. 1: 43–77, 2011.
27 Kaufman and Segura-Ubiergo, 2001.
28 Petras, 1999: 3.
29 Corrales, 2008. Corrales' list of distinct groups voting left include: radicals, protectionists, hyper-nationalists, commodity nationalists, crusaders, big-spenders, egalitarians, equalizers, multiculturalists, and macho-bashers. Each of these groups had distinct identities and agendas.
30 Levitsky and Roberts 2011.
31 The terms applied to this grouping include "moderate," "social democratic," "more instutionalized" or "non-rentier" states.
32 The terms applied to this grouping include "radical," "contestatory," "populist" or "neopopulist," "non-institutionalized" or "rentier states."
33 Kurt Weyland, Wendy Hunter and Raúl Madrid, eds., *Leftist Governments in Latin America* (New York: Cambridge University Press, 2010).
34 See for example, Javier Corrales, "The Repeating Revolution: Chávez' New Politics and Old Ecomomics." In *Leftist Governments in Latin America*, Kurt Weyland, Wendy Hunter and Raúl Madrid, eds. (New York: Cambridge University Press, 2010).
35 George Gray-Molina, "The Challenge of Progressive Change under Evo Morales." In Kurt Weyland, Wendy Hunter and Raúl Madrid, eds., *Leftist Governments in Latin America* (New York: Cambridge University Press, 2010).
36 María Fernanda Enríquez Szentkirályi, "Social Movements and Framing Decisions: Ecuador's Campaign for the Rights of Nature." Ph.D. Dissertation, University of Connecticut, 2014.
37 This is the central claim of Gustavo Flores-Macías (2012) whose account of politics and policy after neoliberalism works just as well to help understand the character of reform under neoliberalism. The central ideas of institutionalization and its impact on governance and policy-making date back to Scott Mainwaring and Timothy Scully, eds., *Building Democratic Institutions: Party Systems in Latin America* (Stanford: Stanford University Press, 1995).
38 Munck, 2016.
39 Heritage Foundation. Data available at http://www.heritage.org.
40 Rudiger Dornbusch and Sebastian Edwards, eds., *The Macroeconomics of Populism in Latin America* (Chicago: University of Chicago Press, 1991).
41 Data available at http://www.cepal.org.
42 CEPAL Fiscal Measures of the Crisis. Available at http://www.cepal.org/notes/61/indicadores04.html (accessed October 16, 2017).
43 Arturo Porzecanski, "Latin America: The Missing Financial Crisis," Economic Commission for Latin America and the Caribbean Studies and Perspective Series, no. 6, Washington DC, 2009.

44 Kaufman and Segura-Ubiergo, 2001; Peter Kingstone and Joseph Young, "Partisanship and Policy Choice: What's Left for the Left in Latin America?" *Political Research Quarterly* 62, no. 1, 2009.
45 Lustig, 2009.
46 José Merino, "No Such Thing as a Social Advantage for the Left?" In *Leftovers*, Jorge Castañeda and Marco A. Morales, eds. (New York: Routledge, 2008).
47 Huber and Stephens, 2012.
48 Candelaria Garay, *Social Policy Expansion in Latin America* (New York: Cambridge University Press, 2016).
49 Jennifer Pribble, *Welfare and Party Politics in Latin America* (New York: Cambridge University Press, 2013).
50 Jessica A.J. Rich, "Grassroots Bureaucracy: Intergovernmental Relations and Popular Mobilization in Brazil's AIDS Policy Sector," *Latin American Politics and Society* 55, no. 2: 1–25, 2013.
51 Maureen Donaghy, *Civil Society and Participatory Governance: Municipal Councils and Social Housing Programs in Brazil* (New York: Routledge, 2013).
52 Crabtree and Durand, 2017.
53 Sara Niedzwiecki and Jennifer Pribble, "Social Policies and Center-Right Governments in Argentina and Chile," *Latin American Politics and Society* 59, no. 3: 72–97, 2017.
54 Birdsall and Székely, 2003.
55 Cuban donations and service volunteers such as doctors.
56 Daniel Ortega, Francisco Rodriguéz, and Edward Miguel, "Freed from Illiteracy? A Closer Look at Venezuela's Robinson Literacy Campaign," Wesleyan Economics Working Papers, no. 2006–025, October 2006.
57 Francisco Rodriguéz, "An Empty Revolution: The Unfulfilled Promises of Hugo Chávez," *Foreign Affairs* 87, no. 2, 2008.
58 Nora Lustig, "Poverty, Inequality and the New Left in Latin America," *Woodrow Wilson Center Update on the Americas*, October 2009.
59 Natasha Borges Sugiyama, *Diffusion of Good Government: Social Sector Reforms in Brazil* (South Bend, IN: University of Notre Dame Press, 2012).
60 Tracy Fenwick, *Avoiding Governors: Federalism, Democracy, and Poverty Alleviation in Brazil and Argentina* (South Bend, IN: University of Notre Dame Press, 2015).
61 Brazil and Chile also developed innovative health plans designed to address inequities in the delivery of health care for the poor. Brazil's *Programa de Saude da Família* (Program for Family Health) was designed to extend basic health care into poor neighborhoods through the establishment of community health care teams that included a doctor, nurse, nurse's aid and health care agents. Chile's *Plan Auge* (Plan de Acceso Universal de Garantías Explícitas, Explicit Health Guarantees Plan), launched in 2002, is a program with the ambitious aim to guarantee affordable health care to all Chileans, financed from small increases in VAT taxes and health care co-payments. Both have had positive impacts in building long-term human capital and are sustainable financially.
62 For an extended discussion of the role of the state in leftist governments in the 2000s, see Gustavo Flores-Macías, 2012.
63 It is important to remember of course that the state had never gone away and that the "return of the state" conceals the ongoing role of government in the economy throughout the neoliberal period. Similarly, Javier Corrales, 2003 points out the neoliberal goal was not the elimination of the state, but to produce a leaner, more efficient state with more appropriate and more effective spending priorities.

64 Allison Post, *Foreign and Domestic Investment in Argentina: The Politics of Privatized Infrastructure* (New York: Cambridge University Press, 2014).
65 George Gray-Molina, 2010.
66 Andrés Mejía Acosta, *Informal Coalitions and Policymaking in Latin America: Ecuador in Comparative Perspective* (New York: Routledge, 2009).
67 María Sol Parrales, "The Re-Shaping of Business–State Relations in Latin America." Paper presented at the Annual Conference of REPAL, Universidad del Pacífico, Lima, Peru, April 27–28, 2017.
68 Javier Corrales, 2010.
69 Diana Tussie and Pablo Heidrich, "A Tale of Ecumenicism and Diversity: Economic and Trade Policies of the New Left." In *Leftovers*, Jorge Castañeda and Marco A. Morales, eds. (New York: Routledge, 2008).
70 Silva, 1998.
71 Nelson, 2009.
72 Eduardo Lora and Francis Fukuyama, eds, *The State of State Reform*, Latin American Development Forum. Washington DC: World Bank Group, 2007.

5   Latin America's Golden Era?

With Hélène Maghin and Eva Renon

The period from roughly 2003 to 2012 was a "golden era" in Latin America – a time when growth improved markedly, poverty and inequality fell dramatically, and macroeconomic stability prevailed everywhere. Latin America had long been the global champion of both exclusion (economic, social and political) and macroeconomic instability (particularly debt and inflation). During this golden era, Latin America offered instead growth without inflation[1] and declining poverty and inequality. The latter was particularly striking as it came at a time when growth in the rest of the emerging economies, such as China or India, was leading to rapidly rising inequality. Was this the dawning of a new age in the region?

The short answer is "no." By 2012–2013, growing tensions revealed that the gains of the golden era had been temporary, and at worst illusory. While average per capita growth in the region between 2003 and 2012 had been slightly over 3% per year (four times the average for 1996–2002), the rate had slipped to under 2% for 2013–2014 and turned negative in 2015–2016. Macroeconomic conditions worsened as well as debt, deficits and inflation all began to rise. With government spending tightening, unemployment rising, and real wages stagnant or falling, democratic politics also showed increasing signs of strain across the region.

The extent of the shift is mostly clearly visible in the dismal fortunes of the two exemplars of the left during the golden era. Venezuela had been the leader of the anti-Washington Consensus bloc, offering financing to allies all across the region and even providing fuel assistance to low-income Americans. Brazil trumpeted the success of the "Brasília Consensus" as an alternative to the Washington Consensus, advised other moderate leftist parties in the region such as the FMLN in El Salvador, and offered extensive development and technical assistance to other developing countries, particularly in Africa. But, as of 2017, both countries were experiencing deep economic and political crises, models of chaos, corruption and democratic reversion rather than inclusive forms of development.

As in the previous chapter, the central question is: What happened? The last chapter explored the rise of the left and assessed its performance, both relative to the right and comparing between two modal approaches to development and governance. The central conclusion was that the differences were not that marked, although the contestatory left's model was more conflictual and more hostile to the private sector. But, virtually all Latin American economies performed well and all Latin American governments made efforts to address poverty, inequality and social inclusion. Some Latin American democracies eroded somewhat on civil and political liberties, primarily in the contestatory regimes where new forms of popular or participatory democracy emerged designed to overcome long-standing discrimination. But, on standard measures such as Freedom House or Polity IV, all remained scored as Free or Partly Free (Freedom House) or democracies (Polity IV). The overall economic policy orientation did change in the contestatory regimes, particularly on property rights and regulation of foreign capital. But for most Latin American countries, not much changed. The biggest shift was regional, between the difficult reform years of the 1990s and the dramatic improvements in macroeconomic performance, poverty and inequality that invited claims of a golden age.

If it was not partisan politics that mattered most, what did? The unambiguous answer is the commodity boom combined with low interest rates in the developed economies. Together, they led to an abundance of foreign capital, through both export revenues and foreign investment. These "good times" gave policy makers unusual ability to invest in social policies and expand a wide range of government services unconstrained by the need to placate foreign investors.[2] Commodity prices began to rise sharply in 2002–2003 along with rapid Chinese growth and that country's consumption of a wide array of goods. Chinese growth drove all prices up both directly and indirectly.[3] The "super cycle" helped move a large number of formerly lower income countries to middle income status and lifted hundreds of millions of people around the world into the "new middle classes."[4] By 2010, however, the cycle reached its inevitable end and began a gradual decline back to the normal pattern identified by Raúl Prebisch (discussed in Chapter 2) of declining commodity prices relative to manufactured goods. With steady downward movement of prices through the 2010s, the good times came to an end as well, most acutely in those economies most dependent on commodity exports.

The second question then is to what extent were the changes during the golden era real? Were growth, macroeconomic stability and social inclusion simply artifacts of unusually good times or did the region change socially and politically in important ways? What are the prospects for development if the good times are over? To what extent did investments in education and research and technology help strengthen the "knowledge economy" necessary to compete in the global market? On the social side, to what extent was the good news of declining poverty and inequality a product of a newfound commitment to equity and meaningful citizenship, or just a product of a region flush with cash? Have Latin American politics become more inclusive?

To address these questions, this chapter looks at the two sides of the golden era: social inclusion and economic performance. It considers the extent to which Latin American governments made efforts to deepen the meaning of citizenship by developing policies of inclusion with potentially durable consequences. Subsequently, it considers the economic picture, looking at both the macroeconomic changes, but also focusing on the micro level limits to the region's capacity for growth. Finally, it ends by presenting two "optimistic" cases of technological development and innovation that highlight the region's potential to foster new models of growth.

The chapter advances three claims about the golden era and its implications for development in the region. First, it argues that Latin American governments made significant and real efforts to deepen citizenship in the region through inclusionary social policies. These were not simply artifacts of good times. In fact, many of the inclusionary efforts find their roots in the 1990s in much less permissive times. There is no question these efforts expanded in the boom years, but they often entailed innovative ways to deliver benefits that went well beyond easy spending. Second, growth was modest at best in the region and almost no Latin American countries used the commodity boom surpluses to protect against the inevitable end of the cycle or to invest in strengthening the underlying competitiveness of their economies. Instead, Latin America structurally experienced a "premature deindustrialization"[5] as high value added manufacturing stagnated or declined and Latin America lost ground to new manufacturing competitors, notably China. The problem lies in firms' investment behavior and capacities at the micro level which translate into weak global competitiveness that prevents even the most advanced Latin American economies from moving up the "knowledge economy" ladder. Finally, it argues that the failure to generate good jobs based on high value added production and high labor productivity presents an important challenge to keeping the social inclusion trend moving forward. Technological advancement, innovation, and investment in human capital are the requirements for producing the jobs that lead to growth with rising wages. Unfortunately, Latin American economies did not emerge from the boom years in a strengthened position in global competition. In the final analysis, the social changes are real, but the lack of economic progress may generate political tensions that are hard to resolve.

Has Latin America Become More Inclusive?

The question of whether Latin America became more inclusive over the boom years faces the slippery challenge of what the term "inclusive" means. The literature on "inclusive growth" offers several possible ways to define it, but here I choose to emphasize what Luiz Carlos Bresser Pereira called "the citizenship problem."[6] For Bresser Pereira, the citizenship problem was one in which members of Latin American society were voters, but not citizens. The restoration of democracy and expansion of the electorate all across the region conferred voting rights. But, for most Latin Americans, those rights were not accompanied by meaningful qualities of citizenship. To be an effective citizen, individuals needed sufficient freedom from economic insecurity to know about, demand and enjoy social and political rights. The problem, as Bresser Pereira observed, was that people worrying about basics like having enough to eat or basic housing, health care and education simply did not have the capacity to act as citizens.

Focusing on citizenship as sufficient freedom from insecurity to both know one's rights and to demand them also begs the question of whether the state is responsive to those demands. Citizenship implies an individual imbued with rights and a state and polity responsive to citizen needs and demands.[7] To see whether inclusion, conceived as deepening citizenship, strengthened over the boom years, one can look at changing social and economic indicators that point to reduction in insecurity, such as poverty, inequality, wages and unemployment. Those indicators, however, are highly sensitive to the performance of the economy. They may reflect rising market incomes that can reverse as quickly as they rose. But, one can, then, also look at indicators of explicit policy effort or innovations in policies that address basic insecurity, such as housing, health, education, and social assistance. The record is clear on both sides of this equation: the booming economy contributed significantly to improved social and economic indicators, but the improvements coincided with, complemented and in many ways actively depended on explicit policy efforts by government officials.

Poverty and Inequality in the Golden Era

The single most striking fact of the boom years was the decline in poverty in the region. In 2000, the poor broadly defined (earning between 0 and $4 per day) constituted the largest group in Latin American society – over 41% of the population. By 2012, that group had shrunk almost in half (25% of the population) and was the smallest in the region.[8] Breaking it down into lower levels of income, with $1.25 per day as the threshold for indigence and $2 per day as the threshold for poverty (the most widely used standard), the region witnessed striking changes. As of 2000, only Chile and Uruguay had fewer than 10% of their population living with less than $2 per day and only Argentina, Costa Rica and Mexico had less than 15%. By contrast, Bolivia, Colombia, Ecuador, Honduras and Nicaragua had over 30% (and nearly 40% for three of them). By 2012, only four – Bolivia, Colombia, Guatemala and Nicaragua had poverty rates over 10%. Bolivia's rate had fallen from 38% of the population to

13% while Colombia's had fallen from 32% to 12%. Five Latin American countries had poverty rates below 5% (Argentina, Chile, Costa Rica, Mexico and Uruguay). The same trend is visible for indigence. In 2000, eleven of the seventeen countries in this set had indigence rates over 10%, including three with rates ranging from 18–27% (Colombia, Ecuador and Bolivia). By 2011–2012, only five had rates of indigence above 5%. The situation for Colombia, Ecuador and Bolivia improved dramatically, falling to 5.5%, 4% and 8% respectively.

As poverty and indigence fell, so did inequality. The GINI coefficient is a flawed measure of inequality, not least because its focus on deciles of the population fails to capture changes at the very top 1% where most income and wealth is concentrated. But, shifts in GINI do provide some evidence of narrowing between lower deciles and upper ones and again the evidence of change over the first decade of the 2000s is clear. On average, the GINI coefficient fell by 5% over the region and in every country except the two most equal in the region, Costa Rica and Uruguay, where it barely changed. Seven of the cases saw changes over 5% between 2000 and 2010, with Bolivia's GINI declining over 16% over the period.

While GINI is a crude measure of inequality, other critical indicators of protection from insecurity tell a complementary story. Amartya Sen's conception of human welfare rests on his notion of "capabilities" – that is the freedom of individuals to live the life they choose or value.[9] The widely used Human Development Index (HDI) arose out of the effort to measure well-being more broadly than GDP or GDP/capita. Here again, the shifts in Latin America from 2000–2013 are telling. HDI rose on average by 10% across the region with life expectancy rising by over three years on average and mean years of schooling rising by 20%. Infant mortality rates fell from 26 per 1,000 live births in 2000 to 16 by 2013. Mortality rates for children under five years fell from 32 per 1,000 live births in 2000 to 18 by 2013.

All of these indicators point to substantial improvements in the quality of life and the freedom from insecurity, but they may simply reflect the higher rate of growth and higher market incomes during the boom rather than explicit policy effort. To see policy effort, we need to consider other ways of understanding how governments in the region affect equity and poverty outcomes. The discussion below considers three different ways of thinking about policy contributions to falling poverty: rising wages and wage equality as a function of government policy, specifically labor market (such as the minimum wage) and education reform; studies that measure aggregate policy effort; and explicit ways that governments transfer resources directly to the poor in the form of social assistance. These three different views all make clear that declining poverty and inequality were not simply products of the good times, but the results of state officials actively trying to improve the lives of the poor.

As noted in Chapter 3, "bootstraps" are the most important tool for poor people to lift themselves from poverty,[10] i.e. access to labor markets and the ability to earn a decent wage is central to concerns about equity. As noted in Chapter 4, neoliberal reforms had not produced rising wages for most Latin Americans through the 1990s. Indeed, contrary to the expectations of Hecksher–Olin theory, it had produced benefits for skilled workers, but not the much larger majority of relatively unskilled labor.[11] Yet, the 1990s also witnessed increased investments in education, and by the 2000s these reforms had begun to pay off. The results showed up primarily in declining wage inequality. Education policies during the 1990s in Latin America focused primarily upon reversing the highly regressive nature of education spending in the region. As a result, policy efforts focused on increasing primary school enrollments and primary education spending. This then translated into a surge in secondary school enrollments during the following decade. The increase in the supply of secondary-school educated workers led to a drop in the skill premium as workers with a secondary school education became less scarce. A notable consequence was significantly reduced wage earning inequality. Declining wage inequality, in turn, has proven to be the principal cause of the declining concentration of household incomes.[12]

Minimum wage increases also contributed to declining inequality by luring informal sector workers into the formal sector. Luis Beccaria, Roxana Maurizio and Gustavo Vázquez note that the decline in informality began in the 1990s, but then intensified in the 2000s[13] as minimum wages rose, helping to both formalize informal sector workers as well as drive up wages of skilled workers.[14] In short, investment in education and raising the minimum wage – both conscious policy choices – played a critical role in equalizing and raising wages.

These policy choices were not isolated. They were elements in broad policy re-orientations in the region. Reviewing the great breadth of policy change is beyond the scope of this book, but another way to see the extent of policy efforts is to look at aggregated measures of government efforts to address poverty and inequality. Two important efforts to examine government commitments are the Social and Economic Rights Empowerment Initiative[15] and the Commitment to Equity Institute.[16] The Social and Economic Rights Empowerment Initiative takes as its starting point the International Covenant for Economic, Social and Cultural rights and produces an index of social and economic rights fulfilment (SERF) that measures both the extent to which individuals enjoy social and economic rights as well as the extent to which the state is attempting to meet its obligations within its capacity to do so. That is, the measures of performance build in estimates of the state's actual capacity to ensure rights (as opposed to relative to some idealized standard or using rich countries as a baseline). This point is critical for evaluating state performance. It is unreasonable to expect Bolivia or Guatemala to provide social and economic rights at the same level or quality as Sweden or Norway and entirely unsurprising and virtually meaningless to observe that they do not. But, asking how Bolivia or Guatemala fare relative to their own capacity and resources (primarily measured by GDP/capita) provides stronger estimates of the extent to which policy makers are directing resources to meet rights obligations. The index specifically examines rights to food, shelter, education, work, social security and freedom from discrimination.[17] The data tell a clear story: between 2000 and 2010, every Latin American country but Panama improved its SERF score, attesting to active efforts to direct state resources to enhancing the fulfilment of social and economic rights (See Table 5.1). What also stands out is that no Latin American country scores 100, that is they are all underperforming relative to their economic resources.

The Commitment to Equity project tells a similarly positive story about Latin America in the 2000s. The CEQ is a comprehensive project to look beyond measures of government spending, which can be misleading. For example, social security is regressive in every Latin American country, but in many cases it is the largest component of social spending. As a result, rising social expenditures can come from increasing payments to a narrow, privileged labor elite or alternatively from demographic changes that lead to more retirees, but neither example demonstrates a commitment to equity. Instead, the CEQ examines how citizens fare after collecting all taxes (direct and indirect) and effecting all transfers (direct and indirect). In short, does the combined effect of spending and taxing address both poverty and equality? The benefit of the CEQ project is that "policy architectures"[18] can vary significantly and governments can find very different ways to deliver similar benefits. Latin American governments differ in the direct taxes they levy, such as the income tax, as well as indirect taxes, like sales tax or VAT. They can deliver very different levels or forms of direct transfers, such as social assistance, as well as providing indirect transfers such as housing subsidies. Finally, government spending is a form of benefit as government payment eliminates or reduces the direct costs to households. Health and education spending are the most important forms of such payments. All of this happens on top of the direct market income individuals earn. The conclusions from studies to date in the 2000s of thirteen of the seventeen cases covered in this book is that overall fiscal policy, despite notable differences in the tax and benefit mix, the overall effect is equalizing and poverty reducing.

Both of these projects tell an aggregate story of an explicit commitment to enhance the well-being and deepen the meaning and quality of citizenship over the 2000s. Neither explains why that is the case, or explores in detail the specific policy mechanisms of how governments have tried to improve equity. Social policies are complex and varied and it is beyond the scope of this book to review them in detail. But, it is worth considering two areas of policy that show the extent of government efforts to protect citizens against old age and to build human capital. The first is the extraordinary spread of non-contributory pensions across the region. The second is the

Table 5.1 Social and Economic Rights Index, 2000–2010 Change

Country	1995	2000	2005	2010	2000–2010 Change
Argentina			88.32	91.75	10%
Bolivia	67.8	66.31	70.84	72.55	9%
Brazil	81.4		83.57	88.13	6%
Chile		87.61	89.49	91.49	4%
Colombia	74.18	76.34	80.41	83.69	9%
Costa Rica	80.85	87.07	90.19	91.91	5%
Ecuador	68.41	73.5		84.16	14%
El Salvador	68.23	71.5	76.5	81.58	14%
Guatemala	54.53	59.12	59.93	69.05	16%
Honduras	60.61	64.94	70.15	80.01	23%
Mexico	71.96	75.85	81.35	86.71	14%
Nicaragua	69.03	69.62	76.6	76.72	10%
Panama				76.07	–1%
Paraguay		77.42	83.51	83.17	7%
Peru		73.69	74.87	77.39	5%
Uruguay			91.24	94.23	3%
Venezuela	70.2	73.98	77.6	81.85	10%
Average	69.75	73.62	79.64	82.97	9%

Source: Sakiko Fukuda-Parr, Terra Lawson-Remer, Susan Randolph, International SERF Index Data, 2015 Update (http://serfindex.uconn.edu/2015-international-serf-index-downloads/).

Note: Data for closest year to 2000 for missing data.

dramatic expansion of conditional cash transfers (CCTs), such as *Bolsa Família*, discussed in Chapter 4.

One of the purposes of social policy is to protect citizens against a variety of risks, including the risk of old age. Pensions emerged in Latin America in waves with the earliest and largest industrializing countries acting as the pioneers.[19] As in Europe and the US, the rise of an organized, industrial working class played a key role in encouraging the development of a pension system. Unlike Europe and the US, however, formal sector workers remained a minority of the workforce for virtually the entire region so even the pioneers, such as Argentina, Brazil or Mexico, never established coverage for very large segments of the workforce. Contributory pensions – that is pensions into which workers and employers actively contributed over the period of a worker's employment – constituted a significant portion of social spending in almost all Latin American countries, yet provided insurance against old age for only a narrow minority. In effect, social security in Latin America was in most countries an expensive and regressive system in which the majority of workers were fated to work until they die.

Declining levels of informality over the 2000s helped bring more workers into the contributory system, but informality remains a significant issue in most of the region, especially among the poorer countries. As of 2015, the average size of the informal sector was 53% across the region and in the 60s for most Andean and Central American countries. Latin American pension systems had too few workers paying in, raising fears about the financial sustainability of the systems, and far too many citizens completely unprotected. In the 1990s, encouraged by the IMF and the World Bank, a number of Latin American countries either privatized their pension systems or instituted less ambitious "parametric" reforms to improve financial sustainability, and to make it easier and/or more appealing for uncovered workers to begin to contribute, for example by altering or relaxing the rules for qualifying for a formal pension. By the 2000s, however, it was clear that privatization was definitely not a solution and parametric reforms led at best to improvements at the margin, but were just not sufficient to increase coverage.

Instead, the solution that spread throughout the region over the 2000s was the growth of non-contributory pensions – in effect a form of social assistance financed through taxes rather than worker and employer contributions. By 2012, almost the entire region (fifteen of the seventeen cases) had introduced new pension system reforms that extended benefits to previously uncovered citizens aged sixty-five and over.[20] In many instances, these reforms entailed highly innovative solutions to the problems of financial sustainability and broad coverage.[21] The reforms varied significantly throughout the region. At the high end, countries like Argentina, Brazil, Chile and Uruguay covered over 80% of their elderly (over 90% for Argentina).[22] By contrast, Bolivia expanded coverage to nearly 100% of its elderly population exclusively through non-contributory pensions. On average, over one third of Latin America's elderly received non-contributory pensions and in eleven of the seventeen cases covering more than 50% of the elderly through both systems (Argentina, Bolivia, Brazil, Chile, Colombia, Costa Rica, Ecuador, Mexico, Panama, Uruguay and Venezuela).

Non-contributory pensions were not the only form of social assistance that spread throughout the region that featured highly innovative solutions to poverty and inequality. Conditional cash transfers (CCTs) are designed to alleviate poverty while building human capital. Beneficiaries receive payments, but only upon meeting certain conditions, typically ensuring children are enrolled and attending school regularly and/or receiving regular health checks. In 2001, roughly 38 million Latin Americans received a CCT payment. By 2010, 135 million people did – roughly 25% of the population. By 2008, Venezuela was the only country that did not offer a CCT.[23]

Conditional cash transfers have their critics, not least because they are means tested and targeted rather than universal and there are strong arguments that universal benefits are better economically, socially and particularly politically.[24] Payments that just go to the poor can stigmatize beneficiaries. They are also more vulnerable politically if middle and upper class voters turn against them. In addition, CCT payments tend to be small and have much more limited effects on poverty and inequality than market income. A good job goes a good deal further than a cash transfer. Nevertheless, a variety of studies have shown positive effects over and above simply alleviating poverty. For one, impact assessments of the two largest, *Bolsa Família* in Brazil and *Oportunidades* in Mexico, have shown that they are particularly effective in reaching their target populations – that is, the payments reach most of the eligible poor and pay out very little to non-eligible, non-poor citizens.[25] One thing this shows is how well policy makers designed their policies to avoid manipulation by clientelistic politicians.[26] Studies have also shown positive effects on school enrollment and attendance, child labor, nutrition, as well as women's sense of empowerment as almost all CCTs are paid directly to mothers.[27] Wendy Hunter and Natasha Sugiyama's work on *Bolsa Família* in Brazil showed that it led to women acquiring legal registration cards for the first time, enhancing their status as citizens. Formal IDs in most Latin American countries are vital as they are the key to access for all public services in the country.[28] In short, CCTs helped alleviate the burden of poverty, but they also played an important role in building human capital, strengthening citizenship, and enhancing the social and economic rights delivered by an increasingly responsive state.

The combined evidence all points to a period of real change, not just on indicators that can shift quickly with changing economic circumstances, but in terms of genuine efforts by state officials to protect the most vulnerable citizens from economic uncertainty and risk. CCTs, non-contributory pensions, active efforts on labor market, housing, food, education, and taxation are all functions of state officials making explicit decisions about how to use resources. Many of these efforts find their roots in the 1990s under much more difficult macroeconomic circumstances. But, they intensified and spread through the 2000s, they were expanded and/or maintained by governments of both the right and the left, and in doing so made tens of millions of poor Latin Americans into citizens, arguably for the first time in the region's history.

Limitations of the Golden Era's Social Inclusion

The boom years helped bring a deeper form of citizenship to millions and millions of Latin Americans, but observers note that there are important limitations to the good news – limitations that may make this trend easier to reverse. For one, millions of Latin Americans enjoy new benefits, but millions and millions more were not brought in. This is particularly true for some of the poorer countries in the region, especially in Central America where countries like El Salvador, Guatemala, Honduras and Nicaragua have offered far less protection. Even countries that have expanded coverage face risks as non-contributory assistance, whether pensions or CCTs, need financing. In some of the most generous countries, such as Bolivia or Ecuador, the new benefits were financed with commodity export revenues. In any case, the payments are quite small and in most countries both CCTs and non-contributory pensions represent only small fractions of the minimum wage.

One critical argument is that this expansion of CCTs and non-contributory pensions represented an "easy phase" of redistribution, but that deeper and persistent forms of inclusion require much harder choices and more resources.[29] Alisha Holland and Ben Schneider have noted that the new benefit schemes for the most part required only small budgetary commitments – generally less than 1% of GDP – and were financed primarily off indirect taxes. In most cases, the new benefit schemes did not require developing new institutions, did not remove or reduce benefits for existing recipients in formal labor markets, and did not require raising direct taxes on existing payers. This last point is crucial as Latin American governments in general raise very little tax revenue from income taxes and the challenge of raising taxes, particularly on higher income households where income is concentrated, is exceedingly hard.[30]

Deepening redistribution and thereby extending citizenship confronts two profound challenges. First, the "hard" phase of inclusion requires much more difficult institutional changes. Delivering a cash payment on condition of attending school and getting regular check-ups is relatively straightforward compared to the substantial institutional reform challenge of ensuring quality education and health care. The second problem is political. The under-developed welfare systems in Latin America favor the organized working class and the middle class – "insiders" who are organized, educated and easily mobilized to demand and defend benefits.[31] Insiders enjoy access to public services (such as education, health or contributory pensions) or are wealthy enough to opt out and obtain benefits privately. To extend the welfare state and provide higher value benefits broadly, governments need to find ways to get insiders to support the hard choices and resources commitments. In effect, inclusionary politics will need new policy coalitions linking insiders and "outsiders" in support of much more substantial reform and institutional commitments. In a context of diminishing resources at the end of the boom years, that may prove very hard to do. As James Mahon has observed, the new CCT and non-contributory schemes do not create organized political constituencies – beneficiaries do not become members of any formal organization when they receive benefits. The unorganized poor are not well positioned to mobilize in defense of their rights. As such, the politics of taking away these benefits may be easier than either building new coalitions with existing insiders or reducing or removing the much more expensive (and frequently regressive) benefits insiders receive. With macroeconomic conditions weakening, this may become the choice Latin American governments confront.

In sum, the new inclusionary efforts have had impressive consequences. But, Latin America remains a region with large numbers of poor, and very poor people, high levels of inequality, and the new schemes face limits to their generosity or the breadth of coverage. Moreover, they are vulnerable both to economic downturns and to political conflicts in hard times between insiders and outsiders. The 2000s were genuinely a Golden Era in terms of the efforts to include the poor and the many impressive results, but in the end, it may only have been a thin layer of gold plating. The future of inclusion depends considerably on the economic story.

The Grasshopper, the Ant, and the Coming of Winter

In the classic fable, the Grasshopper and the Ant, Aesop warned of the dangers of playing all summer rather than storing food for the winter, as the Ant did. Inevitably, the coming of winter left the Grasshopper starving while the Ant, which had foregone immediate pleasure in favor of future needs, thrived. In the fable, the desperate Grasshopper sought help from the Ant, but the Ant declined and the Grasshopper died.

The fable is not really a fair metaphor for the region as Latin American governments did not play during the boom years. In fact, a number of governments made explicit efforts to boost the competitiveness of their economies. Many governments created "stabilization" or "sovereign wealth" funds to create reserves that enhanced their ability to stimulate investments and demand, although only Chile ensured theirs was not dependent on commodity export revenues. But, for the most part, Latin American governments privileged immediate consumption over long-term investment. Global economic competition, however, is fierce and countries that can privilege "patient capital" to finance long-term investments in innovation and productivity have a distinct advantage. In that sense, it is fair to ask what did Latin American governments do to prepare for the inevitable end of the commodity boom? The answer, unfortunately, is not enough.

The 2000s offered the region a period of nearly unprecedented macroeconomic good fortune. The boom offered unusually high prices over the course of an unusually long favorable cycle. At the same time, low interest rates in the US and Europe led foreign capital into emerging markets seeking better returns. The result was a dramatic turnaround for the region with rapidly falling debt and unparalleled opportunities to spend without fears of inflation. The most dramatic evidence is Argentina's 2001 default on its foreign debt which produced devastating consequences. But within a short period of time, Argentina rebounded as commodity export revenues removed the need to negotiate for loans or investment and the economy recovered without making concessions to international banks.[32]

The good macroeconomic news was not just due to factors outside government control. Over the 1990s and into the 2000s, Latin American governments reformed their domestic banking systems, greatly strengthening their regulation to protect against financial crises. Ironically, the strong banking reforms protected the region even as the lax regulations in the US and Europe helped produce a severe crisis that dragged down the global economy. The crisis hit Latin America as a short term *trade* shock in 2009 rather than becoming a full blown financial crisis – a first in Latin American history.[33]

The region's financial health gave governments rare levels of discretion about how to use their resources, which translated into the serious commitment to equity. But, the increases in social spending and wages were not matched by significant investments in the future, particularly in infrastructure,[34] which the region desperately needs, or to strengthen the knowledge base of the economy. As a consequence, the end of the commodity boom has left Latin American economies more vulnerable to rising macroeconomic challenges while exposing deep micro level constraints on competitiveness. Ultimately, future prosperity depends on creating jobs based on high productivity, high value added production. The end of the boom exposed how far the region has to go.

The Macroeconomics of the Golden Era

The boom years led Latin America to one of its strongest macroeconomic positions ever. For a region that had suffered from high levels of external debt, pressures on public spending and the constant threat or reality of high inflation, the macroeconomic story alone justifies thinking of the period as a golden era. The data tell a simple story. As of 1999, at the start of the Pink Tide and just before the boom, total debt servicing as a percentage of GDP – a measure of the capacity of the economy to manage its debt – averaged 44% with some cases like Argentina and Brazil bent under much greater burdens.[35] Brazil's total debt servicing cost stood at 115% of GDP while Argentina's stood at 74%. Given that debt servicing has first claim on resources, these burdens placed extraordinary restrictions on public spending. By 2010, average total debt servicing costs in the region had fallen to 15% of GDP with Argentina and Brazil both coming in at a mere 18% of GDP.

Inflation, the other chief villain of Latin American economic history, also pointed in the same direction. Inflation had been a cause of intense and at times violent conflict through most of the 20th Century, and an important contributing cause to regime breakdowns (both authoritarian and democratic) in numerous instances. Neoliberal reforms played a role in bringing down inflation, but the boom years were even better. Average inflation in fifteen of the cases was over 10% in 1999, down from an average of 34% in 1995. Yet, by 2010, average inflation had fallen to a little over 5%. For some countries, this drop in inflation was nothing short of extra-ordinary. In 1985, as Latin America was beginning the difficult transition to democracy and to neoliberal economic reforms, several countries were among the world's worst sufferers from inflation. Bolivia, Brazil, Mexico, Peru, and Uruguay had inflation rates of over 11,700%, 225%, 58%, 163%, and 72% respectively. In 2010, the same five countries had inflation rates of 2.5%, 5%, 4%, 1.5% and 6.7% respectively. The region's terrible history of debt and inflation is sufficient to explain the sense that Latin America had entered into a golden era.

The end of the commodity boom brought an end to the good times of spending without inflation. Instead, macroeconomic stability requires political commitments to keep inflation low and debt manageable, institutions to help ensure financial accountability and transparency, and hard choices about taxing and spending. Several Latin American countries passed reforms in the 1990s and 2000s to create "hard budget" constraints to contain political instincts to spend. For example, Brazil's *Fiscal Responsibility Law* created strict parameters and monitoring to prevent excessive spending.[36] Nevertheless, by 2014 average inflation had begun a slow climb up to over 7% for the region while the total debt servicing had risen from under 15% in 2010–2011 to over 23%. With growth slowing and macroeconomic conditions more challenging, the question of where future prosperity would come loomed large.

Labor Productivity, Innovation and the Middle Income Trap

Neoliberalism argued that getting prices right was sufficient to generate economic development. Critics argued that this was too simple a view and that getting prices right was less important than understanding how local context and binding constraints on development affected growth.[37] For that reason, many development scholars argued that the state needed to play a complementary role that supported innovation and increasing labor productivity. That does not mean a return to ISI and/or state ownership. But, at the very least, it means specific policies and institutions to support innovation, high value added production, and higher labor productivity – three areas where even the most successful Latin American countries, such as Brazil or Mexico, perform poorly.[38] The cost of not fostering high value added, high productivity activity is that Latin American economies have become stuck in the "middle income trap." The problem for middle income countries is that they find themselves in a situation where wages are too high to compete with poorer countries in standardized, labor-intensive production (such as with commodities), but labor productivity is too low to compete in higher value added areas. With the end of the boom, the problem revealed itself starkly. The question is why have Latin American countries fared so poorly? The answer lies partially at the level of firms, and partially in the absence or weaknesses of supportive state institutions.

One of the biggest issues for development facing Latin American countries is that there are very few domestic high-tech exporting firms. Brazil, for instance, has only one of them: Embraer, an aircraft manufacturer. Instead, the production and export of medium and high technology goods is dominated by foreign-owned MNCs.[39] But, the problem is not the ownership of those exporting firms. Rather, it lies in the fact that they invest little domestically in research and development (R&D). Foreign MNCs prefer conducting their R&D in established centers of excellence, so-called "silicon valleys", in other parts of the world, both in rich countries and other middle income countries, including South and Southeast Asia.[40]

Over the 2000s, most foreign MNCs focused on taking advantage of cheap or abundant inputs (for example natural resources or cheap labor) that Latin American countries offer – investments that do little to raise labor productivity and can move relatively easily when cheaper inputs become available.[41] As foreign MNCs invested in lower value-added sectors to decrease their production costs, they also did not focus on upgrading local capacities and skills. As a consequence, FDI was not a driver of technological development in the same way that it was in "success" cases such as South Korea.[42] This is where the problem of ownership becomes relevant. As growth from foreign-owned MNCs has not helped develop domestic technology, domestically owned firms have been and still remain dependent on imports of technology[43] with expenditures on acquiring foreign technology exceeding investments in domestically conducted R&D.[44]

Even when foreign-owned MNCs did engage in productive R&D it did not guarantee a spillover of knowledge to domestic firms. The problem stems both from weak networks linking domestic firms and MNCs[45] and the limited ability of domestic firms to absorb knowledge when the opportunity to learn exists. One way to illustrate the weakness of networks in the region is by looking at information and communication technology (ICT) – one of the leading edges of the high tech, knowledge economy. MNCs in Latin America imported most of their ICT inputs[46] rather than work with domestic producers. As a result, the average productivity gap between MNCs and domestic firms has grown in this sector.[47] The absence of networks at the national level mirrors the lack of networks at the international level as the inclusion of Latin American firms in global value chains has been very low. Global value chains expose firms to the innovation rhythm of MNCs and international standards for goods.[48] The end result is a vicious circle: limited networks in high-tech production keep low the number of domestic firms capable of producing high tech inputs which in turn discourages MNCs from incorporating Latin American firms into national or international value chains.[49] There are examples of domestic firms linked into global networks, and where it happens there is evidence that it supports innovation. For example, the only high-tech exporting firm in Brazil, Embraer, developed through cooperation between domestic engineers and foreign firms, aided by a state supported technological center, the Institute for Aeronautic Technology (*Instituto Tecnológico Aeronáutica*). The presence of Embraer and the institute helped foster the growth of a cluster of technologically sophisticated firms in São José de Campos. Similarly, Brazil's global success in agribusiness finds it roots in strong networks between domestic and foreign firms, supported by R&D through the state agency the Brazilian Agricultural Research Corporation EMBRAPA (*Empresa Brasileira de Pesquisa Agropecuária*).[50]

In addition to network linkages, firms need to be able to absorb new technology in order to upgrade skills and innovative capacity. Their capacity, in turn, depends on high levels of human capital and a predisposition to upgrading technology (i.e. a certain level of technology needs to be already used in the firm).[51] A key factor is the number and quality of engineers, but virtually all Latin American countries produce far too few.[52] Costa Rica stands out as an exception as it took effective advantage of the arrival of an Intel plant in 1997 to promote a substantial increase in the stock of engineers.[53] The shortfall of engineers means that even regional leaders, notably Brazil, use less skilled labor even in higher tech production than global competitors.[54] Together, the absence of networks and weak absorptive capacity have made it difficult for Latin America to raise productivity. Low levels of productivity, in turn, puts limits on potential growth, and makes it harder to recover from macroeconomic shocks[55] and increases the risk of falling in a "low development trap."[56]

Growth in the 2000s was not simply a story of commodities. In the 2000s, productivity in Latin America improved as labor moved out of the informal sector and from agriculture to higher value added work, but largely in services and construction – not manufacturing – and productivity within sectors did not improve much at all.[57] Instead of growth, the 2000s relied much more on increasing inputs, largely in the form of relatively unskilled labor.[58] In other words, while countries like China, India or Malaysia have experienced structural transformations of their economies that support innovation, upgrading of skills and rapidly rising labor productivity, Latin America experienced limited structural change and limits to future prosperity.

Commodity exports by themselves do not doom countries to low value added, low productivity and low innovation. In the 1990s, East Asian economies managed to keep their export competitiveness in traditional-type exports, i.e. commodities, but they also diversified towards high-tech products. In contrast, Latin America rode the boom and focused on its comparative advantage in unprocessed, low value-adding manufacturing and/or low productivity unprocessed commodities.[59] Rapidly rising commodity exports also led to currency appreciation and increasing uncompetitiveness of manufacturing, a problem often referred to as "Dutch Disease." But, countering the effects of Dutch Disease requires that state officials choose policies and support institutions that foster R&D, innovation and improved productivity.[60] Some governments made some efforts (Brazil in particular), but the investments remained very low overall.

No area demonstrates the need to go beyond simply "getting prices right" more than innovation policy. Firms in Latin America are locked in a vicious cycle where low R&D, innovation and productivity create very weak incentives to invest privately in R&D and innovation. As a result, the state needs to play a decisive and effective role.[61] It is not enough to merely increase spending. States also need to find ways to create incentives for the private sector to engage in R&D and innovation. For example, in South Korea, public funding accounted for more than 80% of R&D when the Korean Institute of Science and Technology (KIST) was created in 1967. KIST formulated clear incentives so that private investment surpassed 50% of R&D financing by 1977 and exceeded 80% by 1988. Public research plays a fundamental role in launching and disseminating research. But, it is the subsequent research in the private sector and higher education that is the second step in ensuring sustainable innovation.[62]

In Latin America, the problem is not just low public sector spending, but also that it fails to design incentives that move investment to the second step. In Brazil, public sector investment over the 2000s was more than double the regional average, but it is still limited: no more than $10 per capita is spent on R&D there compared to $200 in South Korea.[63] In the years 1996 to 2004, the private sector accounted for around 40% total spending on R&D while nearly 60% came from the public sector, with higher education spending negligible. The dependence on public spending presents risks as it is hard to maintain during times of fiscal constraint, such as in the wake of the commodity boom. In the final analysis, public investment in Latin America acts as a substitute for private and university spending[64] and as a result is less effective at driving technological advancement and increasing productivity.[65] Nevertheless, there are successful cases of clusters of innovative firms forming around public–private cooperation.

Public–Private Participation in Creating Success stories

There are important examples, however, of success in Latin America which illustrate how the state working with private capital (foreign and domestic) can spur innovation through the creation of clusters of innovative firms. A cluster is a "geographical concentration of industries which gain advantages through co-location" according to Bosworth and Broun (1996) or, alternatively, a "geographic concentration of interconnected companies and institutions in a particular field" according to Porter (1998).[66] That includes suppliers, service providers, financial providers, educational institutions as well as government agencies.[67] Clusters illustrate the way the state can play a supportive role in promoting a "high road" to competitiveness through "collective efficiency" that enables improvements in productivity through product or process innovations.[68] Clusters have potentially far-reaching positive effects beyond their immediate positive impact in terms of innovation and productivity, including backward and forward linkages to new clusters, new infrastructure investments, and new institutions such as export promotion agencies, all of which can benefit other sectors as well. As a result, clusters are potentially highly effective tools for development.[69] Latin America has produced a number of successful clusters.

What follows are two examples: one that shows the possibility for upgrading a commodity, and the other in ICT production.

Salmon Farming in Chile

The Chilean Salmon Cluster is the rare case of an industry that went from non-existence to second worldwide producer in about ten years. Salmon farming started there in 1979. By 1992 it was the world's second largest producer behind Norway.[70] In that period of time, all the phases of production and services were developed from initial experimentation to maturation.[71] The first phase or the "experimentation phase" was largely led by the public sector.[72] The Fundación Chile, originally created by the government to diversify the economy, worked with foreign universities and institutions, mainly American and Japanese, to test the feasibility of salmon farming.[73] In 1982, the state moved to transfer the new technology to Chile through the creation of a state-owned company, Salmones Antartica S.A., that could put the new technology to use.[74] Once the economic advantages of salmon farming with imported technology were clear, the industry was privatized.[75]

Nevertheless, the state continued to play a critical role. CORFO (the Chilean Agency for Economic Development) was essential in promoting scientific and technological development by providing funds or facilitating technological innovation.[76] CORFO's support led to the emergence of many small firms engaged in salmon farming, with foreign investment playing only a minor role until the 1990s.[77] Indeed, the first generation of investors were local entrepreneurs or Chilean economic groups from other sectors. In fact, many of the firms were created by professionals who had worked previously in public sector salmon research programs.[78]

Further development of the cluster depended on continuous government support and the formation of strong linkages between government institutions, R&D centers, firms and banks sharing information and conducting joint actions. The main driver of productivity improvements in the cluster was the diffusion of production knowledge across firms.[79] The salmon cluster increased its collective efficiency as firms cooperated across the cluster to improve products and process. For example, firms upgraded the quality of their workforce by jointly establishing training programs to develop specialized skills. The state encouraged these initiatives through tax exemptions that strengthened the incentives to invest in improving labor productivity.[80] Between 1990 and 2006, US$86 million was invested in R&D, funded almost equally by the public and private sectors, backed by incentives to invest in high technology. The end result was high levels of innovation across the sector.[81]

Fundación Chile and CORFO remained active participants in supporting the cluster through to the maturation stage of development. Thanks to such efforts, salmon farming gradually moved from a dependence on transferred technology to local adaptation and innovation. Fundación Chile has also moved from seeking imported technology to conducting and supporting local research on diversification and technology development.[82] These efforts have enabled productivity growth to be based on improved inputs, better production practices, improved logistics and more efficient supply chains, all of which were either locally developed or adapted to the local context.

The cluster's success has also led to important linkages with external markets and actors.[83] Indeed, going on the international stage through Chilean institutions such as ProChile (government agency promoting exports, founded in 1974) and SalmonChile (association of producers founded in 1986) enabled Chilean salmon to be collectively promoted in new markets as high quality products.[84] ProChile was particularly helpful to SMEs wanting to export by making them go through a training program and then offering them co-financing.[85]

Support for domestic producers allowed them to learn through exporting. Initially, this came from the diffusion of best-practices and imported technology and inputs, mainly from Norway, the global leader. But, it then enabled Chilean producers to adapt technologies and start producing their own inputs such as fishmeal or fish eggs and promote their upgraded products abroad. Although the cluster has developed well and made big productivity gains based on high value-added production, Chile still lags behind Norway in R&D and still imports technology. That means that further growth of the sector is possible,[86] but it depends on investment in local R&D.[87]

The strength of the cluster and the cooperation between state and firms came out clearly in response to the spread of ISA (Infectious Salmon Anemia virus) disease in 2007. The disease led to a decrease in production, with export volumes down by 16% and earnings down by 12% by 2009. Actors in the cluster realized that they needed better understanding of aquaculture and disease prevention.[88] The strong networks operating within the cluster saved the sector. Firms that had experienced diseases in the past shared their knowledge on a national scale.[89] In order to better deal with the issue in the future, actors in the cluster formed new international knowledge links and as a result Chile now participates in an international research program related to sustainable aquaculture.[90] This was also quickly followed by new regulations on environmental and sanitary standards. Since then, firms started focusing their own R&D departments on ensuring a more sustainable industry.[91] The state helped as well by offering tax breaks for R&D investment since 2008, particularly in the food industry for salmon. This strategy began in response to the ISA crisis but also to the growing presence of foreign companies that acquired local firms and that are a risk to indigenous firms.[92] Until now, it has had quite a positive effect, pushing Chilean exporters to innovate in new areas.[93]

On a final note, the salmon cluster has also helped drive development in other areas. For example, salmon farming has also enabled the expansion of sectors associated with it, such as fishmeal, in which Chile has become a major producer and exporter, as well as other kinds of fish farming. It has also driven social and economic development, particularly for the Los Lagos region where the cluster is concentrated. The presence of the cluster has helped Los Lagos emerge as an economic and cultural center around the strength of salmon farming. Social indicators improved as well thanks to the salmon cluster: the poverty index decreased from 40% in 1990 to 24% in 2000.[94] The success of the cluster in Los Lagos has prompted neighboring regions to support expansion of the cluster, while the national government, having seen the benefits of clusters created an institution that coordinates all exporting agricultural clusters, i.e. a megacluster: Chile Potencia Alimentaria y Forestal (Chile Food and Forestry Power).[95] In short, salmon farming in Chile has shown the possibility of innovative, high value-added production that can emerge from collaboration among firms and between the private sector and the state. Clusters demonstrate the possibility of fostering development through active state efforts to encourage and support private sector innovation.

Costa Rica: The ICT Cluster

The ICT (Information and Communication Technology) Cluster in Costa Rica is mainly located around Intel's plant in the Belen county.[96] More than twenty years after the emergence of the cluster, it is considered as having not only survived but also prospered: exports of electric and electronic goods in ICT increased from 3% of total exports in 1985 to 28% in 2003.[97] Additionally, in 2013, Costa Rica had the largest ratio of high-technology exports as a percentage of total exports in Latin America and among the highest in the world.[98] Electronics is now the largest sector in Costa Rica and, in a few years, has taken a clear lead on banana and coffee production which used to be the leading sectors of the country.[99]

An indigenous ICT cluster began to develop in Costa Rica in the 1980s, before Intel's arrival in 1997. It was composed of many local SMEs that were partnering with foreign multinationals to adapt software to local specificities, i.e. product adaptation. In contrast to the salmon cluster it was, therefore, a spontaneous emergence.[100] In 2002, there were still only 100 firms, 75% of which were small and micro firms.[101] In the 1980s, Costa Rica adopted an outward-oriented development strategy based on promoting non-traditional exports and attracting FDI. While initially focusing on attracting FDI from agriculture and unskilled-labor intensive manufacturing, the country made a shift in the 1990s towards skilled-intensive industries as it was losing competitiveness in the former.

The shift depended on active state policy efforts to move away from primary product exports, including duty-free access to modern ICT products from around the world; and an economic liberalization process along with the creation of a free trade zone to attract FDI.[102] Costa Rica also benefited from free primary and secondary education and an excellent public university system. In fact, without the investment in education that took place for almost two centuries, the prospects for growth based on technology would have been impossible.[103] Software development is a service that is both labor and skill-intensive. Thus, the sector absolutely needs appropriately educated and trained human resources (HR) in sufficient quantity.[104]

These advantages and the specific policies were enough for Intel to open a plant in Costa Rica rather than in countries like Argentina or Mexico, which were, in terms of infrastructure for example, more adapted to such investment. Intel's condition was for the government to promote a cluster by investing more in infrastructure, education and changing its international trade policy, i.e. reducing protectionist measures. Intel's investments along with the government's efforts provided an impetus for further development and growth in the ICT and related industries.[105]

Intel became the anchor for the cluster.[106] As a big manufacturer it attracted ICT service providers around it, whether foreign-owned MNCs or domestic firms. Additionally, after a few years, Intel opened a research laboratory. By the year 2012, Costa Rica hosted over 100 multinational corporations as well as 200 local firms, two research universities, two incubators, and several other organizations supporting the cluster. In 2013, the cluster was employing an estimated 10% of the Costa Rican workforce (55,000 people),[107] and had 800 firms, 100 of which were foreign.[108]

The cluster was built and developed with the help of several institutions and universities. In 1998, the Costa Rican Chamber of Information Technology and Communication (Cámara de Tecnologías de Información y Comunicación, CAMTIC) was created as a private, not-for-profit business association that in 2016 grouped around 90% of local software companies. Since then, this association has played a leading role in cluster initiatives to promote innovation and upgrading, as well as in the establishment of international linkages, acting as the cluster's most visible "knowledge gatekeeper." Besides the critical role of CAMTIC, the national agencies to promote exports (PROCOMER—Promotora del Comercio Exterior de Costa Rica, Foreign Trade Corporation of Costa Rica), and inward direct investments (CINDE—La Coalición Costarricense de Iniciativas de Desarrollo, Costa Rica Investment Promotion Agency), also played an important role in supporting the cluster's internationalization.[109] CINDE not only attracted Intel, it worked together with other institutions such as the Inter-American Development Bank, venture capital funds, the Latin American Center for Competitiveness and Sustainable Development of the INCAE Business School and the Harvard Institute for International Development, to ensure that other multinationals invested in Costa Rica, and that investments aimed at increasing the technological sophistication of the cluster continued.[110] Renowned business strategist Michael Porter, the pioneer of cluster development theory, met several times on the subject with then President Figueres (1994–1998), and a promotional approach was designed for the cluster to have as much development benefit for the country as possible.[111]

As a result, the ICT cluster had a strong, institutionalized beginning, but the Costa Rican government initially did not focus its policy-making specifically on the development of the national ICT sector, and instead concentrated on attracting FDI through Export Processing Zones (EPZs).[112] No technological parks were created and the government did not get involved in the formation of small business incubators that would have greatly helped domestic ICT input suppliers to be involved in the production chain. As a result, success was the result of growth in high-tech MNC production, rather than an increase in domestic productivity. While Costa Rican GDP per worker grew by 0.5% per year from 1997 to 2007, average labor productivity in EPZs grew at an average annual rate of 13.5%. That is, EPZs were one of the main drivers of labor productivity growth in the country – a result highly influenced by Intel's operations.

Although domestic firms did get involved in R&D activities to innovate their products or services, the full potential of knowledge spillover from MNCs has not yet been fully realized,[113] because there is insufficient cooperation between local and foreign actors.[114] This is especially true for suppliers of inputs. Indeed, Intel, has attracted a large base of suppliers of services, i.e. forward linkages. There are, however, only limited linkages with the suppliers of input, i.e. backward linkages. Locally acquired direct materials represent only 2% of the total value of Intel exports while locally purchased services are estimated at 8 to 10% of the total value of Intel's exports.[115]

A cluster mainly relying on MNCs and especially one of them, Intel, is quite problematic for sustainable development. In 1999, Costa Rica's GDP grew 8.4%, but excluding Intel's contribution, it would have grown only 3%. Thus, more than 60% of GDP growth in 1999 could be directly attributed to Intel. However, Costa Rica's GDP also shared Intel's downturns. When Intel activity dropped significantly in 2000, the country's GDP growth fell to just 1.4%. Without Intel, GDP would have grown 3%. This experience led to the realization in Costa Rica that companies such as Intel were subject to severe cycles, and consequently, the country needed to diversify its investment projects in other companies, sectors and markets.

As such, some efforts started in the 2000s to integrate more local suppliers in the productive chain and led them to higher value-added production. Policy makers were concerned that in addition to weak networks with MNCs, Costa Rican ICT firms also cooperated very little with private and public educational and research institutions.[116] They often did not have relationships with industry associations or chambers, the national government's trade promotion agency or government ministries.[117]

In response, Costa Rica PROVEE (Proyecto de Desarrollo de Proveedores para Empresas Multinacionales de Alta Tecnología, Supplier Development Project for High-Technology Multinational Companies), a revamped program to help develop local suppliers, was formally launched in 2000. This was the result of joint efforts by several organizations and achieved more than 40 viable linkages of local suppliers with multinational corporations by 2006.[118] The position of Costa Rica in the "quality of local suppliers" index of the World Economic Forum's global competitiveness report shows significant improvements: from 44 in 2001 to 28 in 2010. For the same period of time, the ranking in the "quantity of local suppliers" index improved from 55 to 44.[119]

Such efforts have enabled local firms to hire more from a very specialized labor market and benefit from the spillover given by MNCs as they moved away from labor-intensive, low value-added production.[120] As multinationals started to invest in R&D to produce with more value added, a group of local firms emerged with capabilities for developing advanced software targeted at international markets operating at the technological frontier in several market niches. Some of these local firms have grown in size to become medium or large firms, and have established along the way a presence in other countries to expand their market opportunities, mainly in other Latin American countries. Whether in national production or FDI, a clear shift took place from quantity to quality and while national firms were initially locally or regionally oriented they gradually internationalized.[121] In sum, the Costa Rican experience, like the Chilean one, demonstrates that states, working with local industry, can foster strong networks across state agencies, multinational firms and domestic producers to create islands of quality, innovation and rising productivity. Latin America is not doomed to low value added, low productivity economic activity. But, as of 2017, these clusters are by far the exception and not the rule.

Conclusion

Latin America rode a wave of good fortune on the back of a "super cycle" of high commodity prices and low global interest rates. The tremendously auspicious global economy facilitated an expansion of inclusionary social spending and policy innovations that made the period from roughly 2003–2012 appear as a "Golden Era." But, there were important limitations. Social inclusion reflected real commitments, but it also depended on the commodity boom to finance spending in non-inflationary ways. In effect, good times produced easy money that made the politics of generosity easier. Moreover, even as millions and millions of people enjoyed social and economic inclusion for the first time, millions and millions were left out. Even at its peak, the "Golden Era" was incomplete.

The next stage of deepening inclusion will require harder choices with more complex politics and more challenging politics. It will also require new resources. But, Latin American governments struggle to tax the wealthy and the tax base of the middle classes is too small. In the final analysis, the most likely route to deepening inclusion is spurring growth. On that score, Latin America's weak performance on increasing high value-added production, investment in innovation and technology, and rising labor productivity are worrying signs for the future. Latin American governments have helped foster clusters in various countries, including Chile and Costa Rica, discussed above. Clusters are evidence of the ability to develop effective institutional links among state officials, domestic business and MNCs. They suggest a possible model for growth. But, as of 2017, they are by far the exception in the region, not the rule. The challenge in Latin America is how to connect people's needs and wants for a better life to policy makers in a way that produces policies that create the kinds of changes the region needs. Institutions are the scaffolding that connects people to each other and society to the state and they are the subject of the next chapter.

Notes

1　Except for Argentina and Venezuela.
2　Campello, 2015.
3　Kevin P. Gallagher and Roberto Porzecanski, *The Dragon in the Room: China and the Future of Latin American Industrialization* (Stanford, CA: Stanford University Press, 2010).
4　Francisco H.G. Ferreira and Julián Messina, *Economic Mobility and the Rise of the Latin American Middle Class* (Washington DC: The World Bank, 2013).
5　Dani Rodrik, "Premature Deindustrialization," Washington DC, National Bureau of Economic Research, *NBER Working Paper 20935*, 2015; Luiz Carlos Bresser-Pereira, "The Dutch Disease and Its Neutralization: A Ricardian Approach," *Revista de Economia Política* 28, no. 1: 47–71, 2008.
6　Luiz Carlos Bresser Pereiria, *Economic Crisis and State Reform in Brazil: Toward a New Interpretation of Latin America* (Boulder, CO: Lynne Rienner, 1996).
7　This is consistent as well with Guillermo O'Donnell's conception of the state and the rule of law in *The Quality of Democracy* (O'Donnell, 2004). O'Donnell's critique of Latin American democracy was the unresponsiveness of the state to citizens. This way of presenting the problem is also consistent with Amartya Sen's "capabilities" framework.
8　Ferreira and Messina, 2013.
9　Amartya Sen, 1999.
10　Birdsall and Székely, 2003.
11　Saavedra, 2003.
12　Economic Commission for Latin America and the Caribbean, ECLAC, *Time for Equality: Closing Gaps, Opening Trails* (Santiago de Chile: ECLAC, 2010).
13　Luis Beccaria, Roxana Maurizio, and Gustavo Vázquez, "Recent Decline in Wage Inequality and Formalization of the Labour Market in Argentina," *International Review of Applied Economics 29*, no. 5: 677–700, 2015.
14　Nicolai Kristensen and Wendy Cunningham, *Do Minimum Wages in Latin America and the Caribbean Matter? Evidence from 19 Countries.* Working Paper No. 3870, World Bank, Policy Research, Washington, 2006.
15　Led by Sakiko Fukuda-Parr, Terra Lawson-Remer and Susan Randolph and housed at the University of Connecticut.
16　Led by Nora Lustig since 2008, the Commitment to Equity (CEQ) project is an initiative of the Center for Inter-American Policy and Research (CIPR) and the Department of Economics, Tulane University, the Center for Global Development and the Inter-American Dialogue. The CEQ project is housed

in the Commitment to Equity Institute at Tulane. For more details visit www. commitmentoequity.org.

17 Detailed explanations of the initiative, the index, the methodology and the data are provided at http://serfindex.uconn.edu/about-us/. The score is an average of the score on each of the separate indices.

18 Juliana Martínez Franzoni and Diego Sánchez-Ancochea, *The Quest for Universal Social Policy in the South: Actors, Ideas and Artchitectures* (New York: Cambridge University Press, 2016).

19 Maria Amparo Cruz-Saco and Carmelo Mesa-Lago, eds., *Do Options Exist? The Reform of Pension and Health Care in Latin America* (Pittsburgh, Pa.: University of Pittsburgh Press, 1998).

20 The benefits varied significantly across the region with sharp differences in generosity, the extent to which they were means-tested versus universal, as well as the depth of coverage. Alisha Holland and Ben Ross Schneider, "Easy and Hard Redistribution: The Political Economy of Welfare States in Latin America," *Perspectives on Politics* 15, no. 4, 2017.

21 Camila Arza, "The Expansion of Economic Protection for Older Adults in Latin America: Key Design Features of Non-contributory Pensions," United Nations UNU-WIDER Working Paper 2017/29, February 2017.

22 Brazil differs from the other three in that two crucial non-contributory payments, the BPC (Benefiço da Prestação Continuada, Continuous Cash Benefit) and the Rural Pension, both reforms of the 1990s, were channeled through the pension system, but financed off payroll and other taxes.

23 James W. McGuire, "Social Policies in Latin America: Causes, Character-istics and Consequences." In Peter Kingstone and Deborah Yashar, eds., *Handbook of Latin American Politics* (New York: Routledge, 2011), with coverage ranging from a low of 12% of the poor in El Salvador to a high of 100% under Ecuador's *Bono de Desarrollo Humano.*

24 Martínez Franzoni and Sánchez-Ancochea, 2016.

25 The term for this is "leakage" and one of the main concerns of high leakage rates is that politicians will use benefit payments clientelistically and reward followers rather than targeted beneficiaries. A detailed and nuanced account of this problem in Argentina can be found in Javier Auyero's *Poor People Politics* (Durham, NC: Duke University Press, 2001).

26 Tracy Fenwick, *Avoiding Governors: Federalism, Democracy, and Poverty Alleviation in Brazil and Argentina* (South Bend, IN: University of Notre Dame Press, 2015).

27 McGuire, 2011.

28 Wendy Hunter and Natasha Borges Sugiyama, "Assessing the Bolsa Família: Successes, Shortcomings, and Unknowns." In *Democratic Brazil Divided*, Peter Kingstone and Timothy J. Power, eds. (Pittsburgh: University of Pitts-burgh Press, 2017).

29 Holland and Schneider, 2017.

30 Tasha Fairfield, *Private Wealth and Public Revenue in Latin America: Busi-ness Power and Tax Politics* (New York: Cambridge University Press, 2015).

31 For example, see Garay, 2015.

32 Campello, 2015.

33 Porzecanksi, 2009.

34 Campbell, 2015.

35 Data available from http://www.worldbank.org – this figure is about double the average for all Middle Income countries, attesting to Latin America's continuing status as the world's regional leader for debt. Note that the 2010 figure of 15% is much closer to the Middle Income average of close to 10%.

36   In fact, it was accusations of violating the law that led to the charges against Dilma Rousseff and her eventual impeachment. While the impeachment was a profoundly controversial act and there remain questions about the extent of the violations, the law itself has not been called into doubt.

37   Tariq Banuri, ed., *Economic Liberalization: No Panacea* (New York: Oxford University Press, 1991); Dani Rodrik, *The Globalization Paradox* (New York: Oxford University Press, 2012).

38   Eva Paus, "Latin America and the Middle Income Trap," Working Paper 250, Financing for Development Series, *Economic Commission for Latin America and the Caribbean* (ECLAC), June, 2014.

39   Ben Ross Schneider, "Big Business in Brazil: Leveraging Natural Endowments and State Support for International Expansion." In Lael Brainard and Leonardo Martinez-Diaz, eds., *Brazil as an Economic Superpower?* (Washington: the Brookings Institution Press, 2009).

40   Mario Cimoli, Andre A. Hofman and Nanno Mulder, *Innovation and Economic Development: The Impact of Information and Communication Technologies in Latin America* (Cheltenham, UK: Edward Elgar, 2010).

41   Gustavo Crespi and Plavia Zuniga, "Innovation and Productivity: Evidence from Six Latin American Countries," *World Development* 40, no. 2: 273–290, 2012.

42   James L. Dietz, "Overcoming Underdevelopment: What Has Been Learned from the East Asian and Latin American Experiences?" In James L. Dietz, ed. *Latin America's Economic Development: Confronting Crisis* (Boulder, CO: Lynne Rienner, 1995).

43   João Carlos Ferraz, Michael Mortimore, and Márcia Tavares, "Foreign Direct Investment in Latin America." In José Antonio Ocampo and Jaime Ros, *The Oxford Handbook of Latin American Economics* (Oxford: Oxford University Press, 2011).

44   Mario Cimoli, *Developing Innovation Systems* (London: Continuum, 2000).

45   Luciano Ciravegna, "FDI, Social Ties and Technological Learning in New Silicon Valley Clones. Evidence from the Costa Rican ICT Cluster," *Journal of Development Studies* 47, no. 8: 1178–1198, 2011.

46   Edmund Amann, "Technology, Public Policy, and the Emergence of Brazilian Multinationals." In Lael Brainard and Leonardo Martinez-Diaz, eds., *Brazil as an Economic Superpower?* (Washington: the Brookings Institution Press, 2009).

47   Cimoli, 2000.

48   Pierluigi Montalbano, Silvia Nenci and Carlo Pietrobelli, "International Linkages, Value-Added Trade, and Firm Productivity in Latin America and the Caribbean." In Matteo Grazzi and Carlo Pietrobelli, eds., *Firm Innovation and Productivity in Latin America and the Caribbean: The Engine of Economic Development* (New York: Palgrave Macmillan, 2016).

49   Luciano Ciravegna, *Promoting Silicon Valleys in Latin America* (Abingdon, Oxon: Routledge, 2011).

50   Roberto Mazzoleni, "The Roles of Research at Universities and Public Labs in Economic Catch-up", in Mario Cimoli, Giovanni Dosi, and Joseph E. Stiglitz, eds., *Industrial Policy and Development: The Political Economy of Capabilities Accumulation* (Oxford: Oxford University Press, 2009).

51   Cimoli, Hofman, and Mulder, 2010.

52   Daniel Lederman, Julián Messina, Samuel Pienknagura and Jamela Rigolini, *Latin American Entrepreneurs: Many Firms but Little Innovation*, World Bank Latin American and Caribbean Studies. Washington DC: International Bank for Reconstruction and Development/The World Bank, 2014.

53   Ciravegna, 2011.

54   Schneider, 2009.

55 Eva Paus, ed. *Getting Development Right: Structural Change, Industrialisation, and Convergence* (London: Palgrave Macmillan, 2013).

56 Leopoldo Laborda Castillo, Daniel Sotelsek Salem and José Guasch, "Innovative and Absorptive Capacity of International Knowledge: An Empirical Analysis of Productivity Sources in Latin American Countries," *Latin American Business Review* 12, no. 4: 309–335, 2011.

57 Paus, 2013.

58 Gerardo Esquivel, Nora Lustig and John Scott, "Mexico: A Decade of Falling Inequality: Market Forces or State Action?" in Luis Lopez-Calva and Nora Lusitg, eds., *Declining Inequality in Latin America: A Decade of Progress?* (Washington DC: Brookings Institution Press, 2010).

59 José Gabriel Palma, "Flying Geese and Waddling Ducks: The Different Capabilities of East Asia and Latin America to "Demand-Adapt" and "Supply-Upgrade" their Export Productive Capacity." In Mario Cimoli, Giovanni Dosi, and Joseph E. Stiglitz, eds., *Industrial Policy and Development: The Political Economy of Capabilities Accumulation* (Oxford: Oxford University Press, 2009).

60 In Brazil, Luiz Carlos Bresser Pereira, a leading economist and two time cabinet minister, argued intensely for the need to look beyond the commodity boom. See Bresser Pereira, 2008.

61 There are good examples of where the state played that role, particularly in Brazil. For a discussion of the BNDES' creative approach to promoting global value chains and domestic innovation capacity, see Jazmin Sierra, "Global Champions Are Made at Home: The Brazilian Development Bank and Domestic MNCs." Paper Presented at the American Political Science Association Conference, Philadelphia, PA, September 1–4, 2016.

62 Mazzoleni, 2009.

63 Schneider, 2009.

64 Mario A Gutiérrez, "Economic Growth in Latin America: The Role of Investment and other Growth Sources," *Macroeconomia del desarrollo*, No. 36, New York: CEPAL, 2005.

65 Amann, 2009. Ciravegna, 2011, illustrates what Latin American countries do through the one positive example in the region: Costa Rica. Although Costa Rica's R&D expenditure per capita and percentage of GDP is below the Latin American average and lower than the expenditure of countries with similar incomes per capita such as Argentina, Brazil, Chile or Mexico, it has produced more innovation and patents than them. In contrast to the enumerated countries, universities are very big contributors to R&D alongside the public sector that accounts only for 17% of financing. It is in Costa Rica that GDP per capita has increased the most.

66 Barry Bosworth and Dayna Broun, "Connect the Dots: Using Cluster-based Strategies to Create Urban Employment," *Firm Connections* 4, no. 2, 1996: 1–6; Michael E. Porter, "Clusters and the New Economics of Competition," *Harvard Business Review*, November–December, 1998: 77–90.

67 The World Bank, *Clusters for Competitiveness: A Practical Guide and Policy Implications for Developing Cluster Initiatives*, Washington DC: the World Bank, 2009.

68 Carlo Pietrobelli and Roberta Rabellotti, "Upgrading in Clusters and Value Chains in Latin America: The Role of Policies," Washington, DC: Inter-American Development Bank, 2004.

69 The World Bank, 2009.

70 Hanni Perlman and Francisco Juárez-Rubio, "Industrial Agglomerations: The Case of the Salmon Industry in Chile," *Aquaculture Economics & Management* 14, no. 2, 2010.

71   Tyler Olson and Keith R. Criddle, "Industrial Evolution: a Case Study of Chilean Salmon Aquaculture," *Aquaculture Economics & Management* 12, no. 2, 2008.

72   Paola Perez-Aleman, "CLUSTER Formation, Institutions and Learning: The Emergence of Clusters and Development in Chile," *Industrial and Corporate Change* 14, no. 4, 2005.

73   UNCTAD, *A Case Study of the Salmon Industry in Chile*, New York and Geneva: United Nations, 2006.

74   The World Bank, 2009.

75   UNCTAD, 2006.

76   José Guimon and Evita Paraskevopoulou, "Foreign Knowledge and Cluster Evolution: Evidence from Salmon Farming in Chile and Software in Costa Rica." Paper presented at the 9th Regional Innovation Policies Conference, Stavanger, Norway, October 16–17, 2014.

77   Paola Perez-Aleman, "Standards as Institutions Supporting the Cluster Emergence Process: the Case of Aquaculture in Chile." In Dirk Fornahl, Sebastian Henn and Max-Peter Menzel, eds., *Emerging Clusters: Theoretical, Empirical and Political Perspectives on the Initial Stage of Cluster Evolution* (Northampton, MA: Edward Elgar Publishing, 2010).

78   Perez-Aleman, 2010.

79   UNID, "Understanding Structural Change: The Location of Manufacturing Production." In *UNID Industrial Development Report 2009: Breaking in and Moving Up – New Industrial Challenges for the Bottom Billion and the Middle-Income Countries* (New York: UN, 2009).

80   UNCTAD, 2006.

81   Pietrobelli and Rabellotti, 2004.

82   UNCTAD, 2006.

83   Eva Gálvez-Nogales, "Agro-based Clusters in Developing Countries: staying Competitive in a Globalized Economy," *Agriculture Management, Marketing and Finance Occasional Paper*, No. 25, Rome: Food and Agriculture Organisation of the United Nations, 2010.

84   Pietrobelli and Rabellotti, 2004.

85   José Guilherme Reis and Thomas Farole,"Policy Options for Competitiveness and Case Studies." In José Guilherme Reis and Thomas Farole, eds., *Trade Competitiveness Diagnostic Toolkit* (Washington, DC: World Bank, 2012).

86   Thomas Bjørndal, "The Competitiveness of the Chilean Aquaculture Industry," *Aquaculture Economics & Management* 6, no. 1–2, 2008.

87   Gálvez-Nogales, 2010.

88   Adolfo Alvial, Frederick Kibenge, John Forster, José M. Burgos, Rolando Ibarra and Sophie St-Hilaire, *The Recovery of the Chilean Salmon Industry: The ISA Crisis and its Consequences and Lessons*. Report from the Aqua-Culture Alliance, February 23, Puerto Montt, Chile, 2012. Available online at http://www.aquaculture.org, (accessed August 1, 2017).

89   P. Ibieta, V. Tapia, C. Venegas, M. Hausdorf and H. Takle, "Chilean Salmon Farming on the Horizon of Sustainability: Review of the Development of Highly Intensive Production, the ISA Crisis and Implemented Actions to Reconstruct a More Sustainable Aquaculture Industry," In B. Sladonja, ed., *Aquaculture and the Environment – a Shared Destiny* (InTech, 2011).

90   Guimon and Paraskevopoulou, 2014.

91   Ibieta et al., 2011.

92   Guimon and Paraskevopoulou, 2014.

93   Perez-Aleman, 2005.

94 UNCTAD, 2006.
95 Gálvez-Nogales, 2010.
96 The World Bank, "The Impact of Intel in Costa Rica: Nine Years After the Decision to Invest," World Bank Group MIGA (Multilateral Investment Guarantee Agency), 2006.
97 Luciano Ciravegna, "The Silicon Valleys of Latin America – Searching for 'Shared Value' Development Models," *The European Business Review,* February 2013, available online at http://www.europeanbusinessreview.com/the-silicon-valleys-of-latin-america-searching-for-shared-value-development-models (accessed August 1, 2017).
98 José Guimon, "Knowledge-intensive Clusters around Multinational Companies in Costa Rica," The Innovation Policy Platform (Washington, DC: World Bank, 2013).
99 The World Bank, 2006.
100 Guimon and Paraskevopoulou, 2014.
101 Brian Nicholson and Sundeep Sahay, "Human Resource Development Policy in the Context of Software Exports: Case Evidence from Costa Rica," *Development Informatics Working Paper Series,* No. 23, 2005.
102 Ricardo Monge-González and John Hewitt, "Innovation, R&D and Productivity in the Costa Rican ICT Sector: A Case Study," IDB Working Paper Series No. IDB-WP-189. Department of Research and Chief Economist, Inter-American Development Bank, 2010.
103 Andrés Rodriguez-Clare, "Costa Rica's Development Strategy based on Human Capital and Technology: How it got there, the Impact of Intel, and Lessons for Other Countries," *Human Development Report 2001* (United Nations Development Program (UNDP), 2001)).
104 Nicholson and Sahay, 2005.
105 The World Bank Group, "The Impact of Intel in Costa Rica: Nine Years After the Decision to Invest," World Bank Group MIGA (Multilateral Investment Guarantee Agency), 2006.
106 Scott Tiffin and Isabela Bortagaray, "Fostering Innovation: Technological Innovation in Urban Clusters." In Jerry Haar and John Price eds., *Can Latin America Compete?: Confronting the Challenges of Globalisation* (Berlin: Springer, 2008).
107 Ciravegna, 2013.
108 Guimon, and Paraskevopoulou, 2014.
109 Guimon, and Paraskevopoulou, 2014.
110 Ciravegna, 2013.
111 The World Bank, 2006.
112 Monge-Gonzalez and Hewitt, "ICT Sectors and Clusters, Local Firm Performance and Employment Generation in Latin America," Fundación Comisión Asesora en Alta Tecnologia, final report, San José, Costa Rica, 2015.
113 Ricardo Monge-Gonzalez, John Hewitt and Federico Torres-Carballo, "Do Multinationals Help or Hinder Local Firms? Evidence from the Costa Rican ICT Sector," International Development Research Centre (IDRC) Working Paper, 2015.
114 Ciravegna, 2013.
115 Pietrobelli and Rabellotti, 2004.
116 Brian Nicholson, "Human Resource Development Policy in the Context of Software Exports: Case Evidence from Costa Rica," *Progress in Development Studies* 8, no. 2: 163–176, 2008.
117 Monge-González and Hewitt, 2010.
118 The World Bank Group, 2006.

119   Guimon, 2013.
120   Pietrobelli and Rabellotti, 2004.
121   Luis Lopez, Sumit Kundu and Luciano Ciravegna, "Born Global or Born Regional? Evidence from an Exploratory Study in the Costa Rica Software Industry," *Journal of International Business Studies* 40, no.7, 2009.

6 Government, Markets and Institutions
Reflections on Development

A decade and a half after the start of the "Golden Era" there are signs that Latin America's progress may have stalled. The last chapter explored a range of policy efforts and indicators of commitment that showed how Latin American democracy had led to a deeper form of citizenship based in genuine state efforts to respond to real needs. The commodity boom provided a rare windfall of resources, but governments chose to use them to invest in their poorest and most vulnerable. Rising incomes led to the emergence of a new "middle class" able to enjoy services and to consume in ways they never had before. Political reforms over the 1990s and 2000s led to greater mobilization, organization and formal participation of previously marginalized or excluded groups, including women, indigenous and the poor. But, the expansion of social and economic rights rested on an economic base that had not developed and in fact arguably had become more dependent on commodities than before the boom.

As the economy slowed down, growing signs of discontent with democracy have manifested in several Latin American countries. As noted in Chapter Four, Brazil and Venezuela, the two leading examples of leftist reform from the region, both descended into chaos. As of 2017, Brazil is still struggling to find its way out of a political crisis in which much of the political class has been caught up in the vast sweep of the *Lava Jato* corruption scandal. In Venezuela, Nicolás Maduro seems determined to hold onto power by any means, including violence, and to strip any pretense of democracy from the regime. As noted in Chapter Four, Peru continued to be one of the stronger economic stories of Latin America, but resting on a model of extractive industries and commodity exports that produced constant conflicts over mining and its impact on local communities in addition to fiscal pressures as prices fell. Striking teachers and miners led to the government of Pedro Pablo Kuczynski declaring a State of Emergency in July 2017. In Argentina, more than a decade of leftist rule under the Partido Justicialista (Peronist) came to an end as Mauricio Macri of the Republican Proposal Party (Partido Propuesta Republicana, PRO) won the 2016 election. As in Brazil, his first step was a return to a neoliberal policy orientation while his predecessor, Cristina Fernández de Kirchner was indicted on corruption charges. In Chile, anger over the education system led tens of thousands to protest again and again from 2011 on, while anger over the privatized pension system led millions to protest in 2017. In Ecuador, anger over tax increases and social spending cuts, and then again over charges of electoral fraud led to thousands of protestors taking to the streets against President Rafael Correa. In Guatemala, President Jimmy Morales attempted to expel the head of the UN backed commission investigating him on corruption charges, only two years after the impeachment on corruption charges of his predecessor, President Otto Pérez Molina and Vice President Roxanna Baldetti. In short, trouble brewed not far beneath the gilt layer of the "Golden Era" and it did not take long to emerge.

At least three different factors help explain the rising tensions in the region. First, Latin American voters have become less tolerant of corruption while state agencies have become more effective at identifying and prosecuting high officials. Most Latin American countries have long-standing problems with corruption. But, for most of the region's history, corruption has co-existed with impunity. The 1990s and 2000s, however, have witnessed historically unprecedented state and citizen capacity to intensify scrutiny. Judicial reforms in a number of countries have empowered independent prosecutors. Brazil may be the starkest example of the pace of reform on the part of the state charged with identifying corruption far outpacing the political classes' ideas about acceptable behavior. The end result is that several hundred politicians are under investigation as of 2017, with one president impeached, a past president indicted and the interim president, Michel Temer, barely holding onto power in the face of incontrovertible evidence of gross corruption as of late 2017. Yet, for all the public attention and the larger number of high profile cases, Brazil's judicial system still is incapable of handling the scope of the problem in the country leaving citizens aware of and coping with ongoing, but now much more visible, impunity. It is no surprise, then, that the 2016 Latin Barometer survey found that corruption was listed as one of the main problems in thirteen countries in the region.

Another problem generating discord is that governments in some of the countries that pushed the most radical reforms of politics and economics have worked to hold onto power in relatively obvious bids to undermine electoral competition. The parties leading radical reforms always argued that the rules of "procedural democracy" – that is, fair and regular elections, freedom of assembly, freedom of speech, and freedom to compete (competition and contestation) – were less important than participation and inclusion. This was the rallying cry of parties committed to politically including long excluded communities and sharing widely in the wealth of the country. Presidents like Hugo Chávez and his successor Nicolás Maduro in Venezuela, Rafael Correa in Ecuador, and Daniel Ortega in Nicaragua all were elected initially in free and fair elections. All of them used their ability to mobilize the informal sector poor to support constitutional reforms to enhance their command of the polity. While commodity boom revenues poured in, these presidents were able to maintain support, but as the economy shifted and public opinion soured, presidents in all three countries resorted to fraud to secure power for themselves or their hand-chosen successor. In Bolivia, Evo Morales appeared to be moving on the same track before accepting a narrow loss on a 2016 constitutional referendum to allow him to run for an unprecedented fourth term. Morales' stewardship of Bolivia during the boom had led to one of the best growth rates in the region, massive expansive of non-contributory pensions and other social policies and enormously improved political inclusion and participation for the majority indigenous population. Yet, by 2016, Morales faced serious and credible accusations of corruption along with more controversial charges of electoral fraud during the referendum.

The biggest issue producing discontent, however, was the mismatch between the expanded expectations of citizens and the capacity of the state and the political system to meet them. In other words, the reforms and successes of the 2000s had led to millions and millions of Latin Americans wanting and expecting more of their governments. Increased participation and mobilization combined with a host of new social and economic rights taught Latin American voters that they could demand more of their governments exactly at the time that the economic downturn made it harder to meet them. Earlier commentaries on neoliberal reforms argued that their effect was to "hollow out" society and convert citizens into consumers. Studies focused on protests and in particular on labor unions and strikes argued that the evidence showed civil society diminishing. By the 2000s, some argued that in fact the effect of neoliberalism was to motivate and mobilize new groups in society. Others argued that they had been there all along. Whatever the case, Latin America in 2017 has much more mobilizing and organizing capacity than expected by the more pessimistic observers. And these citizens have demands.

A very critical part of this story is to remember that the "Golden Era" was a time of major change in Latin America relative to its own past. But, poverty and inequality remain high and the new "middle classes" are a very vulnerable group. They were able to consume in new ways and enjoyed a new array of *modest* social and economic rights. But, workers earning US$4–10 per day are still vulnerable and indeed are often one income shock away from returning to poverty. To move into a more secure position, they need good, high productivity jobs, but they also need to develop their own human capital. That means quality education and quality health care in addition to affordable housing (with secure property rights), and affordable transportation. That is what Brazil's protestors during the *Vinegar Revolution* meant when they demanded FIFA quality services. The Lula and Dilma governments committed the country to billions in investments to host global sporting events. Emergent middle-class citizens demanded investments in quality for Brazilian citizens, not visiting soccer teams.

It is also important to remember that Latin American governments made genuine and important efforts to provide new social and economic rights to millions of new citizens. But, as noted in the previous chapter, these were still underdeveloped relative not just to other parts of the world, but to the actual capacity of Latin American governments to perform. The previous chapter used the SERF index to show the extent of change over the "Golden Era." But, it also showed that there is a good deal of room for improvement.

In democracies, theoretically, political institutions link citizens to representatives to ensure that their needs and wants shape policy making decisions. In turn, responsive politicians make laws that the executive implements through state institutions. Democratic development happens because the state is responsive and effective in addressing citizens while political institutions function well to aggregate and represent interests in society. Of course, this is an ideal and not even the most democratic, wealthiest societies meet this standard. But, in developing countries, where most of society is poor or vulnerable, the consequences of unresponsive policy makers are high.

The evidence presented in this book so far suggests that neither markets nor states are the answer. At the extremes, certainly neither has proven to be a solution for sustained economic growth and development. Yet, even a balanced model is not sufficient to address the lingering challenges. Ultimately, the region has to solve deeper problems of development: developing and unleashing the entrepreneurial and innovative capacity of the population; expanding the distribution of assets; increasing the availability of capital, including human capital; limiting the arbitrary and disruptive behavior of the state; establishing secure and stable rules that govern society, represent interests, and mediate conflicts; strengthening the forms of representation, transparency, and accountability that are vital to democratic governance. These are not simple problems. They require fundamental changes in the institutions that support both markets and states. Unfortunately, designing good institutions that function the way they are supposed to function is very hard. The difficulty of the task is even greater in that neither policy makers nor scholars really understand how good institutions come into being and why they function or why they do not in the way they are intended. This chapter reviews the role of institutions in the economic reform and development process and considers the state of our understanding of the origins of good institutions.

Why Institutions Matter

Institutions are sets of rules, both formal and informal, that emerge from society and in turn structure social and political interactions. They specify what can be done, by whom and to whom, and they define the sanctions for breaches of the rules of behavior.[1] They may be highly formal and structured, such as a legislature or the judiciary. They may be unwritten, defining the rules of conduct within a given community or culture – invisible and unknown to outsiders, but well known and followed without any formal law or authority behind them for members. Institutions constitute the scaffolding of any society, ordering our interactions and providing stability and certainty about each other's behavior and the consequences of violations of rules of conduct. Without institutions ordering our lives, every exchange, political or economic, would require negotiations about the content of the exchange as well as over the rules of the transaction. Our interactions would require costly mechanisms to monitor each other's behavior for cheating and difficult (and possibly even violent) methods of enforcing agreements. Well-functioning institutions are the sine qua non of democracy and market economies.

Over the course of the 1990s and into the 2000s, scholars and policy makers increasingly identified the importance of institutions for the success of economic development – whether market or state led. In short, neither markets nor states are sufficient to spur development if the key institutions are either missing or do not function as they are intended. For example, Michael Walton of the World Bank observes "it is of fundamental importance to link market and government policies to the institutional context in which it occurs."[2] Evelyne Huber and Fred Solt's criticism of neoliberal reforms acknowledges as well the central importance of adequate institutions

> the rich literature on the political economy of advanced industrial societies has firmly established that the institutional context in the wider sense, including political parties, constitutional structure, and labor and employer organizations is the crucial determinant of economic performance, the welfare state, and poverty and inequality ... these institutions are generally very weak in Latin America.[3]

Both the 1997 CEPAL *World Development Report* and the 1997 Inter-American Development Bank Annual Report emphasize the centrality of institutions. Thus, there is a pervasive agreement that economic development requires a focus on the quality of the rules that undergird society and the economy.

The centrality of institutions can be seen in the prescriptions offered by both critics and advocates. John Williamson and Pedro Pablo Kuczynski – two of the key intellectual figures of the Washington Consensus – defend the original set of policies in the neoliberal agenda, attributing the weaknesses of the region's performance to poor policy decisions and incomplete implementation of the agenda. They do note, however, that a number of critical institutional qualities are necessary for the reform agenda – especially the more difficult post-stabilization reforms. For example, they identify the importance of better prudential regulation of banking systems and the need for institutions capable of doing that. They argue for the need for greater independence of the judiciary from the political system to better uphold the laws. The authors confess that they do not know how to solve these institutional problems, and in fact explicitly eschew any effort to do so, arguing that the politics of solving these more complex questions are best left to others.[4] The same problem is visible in Wolff and Castro in their study of education reform. The authors note that there are no magic bullets for improving education. Instead, policies that promote equity and stability are necessary, but again it is not clear what those are or how to develop them.[5] In fact, as Kaufman and Nelson observe, it is surprisingly difficult to implement policies that equitably address crucial needs, such as health or education.[6] They note that Latin American governments have experimented a great deal, mostly through small, sub-national, incremental efforts. But, there appear to be very weak incentives for politicians to actually address what are typically urgent needs. Instead, the "urgent" reforms fall by the wayside in the face of more salient concerns and resistance from stakeholders defending the status quo. Thus, the institutional setting actually discourages vital reforms rather than supporting them.

Duncan Green and Jorge Castañeda, two critics of neoliberal reforms discussed in Chapter 3, also illustrate the challenge of designing solutions to Latin America's problems. Both authors offer reformist critiques of neoliberalism, drawing heavily on the work of CEPAL. Both accept the value of the market as a mechanism for promoting growth, but believe it needs to be complemented with state action. The state should play an active role in promoting equity and partnering with the private sector to promote an active industrial policy. Roberto Bouzas and Saúl Keifman, writing from a more pro-market perspective, also argue for an active state presence in industrial policy.[7] As discussed in the previous chapter, this is in fact emerging in the balanced programs of countries like Brazil and Chile. Yet, an active industrial policy requires technical expertise, strong links to the private sector to facilitate communication and cooperation, a degree of autonomy from both political pressures and corporate influence,[8] and low levels of corruption to protect against misallocation of resources. Similarly, equity enhancing policies depend both on mustering the political capacity to reflect the needs and concerns of the many as well as the ability to design institutions that effectively deliver the benefits they are supposed to without being compromised by corruption, clientelism or political manipulation for private or partisan gain.

This is not to say that these institutions do not exist at all in Latin America. There are many examples of "good government in the tropics" as Judith Tendler labeled it.[9] As noted in Chapter 4, innovative and effective social policies have emerged in several countries in Latin America. *Bolsa Família* in Brazil, *Plan Auge* in Chile or *Oportunidades/Prospera* in

Mexico are innovative approaches to delivering social benefits and appear to have overcome legacies of clientelistic manipulation, especially in Brazil and Mexico. In Brazil, cities like Curitiba gained international recognition under Mayor Jaime Lerner for the quality of his administration while the development of participatory budgeting – a form of citizen inclusion in a deliberative municipal budget process – has been heralded and imitated around the world. In Costa Rica, small, incremental programs of rural health care delivery have brought about first world levels of infant mortality and maternal care.[10] These examples are important and point to the good will and technical capacity that exists throughout Latin America.

The problem is not in the specific instances, which are many, but in the average and in the aggregate. For example, despite the cases of good governance, corruption is the norm in Latin America. Table 6.1 reports the scores from Transparency International, an NGO committed to fighting corruption, from 2012 and 2016 and their global ranking, along with some key emerging market competitors. A small handful of countries score well. Chile and Uruguay are the only two countries that appear within the ranks of the OECD countries and Costa Rica is not far behind. By contrast, Honduras, Nicaragua, Ecuador, Paraguay and Venezuela are in the bottom 20% of countries in the world. As Table 6.1 illustrates, Latin America has a large number of countries in the lower half of the global rankings.

Other indicators point to the institutional weaknesses of the region. The World Bank's widely cited World Governance Indicators measure six areas of governance quality: political stability and absence of violence, voice and accountability, control of corruption, government effectiveness, rule of law, and regulatory quality. Table 6.2 compares regional average percentile rankings from 2000 to 2013 with some key emerging market competitors. Again, the table shows wide disparities in the region with the usual suspects, Chile, Costa Rica, and Uruguay standing out as particularly favorable with global comparators while the small Central American poor nations and most of the contestatory regimes look much more unfavorable.

Two examples illustrate the importance of well-functioning institutions and help to situate the good examples cited earlier in the larger context. As noted in Chapter 4, Brazil's *Bolsa Família* program has won international awards for its innovative conditional cash transfer. Heads of households received monthly stipends through a system designed to minimize the risk of political manipulation and protect the dispersal of funds from authoritarian or clientelistic practices. Distribution of the funds depended on the condition that school age children enroll in school and maintain good attendance records. The program produced excellent results – the small cash allowance roughly doubled household income for the poorest families in the country while producing virtually 100% enrollment rates for children up to the 8th grade. The program has earned its plaudits. It tells only a portion of the story, however. The negative side of

Table 6.1 Transparency International Scores and Rankings, with Some Comparators

Country	2012	2016	Rank −2016
Chile	72	66	24
Uruguay	72	71	21
Costa Rica	54	58	41
Brazil	43	40	79
Colombia	36	37	90
Peru	38	35	101
El Salvador	38	36	95
Guatemala	33	28	136
Panama	38	38	87
Mexico	34	30	123
Argentina	35	36	95
Bolivia	34	33	113
Honduras	28	30	123
Nicaragua	29	26	145
Ecuador	32	31	120
Paraguay	25	30	123
Venezuela	19	17	166
China	39	40	79
India	36	40	79
Malaysia	49	49	55
Saudi Arabia	44	46	62
South Africa	43	45	64
Vietnam	31	33	113

Source: Data available from Transparency International, available online at www.transpa
rency.org

the story is a school system that suffers from a series of serious shortcomings for the roughly 80% of the population in the public school
system. Brazilian teachers on average are underpaid, undertrained, and
undersupervised. Brazilian schools lack adequate resources, such as
schoolbooks. Violence is pervasive in the school system and the absence of
school counselors or psychologists limits the capacity to deal with the
large number of social problems that manifest in the school system.
Moreover, clientelistic practices lead to high rates of turnover of both
administrative and clerical staff with little to no guarantee of adequate job

Table 6.2 World Bank Governance Indicators, plus Some Comparators

	Voice	Stability	Effectiveness	Regulatory	Rule of Law	Corruption
Argentina	57.07	41.52	51.35	26.17	30.53	40.59
Bolivia	46.56	26.9	37.62	31.25	23.68	32.66
Brazil	60.77	42.34	53.42	56.63	46.04	57.09
Chile	82.21	66.21	85.86	91.75	88.08	90.37
Colombia	40.62	6.11	51.66	57.67	35.96	48.69
Costa Rica	78.96	67.82	63.87	66.71	64.69	71.36
Ecuador	38.73	24.11	24.29	18.23	17.87	22.36
El Salvador	49.98	46.6	47.11	58.13	30.55	45.94
Guatemala	37.86	21.63	30.92	47.24	15.06	33.02
Honduras	37	30.89	30.9	41.39	19.55	21.08
Mexico	54.28	28.83	61.5	62.77	37.02	47.61
Nicaragua	38.74	36.23	21.66	41.14	26.53	28.51
Panama	64.35	44.79	58.93	63.92	49.88	46.05
Paraguay	39.18	22.62	18.05	30.95	17.31	12.29
Peru	49.12	18.66	42.5	62.46	31.04	47.73
Uruguay	80.49	73.02	68.94	64.06	66.26	82.9
Venezuela	27.96	13.92	14.7	11.36	6.21	13.35
China	6.43	29.65	29.65	44.72	40.73	37.56
India	59.73	13.76	13.76	40.89	55.09	40.32
Malaysia	35.74	51.95	51.95	68.05	64.96	63.96
Saudi Arabia	5.33	34.86	34.86	54.62	58.18	53.24
South Africa	67.24	42.6	42.60	67.06	56.39	64.5
Vietnam	8.8	53.69	53.69	28.34	39.64	31

Source: Data available at World Bank, www.worldbank.org

related skills. Unattended classrooms are pervasive and many teachers are absent regularly, in part because inadequate salaries lead them to seek supplementary employment. Perhaps unsurprisingly, the drop-out rate after the 8th grade, when *Bolsa Família's* conditionality no longer applies, is substantial. Roughly 100% of school age children reach the 8th grade, but the high school graduation rate falls sharply as attendance for the latter years is only around 70%. Finally, school funding is sharply unequal, with a substantially disproportionate share going to public universities although only 15% of the population attends university; 25% of all resources benefit the wealthiest quintile of the population while only 16% go to the poorest. Both the federal government and IFIs like the World Bank have supplied funds to improve the financial condition of schools. FUNDEF (Fundo de Manutenção e Desenvolvimento do Ensino Fundamental e de Valorização do Magistério, Fund for Maintenance and Development of the Fundamental Education and Valorization of Teaching), another innovative Brazilian program, guarantees a minimum sum (roughly 140 dollars per pupil) for each student enrolled in a municipality's public school system. The World Bank has supported education reform as well, for example with a US$ 69 million grant to the State of Bahia for a reform program called "Learn to Win."[11] Ultimately, however, severe institutional underdevelopment, funding inadequacies, and a lack of political will or capacity to tackle the fundamental problems afflicting the system offset the benefits of innovations like *Bolsa Família* or FUNDEF. Other studies have shown that after years of efforts to improve education, some results are beginning to show and although Brazil still ranks poorly in global comparisons, it is improving rapidly, but only where strengthened accountability makes sure resources are diverted. Marcus André Melo has argued that political competition plays a critical role in making officials accountable. In its absence education does not improve.[12] Instances of good governance matter and can deliver meaningful benefits to portions of the population badly in need of them. But, the full potential suffers greatly from the overall poor institutional context.

Another way of seeing how institutional innovation and quality can suffer from a larger, weak institutional context can be seen in the regulation of utilities. Regulatory agencies were an institutional innovation that first appeared in the US more than a century ago. They have an unusual character in that they are by design state agencies that maintain an arms' length relationship with government. They occupy a space between government and the private sector. Their purposes include collecting information and fees from private firms as well as setting and enforcing the rules of a sector. The idea is to create an agency that is free from political interference and can therefore set, monitor and enforce rules for a sector so that firms have clear, predictable understandings of how the market in their sector will work: what is permitted and what is not permitted; how prices will be determined; the terms of contracts and how contract disputes will be settled, etc. When they are well designed and function properly, they work to protect firms from opportunistic behavior by politicians, they offer stability and certainty about how the market will function, and they protect consumers from exploitative or predatory behavior by firms. Ideally, they encourage continuous investments and improvements in access, price, and quality of services for consumers. But, the benefits of private investment can quickly disappear if the regulatory agencies do not function the way they are intended. For example, firms operating in a sector do not want governments to "administratively expropriate" their assets by setting tariffs too low to earn a return on investments. Yet, politicians might try to intervene because voters always prefer lower tariffs. Similarly, a new president may want to revoke a contract and favor an alternative operator or insist that the operator purchase parts from firms with political connections. Politicians may demand that private firms hire workers to help with political concerns about unemployment. On the opposite side of the ledger, firms may raise their rates to extract greater profits, especially if they have a monopoly or only limited competition – a relatively common occurrence with utilities. They may try to use their position in the sector and influence politicians and/or the regulator to keep competitors out. Firms may choose to limit investments or service to high-income areas and avoid investments in poor communities that are unlikely to yield profits.[13] In short, private utilities, even when operating in a competitive market, may not lead to efficient, equitable outcomes, either because of government misbehavior or firm misbehavior or both. It is the job of regulatory institutions to protect against these kinds of outcomes.[14]

The US has had a century of adjustment and experimentation to improve the functioning of regulatory institutions.[15] Regulation inherently involves a tension between the preferences of investors and the preferences of consumers and in all developed countries there is a tendency for the emphasis to shift periodically. Even in advanced economies, then, regulation can be tricky. For Latin America, the problem went deeper as regulatory institutions were unfamiliar – a form of governance imported from abroad as part of the utility privatization process. In many cases, the new regulators were trained in advanced economies or had been socialized into the expectations and norms of regulatory institutions. But, they frequently confronted and clashed with a series of foes: fellow regulators who came from the old state owned firm and retained old norms and networks of political connections; legislators who did not know what a regulatory agency was and why they could no longer exercise political influence over the assets and resources of the newly privatized sector; and executives who wanted investments, improvements, *and* low tariffs simultaneously.

The new agencies encountered serious challenges from the beginning. In a number of cases, privatization took place prior to the establishment of the regulatory agency, leaving the rules for the sector poorly defined and subject to manipulation, collusion, and conflicts. In some instances, it led to reluctance of private investors to enter into the sector because of the uncertainty. In some cases, the regulatory agency was purposely designed to limit the autonomy of its decision-making, for example by establishing appointment and replacement procedures that facilitated discretionary removal by the executive. Regulators whose jobs depended on presidential approval are much more vulnerable to political manipulation. In fact, even in cases where regulators did enjoy nominal independence, overt conflicts with presidents led regulators to resign their position, thereby weakening the autonomy of the agency. For example, this occurred in the tele-communications sector in both Bolivia and Brazil. In many cases, regulators struggled with politicians that either did not understand or did not accept the idea of a government agency not subject to government control, and, in many of these cases, regulatory agencies found their budgets under attack. Regulators also struggled with firms that contested their authority, lobbying both the executive and the legislature to evade monitoring and enforcement. In some of these cases, foreign firms that had purchased state assets relied on the governments of their own countries of origin to pressure the Latin American government. For example, both the Italian and the Spanish governments pressed Argentina to keep competitors to Italian Telecom and Telefónica out of the country. Regulatory agencies also struggled with information asymmetries as they confronted the challenges of measuring firms' compliance with the terms of their contracts and efforts to force them to live up to them. In short, privatization of utilities depends on effective regulatory agencies to encourage investments, improvements in access, price and quality, and to protect consumers from predatory or exclusionary behavior. But, in general (again, with important exceptions to the rule), Latin American regulatory institutions struggled against a wide array of challenges that undermined the quality of their performance.[16]

Institutions matter. In the final analysis, neither state led nor market led models of development offer much hope of real improvement unless the basic institutions of the economy and governance function well. The reality in Latin America is that all too often, key institutions do not. The results are weakened democratic governance and sub-optimal economic performance. This includes: less meaningful and less equitable political representation; low quality policy deliberation and unaccountable executives; weak or corrupted judicial systems and support for the rule of law; poor controls on the extent and depth of corruption; inadequate institutions that pro-mote equity and build human capital; underinvestment and misallocation of resources because of instability and uncertainty for actors in markets.

The next section further explores what we know about institutions and considers three different ways at evaluating their effect on economic development. The three are political institutions and their role in shaping democratic governance and effective policy-making; the "self-restraining state" and property rights; and the institutional frame for policy reform and implementation.

Political Institutions and the Politics of Policy Reform

Studies of democracy and economic reform focused their attention initially on the character of political institutions (the presidency, parties, legislatures, electoral rules) as the most important impediment to successfully managing the "dual transition" of democratization and economic reform. New, fragile democracies needed to pass reforms urgently to deal with the economic crisis of the "lost decade." The concern was that both the design and the performance of the key institutions of representation, deliberation, and policy-making were not up to the task. Scholars focused on rules that granted excessive powers to presidents to make policy without consultation, often by simply emitting presidential decrees. Political parties caught the attention of analysts who noted that on average parties did not effectively represent voters and frequently lacked clear programmatic or ideological identities. Electoral rules led to fragmentation of the party system in many countries so that executives faced the difficult challenge of trying to forge policy coalitions among a large number of political parties. In some countries, ideological extremes polarized the legislature and impeded the possibility of negotiation and compromise. In some party systems, electoral rules made individual legislators highly dependent on patronage spending rather than responsive to voter concerns or programmatic/ideological appeals. Pork barrel politics complicated legislative negotiations and undermined efforts to cut government spending. Taken together, the various concerns pointed towards two undesirable outcomes: presidents with extraordinary powers making policy decisions in ways that undermine democracy; or political systems hopelessly mired in gridlock and dependent on destructive amounts of pork and patronage expenditures. A balanced position exists between these two poles, but scholars noted that most Latin American political systems tended towards the extremes.[17]

Presidential Power and "Delegative Democracy"

Presidential power varies across different political systems. Presidents enjoy differing levels of support in the legislature, depending on whether the governing party also tends to hold a legislative majority ("partisan powers"). Presidents also have varying legislative authority to issue laws and to block legislative initiatives ("constitutional powers").[18] Mainwaring and Shugart observed that in practice there is a trade-off. In political systems where legislative majorities are rare, such as Brazil or Chile, presidents enjoy considerable constitutional authority to issue decrees. By contrast, constitutional authority has tended to be limited in countries where the executive tends to be able to rely on stable majorities in the legislature. Mexico and Venezuela before Chávez were notable examples of presidents with reliable legislative support and limited constitutional authority. In some cases, countries had both. Since 1983, Argentina's presidents have tended to have solid majorities in the legislature while also possessing considerable decree authority. Hugo Chávez passed constitutional reforms that granted him extraordinary legislative power while enjoying the support of an unassailable majority in the legislature.

Whether it is the power to issue laws directly or the ability to use a pliable and acquiescent legislative majority, the danger is what Guillermo O'Donnell has called "delegative democracy."[19] O'Donnell, one of the leading democratic theorists of Latin America specifically and developing countries generally, notes that Latin America has a cultural proclivity to elect "great men" and delegate to them the authority to do what is necessary. Thus, voters do not expect legislatures to hold executives accountable for their decisions or to enter into transparent deliberations and negotiations over policy. But, this extraordinary executive autonomy diminishes the quality of democracy, helps foster corruption and secrecy, and often leads to egregious policy errors since there is no mechanism for feedback or criticism, constructive or otherwise. This concern is consistent with leftist critiques of neoliberalism as undemocratic and unaccountable, though it just as easily fits the contestatory left and its retreat from neoliberalism.

There is no question that accountability, transparency, deliberation, and compromise could improve in Latin America. There are too many instances of "delegative democracy" at work in important areas of policy reform. This was especially true in the early years of neoliberal reform where countries facing severe economic crises made drastic changes rapidly and sometimes contradicted explicit campaign promises. Carlos Menem in Argentina relied on emergency laws granting him extraordinary legislative power to confront skyrocketing inflation and brutal recession. Alberto Fujimori of Peru campaigned on an economic security platform against the overt neoliberal Mario Vargas Llosa in 1990. On his victory, he initiated a drastic neoliberal reform program, eventually suspending the Congress, ostensibly because of its obstructionism. Fernando Collor of Brazil initiated his neoliberal reform program by swamping the Congress with so many temporary presidential decrees that he effectively prevented the emergence of any kind of legislative agenda aside from considering and voting on his decrees. Brazil's presidential decrees have the force of law for thirty days and require legislative approval to become permanent law otherwise they lapse. In instances when the legislature did not vote on Collor's temporary decrees or did not approve them, he simply re-issued them.[20] In Venezuela, Hugo Chávez' constitutional reforms so centralized power in the hands of the president that he effectively converted the legislature into a rubber stamp. One of the clearest indicators was that under Chávez the legislature did not offer *any* spending amendments to the budget despite clear legislative power to do so.[21]

On the other hand, the delegative democracy view overstates the case. Latin American legislatures have been far more involved in active negotiation and deliberation than this critical view suggests. Even in cases of high executive authority, legislatures have made their presence known. For example, in both Argentina and Peru, the pace of economic reforms slowed down as crises passed and public reticence to continued rapid reform grew. In both Argentina and Venezuela, legislative majorities from parties with leftist or nationalist identities checked the reform efforts of their respective presidents. In the case of Argentina, Carlos Menem accommodated the concerns of his Peronist Party, slowing reforms and negotiating over key ones such as social security. In Venezuela, Carlos Andrés Pérez ignored the growing signs of anger and resistance from his Acción Democrática (AD) Party. Pérez' team of policy insiders consisted of committed neoliberals trained in various US economics and management programs. Despite technocratic efforts to explain their policies, AD members were deeply uncomfortable with the unpopular reforms and ultimately impeached their own president on corruption charges, effectively ending the neoliberal experiment in Venezuela.[22] In Bolivia, Gonzalo Sánchez de Lozada included reforms that empowered municipalities and indigenous groups as part of a bargain to secure support for his neoliberal restructuring. Even his neoliberal restructuring required legislative bargains as, for example, the Congress insisted on revisions to his privatization of telecommunications to protect local small operators.[23] In Brazil, perhaps the country that has inspired the largest literature on its institutional faults, presidents agreed to restrict the use of executive decrees and have regularly entered into legislative negotiations. For example, President Fernando Henrique Cardoso secured passage of a bill allowing private sector competition in the energy sector by promising not to privatize one of the country's most important national symbols, Petrobras (the national oil company).[24] Scholarly studies of the policy-making process, rather than the more general or abstract studies of institutions, have pointed to substantial legislative involvement. It is impossible to measure precisely the extent of involvement or the balance between delegation and deliberation/negotiation. But, it is possible to note that the more critical view overstates the case for "delegative democracy" in the reform process.

Fragmentation, Personalism and the Impediments to Reform

If excessive, centralized power represents one pole of concern over democratic institutions, gridlock and legislative paralysis represents the other. Fragmentation, the effective number of parties represented in the legislature, complicates legislation by making it harder to forge a legislative majority. The higher the number of parties, the less likely any one will have a majority of seats and the higher the number of parties that will have to agree to participate in a coalition to produce a majority. The "incentive to cultivate a personal vote" or personalism only complicates the matter.[25] In electoral systems with high degrees of personalism, politicians depend on their ability to cultivate personal followings based on their identity, or their link to a specific group or geographical location, or on the specific benefits for voters for which they can claim credit. They depend much less or not at all on their party. Such politicians need access to patronage resources or the ability to amend the budget in order to directly and overtly serve their voting base. Programs, ideology, party reputation all matter very little. Such politicians complicate bargaining because coalitions need to be stitched together from large numbers of individual legislators rather than a more manageable number of political party leaders. The two qualities, separately or combined, create dangers of gridlock where executives are unable to pass essential reforms through the legislature. Boliver Lamounier, referring to Brazil, described what he called "hyperactive paralysis" – a situation in which there is a great deal of political activity as presidents and legislators bargain ceaselessly, but ultimately little or nothing gets done.[26] Gridlock, or paralysis, sets in because legislators prevent budget cuts or shifts in spending priorities and defend the narrow sectoral interests of well-organized groups who prefer the status quo to reforms, no matter how important or beneficial they may be for society at large.

Initially, studies of neoliberal reforms claimed that the only way to implement them was through concentrated executive power forcing drastic, irreversible policies through and/or crises that would break the power and will of the special interests opposing them.[27] As with arguments about delegative democracy, more specific studies of reforms and policy-making processes suggest that the general argument overstates the case. Brazil, the paradigmatic fragmented, personalistic system "muddled through gridlock" to produce extensive political and economic reforms. Among the many reforms, some of the major ones included: liberalizing trade despite the largest and most diverse domestic industry in the developing world; privatization of important productive firms in sectors like steel, mining and aviation, as well as vital utilities such as telecommunications and electricity; "flexibilization" (i.e. loosening of investment rules and restrictions on private enterprise) of the oil industry; significant reforms of the social security system; deep overhauls of the financial system, including measures to establish standards of fiscal restraint for states and municipal governments, tighter prudential regulation of banks, and privatization or closure of unprofitable state owned banks; tax reforms that substantially increased federal revenue collections; and innovative social reforms in health and education. This occurred despite as many as nineteen parties represented in Congress, with at least five major parties at any given time, spread across the ideological spectrum and with very strong incentives to cultivate personal votes. If there were any political system in Latin America that pointed to policy stalemates in gridlock, it was Brazil. Yet, despite a sizable literature detailing the country's institutional challenges, successive presidents built on a record of gradual, incremental reforms ultimately resulting in one of the most innovative and highest quality policy records in the region.[28] In response, a new framework labeled "coalitional presidentialism" emerged to explain how multiparty presidential systems functioned like parliamentary systems, using cabinet posts and other concessions as a means to enhance governability.[29] This new literature became the dominant way of understanding Brazil's success. The collapse of the Dilma government in 2015–2016, in the face of growing inability to cope with corruption and growing social and economic discontent, called into question "coalitional presidentialism" as a way to explain policy performance. As Argelina Figueiredo and Fernando Limongi have suggested, Brazil's legislative difficulties perhaps are best understood as a function of the difficulty of the policies and not of institutional defects.[30]

This last point bears repeating. The set of reforms passed across Latin America were complex, difficult reforms. Some of them entailed inflicting painful costs – for the poor or for workers as well as for narrow, organized interests. The political economy literature and neoliberal advocates tended to focus on legislatures as obstacles to necessary reforms as if "there were no alternative." However, even if all agreed that these reforms were the best alternative, it does not mean that passing them would be democratic. Legislatures, organized interests, and the public – misinformed or not – all have democratic rights to resist policies that they believe are unwise or directly hurt them. It can make for a messy process. But, the fact that legislatures resisted, delayed, or "morselized" reforms that after all dramatically altered the nature of state, market and society perhaps needs to be understood as democracy functioning as it was meant to, not as an obstacle to the correct policies. For critics of neoliberal reforms, again the fact that legislatures reflected popular concerns or the concerns of organized interests, suggests that the neoliberal reform process may not have been as undemocratic as the critical view suggests. Certainly, the voting behavior discussed in Chapter 4 complements that view.

In sum, Latin American political institutions are weaker than they need to be to strengthen democratic governance in the region. Meaningful representation, thoughtful deliberation, transparent and accountable policymaking all could improve. Of course, observers of the US policy reform process in the wake of the 2008 financial crisis could make the same claims. Fiscal stimulus, bank bailouts, health care reform, and deficit reduction measures under both Presidents Obama and Bush do not appear to conform to an ideal of deliberation, transparency or accountability and the legislative chaos under Donald Trump is hardly a model for any country in the world. Latin America certainly falls short of an ideal of democratic governance. But, in fairness, Latin America's political institutions also probably get less credit than they deserve for functioning at least moderately well in the face of serious economic challenges and complex, fundamental policy reforms. At the very least, they performed much better than expected in the 1980s and into the early 1990s and continue to offer examples of reasonably good government, especially in places like Costa Rica or Uruguay. Thus, the early concerns about political institutions may have overstated the extent of the problem for democratic governance and economic policy-making. However, other institutional features continue to raise concerns.

The Self-Restraining State and Property Rights

Economists trying to understand the process of economic development and the conditions under which markets function well have increasingly turned their attention to institutions and the character of the state. Institutional economists have been the vanguard of a critique of neoclassical economics – the dominant approach within the profession. For institutionalists, neoclassical economics works well to explain resource allocation in a developed market economy. But, neoclassical economics cannot account for the emergence of markets or why they function well. As Douglass North notes, they treat economic problems as timeless and frictionless. In order to understand the successful emergence of market society, institutional economics looks to history, political science, sociology, law (and more recently neuroscience) for help in understanding the underlying institutional scaffolding of markets and the proper relation between the state and markets.

For economists, institutions arise to reduce uncertainty in a world of complexity and imperfect information. Institutions make exchange predictable in that they set the rules of interaction (including, for example, by assigning property rights) and they establish enforcement of those rules (such as enforcement of contracts) so that actors can clearly decipher the incentives facing them and the consequences of violating the rules. But, to function well and support regular, fair and efficient economic exchanges, the rules have to be stable. Political order, therefore, is a fundamental requirement for markets to operate well.

In modern societies, states play the central role in facilitating economic exchanges. States are the only organizations that can establish a system of property rights, ensure that those rights are secure, enforce exchange agreements, and provide a measure of political and macroeconomic stability. As Douglass North, William Summerhill and Barry Weingast observe, the fundamental political problem of an economy is that any organization strong enough to do this is also strong enough to violate some or all citizens' property rights. Such an organization could confiscate all its citizens' wealth or turn on one set of citizens in favor of another or at the behest of another. In short, efficient markets need a balance between a state strong enough to secure property rights and enforce agreements, but that is "self-restraining." That is to say, the state is bound (as are its officials) by shared norms about the limits of its actions. For North et al., citizens must believe that the institutions of their society are appropriate for their society; they must accept that the decisions made within these institutions are legitimate; and they must believe that the distribution of property rights is legitimate and that they are willing to react to state efforts to violate them.[31] A self-restraining state that establishes secure property rights and effective enforcement is a key to efficient markets.

Both democracy and efficient economic exchange break down when property rights are undefined or their distribution is open to question.

Authoritarian rulers may protect the property rights of some favored group (whether economic, geographic, racial, etc.) and use that base of support to repress others. Poorly defined property rights encourage corruption and "rent-seeking" as actors invest resources to capture a right. This was the neoliberal critique of state involvement in the economy where domestic businesses invested to shape regulations or influence protectionist policies for their own enrichment, but at the expense of society. Of course, illegitimate institutions and undefined or illegitimate property rights systems can spark political disorder as groups in society fight to alter them. One could describe Hugo Chávez, for example, in these terms. Chávez' critique of the unfairness and illegitimacy of the Punto Fijo system was a critique of a prevailing distribution of property rights and illegitimate institutions that enforced those rights at the expense of the rest of society. Given the opportunity, voters supported a radical re-configuring of their political and economic system, but have not produced a stable or efficient alternative. Indeed, Javier Corrales has argued that these "radical claims to accountability" rest on commodity revenues and systematic efforts to close down voice and opportunity for opponents. Both Bolivia and especially Ecuador are hinting at continued political and economic unrest while Venezuela has descended into unambiguous authoritarianism on the back of a disastrous economy.

Looking more carefully at property rights offers a powerful view of the limits of economic development in Latin America. Hernando de Soto, a Peruvian economist, became interested in the informal sector of Lima in the 1980s. *The Other Path*, the book that came out of that study is over twenty years old as of this writing, but it is still very relevant for Latin American economic development. The informal sector poor have often been portrayed as a blight, or undesirables, or "marginals." Various leaders in Latin America have made efforts at different times to clean out their shanties and shut down their informal enterprises. De Soto saw them differently. What he observed was extraordinary dynamism, creativity and entrepreneurial spirit. At the time of his writing, de Soto noted that the informal sector comprised 48% of the economically active population, putting in 61.2% of all work hours and contributing 38.9% of the country's GDP. Informals accounted for 47% of Lima's population and 42.6% of all housing amounting to over US$ 8 billion invested in these illegal structures as of 1987.[32] The problem of the informal sector is that this vast population, their dynamism and entrepreneurial spirit and their contribution to the wealth of the country all take place outside the sanction of formal laws. That makes a considerable difference.

De Soto is often dismissed for his singular focus on property rights as *the* answer. Moreover, his work in the government of Alberto Fujimori to institute a land titling program demonstrated the limits to its effectiveness as a way to promote development. But, this critique ignores the nuances of de Soto's efforts to understand the economic problem of the poor. Along with a team of graduate students, de Soto conducted extensive interviews in the informal sector of Lima to document the costs and challenges of mounting a business or buying a home when the law does not recognize the property rights of the poor or protect them from predatory behavior. In fact, de Soto's study demonstrates that the law itself pushes the poor into informality. For example, a team of de Soto students initiated a simulation to open a small garment factory with a single proprietor in accordance with all bureaucratic procedures. The exercise required 11 different permits, resulted in ten separate demands for bribes, took 289 days to secure all formal permission and cost US$ 1,231 or thirty two times the monthly minimum wage.[33] Housing was even more discouraging. An experiment to determine the cost and time required to acquire unused land and legally construct housing on it showed that it took an extraordinary 83 months – over six years – and US$ 2,156 or the equivalent of four years' wages at minimum wage.[34] These are only two of many indicators of the extraordinary penalty that legality in unjust societies inflicts on the poor.

Unable to participate in the formal, legal world of housing, employment, or enterprise, the poor move into illegality and craft their own, informal institutions to regulate their lives. But, illegality generates a considerable number of penalties. First, illegals do not enjoy the protection of vital social policies such as access to health care, disability or unemployment insurance, or pensions. Nor do they pay taxes or contribute to state funded health care or pensions. Informals do pay taxes indirectly through their transactions with legal enterprises (such as purchasing gasoline). Thus informals contribute partially to the maintenance of a legal framework that affords them no protection and in many ways actively discriminates against them. Informals also pay exorbitant costs for illegal access to utilities, such as water and electricity, as well as transportation. Furthermore, informals pay costs associated with avoiding detection by legal authorities and protection money to secure them from violence in the absence of reliable police protection. All the makeshift mechanisms that the poor invent for survival and interacting both with each other and with the formal sector are costly in and of themselves and constitute drags on their productivity and the national wealth, not to mention the quality of democracy. Institutional reforms that would reduce the cost of legality by clearly assigning and protecting property rights for the poor promise considerable economic and political gains. Unfortunately, as long as the prevailing system of property rights and the legal institutions that govern them protect the interests of the minority of middle and upper class members of society, moving into legality is impossible.

For de Soto, one of the greatest costs of informality, both for the poor and for the economy in general, is the inability to convert assets into capital. Since informals do not hold titles to their illegally constructed homes on land that is being squatted, they cannot use them as collateral with a bank. The result is an enormous stock of *potential* capital – the basic material for spawning economic growth – that cannot be translated into actual capital for investment. As Birdsall and Székely note, the only real way for the poor to improve their situation is to be able to leverage themselves up out of poverty by their "bootstraps, not bandaids."[35] Throwing money at the poor does not permanently solve the problem. Investing money in the development of human capital and helping the poor develop tradable assets is the only way to help the poor help themselves. For de Soto, illegality is a fundamental barrier to the ability of the poor to help themselves. Ultimately, the various costs of informality translate into lost productivity, diminished tax revenues, gross inefficiency and unproductive allocation of resources, and the perpetuation of deep social and economic injustices.

A fair and efficient distribution of property rights is but one dimension of a healthy relation between a self-restraining state and the market. But, it leaves unresolved the issue of how a society develops a self-restraining state? How does a fair, equitable property rights system come about? What produces the consensus on norms of accountability and public officials acting within agreed upon constraints? Institutional economists and political scientists have been working on this question, but in truth we are at best only marginally closer to having a satisfactory answer to these questions in 2017 than when Douglass North first began to pose them for economists in the 1980s. New work has gained wide attention offering answers to the link between institutions and development. For example, Daron Acemoglu and James A. Robinson's *Why Nations Fail* has gained wide readership for its argument about inclusionary and extractive orders.[36] Coming from a very different tradition, theoretically and methodologically, others have offered arguments about "political settlements" as intra-elite bargains about the organization of politics and the economy and can be inclusionary or exclusionary, or developmental or not.[37] These are evocative works and help frame analytical efforts to account for development outcomes. Yet, in the end, even if we agree that self-restraining states, inclusionary orders, or inclusionary political settlements do accurately explain outcomes, we do not know where they come from. Only a handful of countries have gone from poor to upper income in the modern world (primarily South Korea and Taiwan) and political economy is no closer to understanding why those countries and not others.

The "Politics of Policies" and the Importance of "Development" for Development

Yet another exploration of the importance of institutions for economic development is the ambitious and comprehensive study of the "politics of policies" of the Inter-American Development Bank.[38] The 2006 study brought together a large team of economists and political scientists – country specialists as well as general scholars of institutions and economic development. The purpose of the study was to determine the institutional factors that explain the quality of policy. The authors defined quality of policy as being a systemic feature rather than a function of any given specific policy. That is to say, that rather than study a set of specific policies, they looked at the policy-making system to determine the quality of the outputs produced by that system. Policy quality was measured as an index with six components: 1) stability and predictability of the rules – frequent policy changes increase uncertainty, provoke conflicts in both the market and the political arena, and ultimately discourage investors; 2) adaptability – the capacity of the system to alter policy in the face of changing circumstances; 3) coherence – the extent to which policies are consistent with related policies and are designed and implemented in a coordinated manner; 4) quality of implementation and enforcement – the effectiveness of efforts to implement and enforce policies passed by the government; 5) efficiency – the extent to which resources are put to their best use; and 6) public regardedness – that is to say that the policies passed focus on the public interest rather than providing extensive loopholes, exemptions and special treatment for narrow, organized interests. To determine the influences on the quality of policy, the authors conducted detailed studies of thirteen countries and a variety of sectoral studies, including budget processes, tax policy, privatization and regulation, as well as education, health and social insurance. Among the institutional variables they considered were the political institutions discussed above (electoral rules, legislative, executive and political parties) as well as key administrative institutions including regulatory agencies, the civil service, the judiciary, and technical support staff for the legislature.

It is difficult to reduce a vast undertaking such as this to a single claim. But if there is a central claim to the report, it is that good policy ultimately rests on the capacity of the system to facilitate "inter-temporal" cooperation. Institutional features that facilitate reaching and enforcing agreements enhance the quality of policy over time. Those that impede cooperation or encourage reneging on agreements undermine it. In addition, the authors offer a series of "messages." Among the central ones for the purposes of this chapter are: first, policy processes matter and as a result there is no such thing as a "universal" policy prescription that works independently of time and place. Second, the quality of the process matters more than the content. A sub-optimal policy that is stable, cohesive and credible is better for development than some "ideal" policy that lacks these systemic qualities. Finally, policies need to be understood holistically, with reference to specific countries' histories, contexts, and institutional arrangements. Note the distance this view has come from the early expectations of neoliberalism.

On the key institutional dimensions, the authors make several observations. First, they find little relation between political institutions such as electoral rules or the extent of executive powers and the quality of policy. This is not surprising given the discussion above. Arguments about these political institutions have tended to overstate their constraints on policy making. Nevertheless, the authors did find that well-institutionalized parties with national and programmatic orientations improve the quality of policy. The study also found that a well-developed civil service, independent judiciary, and strong legislative technical capacity mattered a great deal. In fact, the authors show that these institutional qualities are associated with higher rates of growth, per capita GDP growth, welfare improvements and reduction of poverty. The authors use simple statistical tests for the correlation with the policy index (the aggregate score for all their measures of concern) and find that after controlling for wealth in 1980, the correlations with GDP per capita growth, increases in the United Nations Human Development Index, and an index of welfare developed by Amartya Sen are 0.509, 0.614 and 0.730 respectively and all highly significant statistically.[39]

They also note that there is a strong correlation among the institutional features and therein lies the central question. Countries with well-institutionalized, national parties also tend to have independent judiciaries, highly professional civil services and legislative technical capacity. These are the same institutional features that we associate, virtually by definition, with developed countries. In other words, the explanation for higher quality policy and better development is better development. Although the authors themselves do not see it this way, ultimately the Inter-American Development Bank report can be reduced to the claim that something that for lack of a better term we may call "institutional development" is really what explains policy quality. The authors clearly state that the analysis of political institutions and policy-making processes cannot explain specific policies – only the overall policy quality over an extended period of time (from the 1980s on). But, policy quality is essentially a function of institutional qualities that are very stable over time. We are left then with the same question we asked about the self-restraining state: Where do good institutions come from?

By Way of Conclusion: The Origins of Institutions and a Bias for Hope

Institutions clearly matter for economic and political development. Institutions link voters to leaders and constrain the behavior of elected officials. They work to represent the interests of common citizens and make the political system responsive to those concerns. Political institutions are important for the quality of deliberations and the checks on arbitrary, abusive, or reckless behavior. Institutions help in the design, implementation and enforcement of policy. Institutions matter for the assignment and protection of property rights and the integrity of contracts. The rule of law and its protection of citizens, both as market actors and as members of a society, rest on the quality of institutions. Social policies designed to develop human capital depend on institutional quality. Ultimately, growth and equity depend on a strong set of institutions that preserve a balance between markets and states and among citizens of differing ethnicity, race, gender and economic status. Where appropriate institutions do not exist, do not function as intended, or protect privilege, corruption, and injustice, neither markets nor democracy develop particularly well.

The evidence from Latin America is fairly clear. Chile, Costa Rica and Uruguay come out on top on virtually every measure of institutional quality. It is not an accident that these three are also consistently the most democratic countries in the region. Brazil, like Chile, scores highly on the quality of its civil service and the technical capacity of its legislature. Again, it is not a surprise that both countries are sources of creative policy solutions to deeply ingrained problems, despite Brazil's chaotic contemporary crisis. Nor is it a surprise that Chile, Costa Rica, and Uruguay are also among the countries slowly finding a working balance between market-led and state-led development. Brazil is also well positioned to be part of this group once its corruption crisis resolves (though that may take some time and leave a significant legacy of destructive consequences in its wake).

The problem of development, then, is not a question of markets versus states. Policies matter, but the institutional framework in which policies are designed, implemented and enforced matters more. The institutional scaffolding that supports economic and political exchanges matters more. The evidence from Latin America is troubling on that score. It seems to suggest that to develop successfully, the institutions must be "developed." But, it simply is not clear why or how that happens. Chile's strong commitment to the rule of law is visible everywhere. The subway in Santiago is clean, well ordered and remarkably punctual. Signs indicate the arrival times for the next train and warn about prohibitions against running in stations or walking "down" the "up" staircases. By contrast, Buenos Aires' subway stations are breaking down, trains arrive without apparent connection to expected times, and the station clocks post the time incorrectly. Caracas' stations are a battleground of aggressive and disordered behavior. In Chile, government records are well ordered and easily accessible. In Bolivia, legislative committees rarely meet and do not make transcripts of their hearings. The congressional library is rarely open. These differences affect the quality of life and the standard of living, but it is not known what it would take for Argentina, Bolivia or Venezuela to become Chile – only that being Chile makes a difference.

On the face of it, it would seem like the answer is simply to import the desired rules and institutions. In fact, this has been the practice for a long time in Latin America and it has not been effective. It is not enough simply to import rules, laws or institutions from abroad. As the earlier discussion on the self-restraining state indicated, there needs to be a consistency between the institutions and the beliefs underlying them. Otherwise, the formal functioning of the institution will be undermined by the behavior of people following a different set of informal rules. For example, Dan

Brinks has studied police killings in Argentina, Brazil, and Uruguay, trying to understand the persistence and intensity of that violence (especially in São Paulo, Salvador, and to a lesser extent Buenos Aires). Once again, Uruguay is an outlier with low levels of police violence and higher conviction rates than in Argentina and Brazil.[40] Despite clear laws prohibiting police killing and strong penalties, police killing of civilians is pervasive. Prosecutors routinely decline to prosecute these cases and even when they do, judges do not convict them. Brinks demonstrates that beneath the surface of the formal law lie strong beliefs about "undesirables" and the legitimacy of police violence against them. Thus, an imported legal standard critical for deepening democracy founders as it confronts entrenched informal rules that stipulate limits on police violence against middle-class citizens, but permit violence against the poor or racial minorities.

The need for consistency between underlying norms and the social, political and economic institutions presents one of the most serious challenges to understanding the process of economic development. Chileans' orderly subway stations remain so because they are populated by people who believe in the values embedded in the rules. It is this fit between formal rules and informal practices or beliefs that is so hard to explain. How do societies develop the institutions best suited toward economic and democratic development so that they are consistent with the beliefs of the society? Some would argue that in fact if the rules change, then so too do the incentives and eventually people will conduct themselves accordingly. There are numerous examples of institutions that do work well that way. Brazil's *Bolsa Família* pays a stipend to families if their children attend school regularly and people have responded accordingly. Some argue that it has to do with wealth or economic classes. In effect, economic growth empowers new groups in society who in turn are in a better position to articulate their demands, balance the economic power of elites, and hold leaders accountable. Again, this is a plausible argument and certainly organized groups, such as unions or indigenous organizations, played an important role over the past several decades, both in transitions to democracy and deepening of the quality of democracy. Others have argued that cultural traits are crucial and relatively independent of institutions or economic classes. Unfortunately, all these approaches offer plausible approaches to understanding the problem, but as a field, we do not have anything approaching a consensus on the question.

In recent years, institutional economists have offered intriguing new ideas about how to think about the problem of institutions, cultural change, and economic development. For example, Avner Greif's *Institutions and the Path to the Modern Economy* seeks to understand how culture shapes societal solutions to exchange problems in ways that affect the possibility of economic development.[41] Greif compares Mediterranean societies in the 1400s, focusing on the Maghreb of Northern Africa and Italian city-states such as Venice. By the 1500s, Italian city-states had developed political and economic institutions that differed substantially from the Muslim Maghribi and ultimately constituted the basis for successful democratic, capitalist development. The wealthy and very successful Maghribi traders, by contrast, developed institutions that functioned well and permitted growth and political stability, but impeded the emergence of democracy and prevented the Maghribi from pursuing new opportunities for trade and the accumulation of wealth. As a result, the Italian city-states forged a path to success in the modern world while Northern Africa steadily declined in relative terms.

The central problem in Greif's analysis is how to manage economic exchanges over large, far-flung territories when you do not personally know the people with whom you are engaged in trade. How do you prevent cheating? The culturally homogenous and cohesive Maghribi managed it through social solidarity and an agreement to ostracize cheaters enforced through shared values and extensive family and kin networks. Greif reviews a 100 year period and finds almost no examples of cheating because the extended social networks and solidarity made monitoring relatively inexpensive and the penalties for violating contracts very costly. On the other hand, the Italian city-states were characterized by heterogeneity, with traders unrelated by family ties and unconstrained in their efforts to cheat each other – something that was pervasive. The absence of social solidarity meant that traders had to invent impersonal mechanisms to monitor and enforce agreements. Out of this problem emerged the precursors of modern contracts, banking and states that could secure property rights and enforce contracts. Both solutions permitted successful trade and both were functional, stable, and culturally consistent with their respective societies. The problem is that one set of institutions was perfectly suited to modern economic development and the other sharply constrained the possibilities.

Greif's work shows the way that institutions emerge holistically from societies and the fact that as long as they are functional, they may persist even though they become sub-optimal over time. But, the problem of how to account for changes remains. Douglass North, the dean of the institutional economists, has been particularly provocative and innovative in his efforts to solve the problem.[42] North has increasingly turned away from mainstream economics, especially neoclassical economics, drawing on history and political science for example to understand the process of economic change.

More recently, North has turned to neuroscience and theories of cognition and learning to understand culture, institutions and economic development. North notes that the world is characterized by enormous uncertainty and complexity. But, he observes that neuroscientists have demonstrated that humans are hard wired to impose order on the world around us. Our efforts to make sense of the complexity around us are designed to reduce uncertainty – to make things appear knowable and manageable.

If North is right, then some form of social learning is the key to developing the institutions that are vital for democracy and economic development. The stakes are tremendous. Millions of Latin Americans remain poor and the end of the "Golden Era" threatens to impoverish millions more who had hoped to escape poverty. Life for the poor can be tenuous and brutal. Many of them lack basics such as access to quality health care or secure housing. Child labor and violations of children's human rights are pervasive. Basic injustices in the rule of law are a daily feature of life, including fear of police violence that at times matches fear of violent criminals. Economic growth and innovative social policies have emerged in some regimes. But, even so, many countries in Latin America are not among them and the results are still uneven and constrained even among the ones that are growing well and designing innovative, progressive policies. Latin America has made enormous progress over the last century, and arguably even over the last decade, but much remains to be done. Discussions of institutions and their origins can seem abstract, but they are vital for the quality of life of tens and tens of millions of people.

Greif and North's emphasis on culture and the correspondence between a society's beliefs and values and its institutions can appear discouraging. If development cannot occur without the appropriate institutions and those cannot appear unless the underlying beliefs are consistent, then is there any possibility for development in anything but the long term at best? Some evidence deepens the basis for pessimism. For example, interpersonal trust affects the ability of civil society to work together cooperatively to solve problems of collective concern and to hold government accountable. Yet, surveys indicate that Latin Americans report very low levels of interpersonal trust.[43] Other survey evidence points to the existence of deeply hierarchical and authoritarian values.[44]

Yet, other sources of evidence point to "a bias for hope."[45] Studies of attitudes toward democracy, hierarchy and trust suggest that education matters a great deal.[46] Increasing investment in education and rapidly rising school enrollments have been among the landmark accomplishments of the past 20–30 years. As people become more educated, they report greater adherence to democratic values, tolerance for others, and belief in human rights. Generational change has been occurring as well, with younger generations more deeply socialized into democratic norms than their elders. The evidence of voting behavior also points to important changes. Over the course of the 1990s and into the 2000s, Latin American voters have increasingly demonstrated an ability and a willingness to hold elected officials accountable for their performance in office. Governments in the region have made efforts to tailor their programs in accordance with voters' preferences. Voters across Latin America have shown less tolerance for corruption even as state agencies have grown in their capacity to identify and prosecute corrupt practices. In a number of Latin American countries, the press has played an active role in uncovering unsavory corruption scandals. One of the most promising outcomes of the "Golden Era" is the tens of millions of people who have come to enjoy new social and economic rights – rights that may be very hard to withdraw, even in hard economic times. The end of the commodity boom may make it harder for politicians to deepen inclusion, but it may prevent them from rolling it back. In short, learning takes time and solving the deeper institutional aspects of development poses considerable challenges. Latin American governments still face a host of troubling problems. But, many important and promising changes have come out of the past three decades. There has always been, and will always be, variation in the experiences across Latin America. Some of the promising trends, however, suggest that the region may be able to find a good road – one that offers hope for a wealthier, more equitable, just future.

Notes

1 The definition used here draws on James Johnson, "What the Politics of Enfranchisment Can Tell Us about How Rational Choice Theorists Study Institutions." In *Preferences and Situations: Points of Intersection between Historical and Rational Choice Institutionalism*, Ira Katznelson and Barry R. Weingast, eds. (New York: Russell Sage Foundation, 2005).
2 Walton, 2004: 166.
3 Huber and Solt, 2004: 162.
4 John Williamson and Pedro Pablo Kuczynski, eds., *After the Washington Consensus: Restarting Growth and Reform in Latin America* (Washington DC: Institute for International Economics, 2003).
5 Wolff and Castro, 2003.
6 Robert Kaufman and Joan Nelson, eds., *Crucial Needs, Weak Incentives: Social Sector Reform, Democratization and Globalization in Latin America* (Washington DC: Woodrow Wilson Center Press, 2004).
7 Roberto Bouzas and Saúl Keifman, "Making Trade Liberalization Work." In *After the Washington Consensus: Restarting Growth and Reform in Latin America*, John Williamson and Pedro Pablo Kuczynski, eds. (Washington DC: Institute for International Economics, 2003).
8 These two qualities of connection and autonomy constitute what Peter Evans has called "embedded autonomy" and which he has argued was a critical component of East Asian economic successes as well as integral to Brazil's more localized successes. *Embedded Autonomy* (Princeton: Princeton University Press, 1995).
9 Judith Tendler, *Good Government in the Tropics* (Baltimore: Johns Hopkins University Press, 1998).
10 McGuire, 2010.
11 Bernd Reiter, *Negotiating Democracy in Brazil: The Politics of Exclusion* (Boulder, CO: Lynne Rienner Press, 2009).
12 Marcus André Melo, "Checking the Power of Mayors: Explaining Improvements in Brazilian Educational Outcomes." In *Democratic Brazil Divided*, Peter Kingstone and Timothy J. Power, eds. (Pittsburgh: University of Pittsburgh Press, 2017).
13 See the review of the struggles over regulation of utilities in Luigi Manzetti and Carlos Rufin, "The Political Economy of Regulatory Policy." In *The Handbook*

of Latin American Politics, Peter Kingstone and Deborah Yashar, eds. (New York: Routledge Press, 2011).

14 Note that the aggregate and average strength of governance institutions in the United States does not mean that there are not examples of bad performance. The Minerals Management Service (MMS) of the Interior Department is a regulatory institution that was supposed to monitor and enforce the rules governing deep-sea drilling for oil. As millions of barrels of oil have seeped out of the Deepwater Horizon Rig owned by British Petroleum, it has come to be understood that pervasive collusion between the MMS and private operators led to an almost complete lapse of regulation and enforcement of safety principles. The calamity that has hit the Gulf of Mexico and the coastal communities devastated by it is an all too vivid illustration of the importance of adequate institutions.

15 Peter H. Schuck, "Law and Post-Privatization Regulatory Reform: Perspectives from the U.S. Experience." In *Regulatory Policy in Latin America: Post-Privatization Realities*, Luigi Manzetti, ed. (Miami: North-South Center Press, 2000).

16 The political choices, their consequences and the subsequent struggles over adjustment of regulatory schemes is discussed in Murillo, 2009.

17 See for example, Scott Mainwaring and Matthew S. Shugart, *Presidentialism and Democracy in Latin America*, Cambridge University Press, 1997, or Scott Mainwaring, *Rethinking Party Systems in the Third Wave of Democratization*, Stanford University Press, 1998.

18 Scott Mainwaring and Matthew Shugart, eds., *Presidentialism and Democracy in Latin America* (New York: Cambridge University Press, 1997).

19 Guillermo O'Donnell, "Delegative Democracy," *Journal of Democracy* 5, January 1994.

20 Timothy J. Power, "The Pen is Mightier than the Congress: Presidential Decree Power in Brazil." In *Executive Decree Authority*, John Carey and Matthew Soberg Shugart, eds. (New York: Cambridge University Press, 2002).

21 Jose Puente and Abelardo Daza, "The Political Economy of the Budget Process in the Andean Region: The Case of Venezuela." Paper Presented at the Meeting of the Latin American Studies Association, Montreal, August 2007.

22 Javier Corrales, *Presidents without Parties: The Politics of Economic Reform in Argentina and Venezuela in the 1990s* (University Park, PA: Penn State Press, 2002).

23 Gray-Molina et al., 1999.

24 Kingstone, 1999.

25 Stephan Haggard and Mathew D. McCubbins, eds., *Presidents, Parliaments and Policy* (New York: Cambridge University Press, 2001).

26 Bolivar Lamounier, "Brazil: The Hyperactive Paralysis Syndrome." In *Constructing Democratic Governance: Latin America and the Caribbean in the 1990s*, Jorge J. Dominguez and Abraham F. Lowenthal, eds. (Baltimore: Johns Hopkins University Press, 1996).

27 Stephan Haggard and Robert Kaufman, *The Political Economy of Democratic Transitions* (Princeton: Princeton University Press, 1995).

28 Peter Kingstone, "Muddling Through Gridlock." In *Democratic Brazil: Actors, Institutions and Processes*, Peter Kingstone and Timothy J. Powers, eds. (University Park, PA: Penn State Press, 2002).

29 Timothy J. Power, "Optimism, Pessimism, and Coalitional Presidentialism: Debating the Institutional Design of Brazilian Democracy," *Bulletin of Latin American Research* 29, no. 1 (January): 18–33, 2010.

30 Argelina Cheibub Figueiredo and Fernando Limongi, "Presidential Power, Legislative Organization and Party Behavior in Brazil," *Comparative Politics*, January 2000.

31 Douglass North, William Summerhill and Barry R. Weingast, "Order, Disorder and Economic Change: Latin America versus North America." In *Governing for Prosperity*, Bruce Bueno de Mesquita and Hilton Root, eds. (New Haven: Yale University Press, 1999): 25.

32 Hernando de Soto, *The Other Path: The Invisible Revolution in the Third World* (New York: Harper & Row, 1989).

33 De Soto, 1989: 134.

34 De Soto, 1989: 139.

35 Birdsall and Székely, 2003.

36 Daron Acemoglu and James A. Robinson, *Why States Fail: Power, Prosperity and Poverty* (London: Profile Books, 2012).

37 Jonathan Di John and James Putzel, "Political Settlements." Governance and Social Development Resource Centre, Department of International Development (DFID), Issues Paper, June 2009; Mushtaq Khan, "State Failure in Weak States: A Critique of New Institutionalist Explanations." In John Harriss, Janet Hunter and Colin Lewis, eds., *The New Institutional Economics and Third World Development* (London: Routledge, 1995).

38 *The Politics of Policies: Economic and Social Progress in Latin America* (Washington DC: Inter-American Development Bank, Annual Report, 2006).

39 *The Politics of Policies*: 140.

40 Daniel Brinks, "The Rule of (Non)Law: Prosecuting Police Killings in Brazil and Argentina." In *Informal Institutions and Democracy in Latin America*, Gretchen Helmke and Steven Levitsky, eds. (Baltimore: Johns Hopkins University Press, 2006).

41 Avner Greif, *Institutions and the Path to the Modern Economy: Lessons from Medieval Trade* (New York: Cambridge University Press, 2006).

42 Douglass C. North, *Understanding the Process of Economic Change* (Princeton: Princeton University Press, 2005).

43 World Values Survey databank, available at http://www.worldvaluessurvey.org

44 Almeida, 2008. Ronald Inglehart and Wayne E. Baker, "Modernization, Cultural Change, and the Persistence of Traditional Values," *American Sociological Review* 65, no. 1, February 2000.

45 The phrase is from Albert Hirschman, *A Bias for Hope: Essays on Development and Latin America* (Boulder, CO: Westview Press, 1986).

46 Alejandro Moreno, "Mass Belief Systems and Democracy in Latin America." In *Citizen Views of Democracy*, Roderic Ai Camp, ed. (Pittsburgh: University of Pittsburgh Press, 2001).

Index

Note: references to tables are in **bold**